Let Love Lead
On a Course to Freedom

Gary L. Lemons, Scott Neumeister, and Susie Hoeller

Copyright © 2019 Gary L. Lemons, Scott Neumeister, and Susie Hoeller

ISBN: 978-1-64438-807-5

All rights reserved. No part of this publication may be reproduced, stored in a retrieval system, or transmitted in any form or by any means, electronic, mechanical, recording or otherwise, without the prior written permission of the author.

Published by BookLocker.com, Inc., St. Petersburg, Florida.

Printed on acid-free paper.

Library of Congress Cataloging in Publication Data
Lemons, Gary L.; Neumeister, Scott; Hoeller, Susie
Let Love Lead on a Course to Freedom by Gary L. Lemons, Scott Neumeister, and Susie Hoeller
RELIGION / Biblical Commentary | SOCIAL SCIENCE / Feminism & Feminist Theory | EDUCATION / Philosophy, Theory & Social Aspects
Library of Congress Control Number: 2019906803

BookLocker.com, Inc.
2019

First Edition

Contents

Preface - If Anyone Had Ever Told Me ... "A Litany for Survival"
Gary L. Lemons vii

Introduction - At the Pedagogical Intersection of Faith, Hope and Love
Gary L. Lemons 1

Part I - Where the Personal, Pedagogical, and the Biblical Merge 15

    Chapter 1 - A (His)Story of Love: Autocritography as a Writing Sanctuary
    Gary L. Lemons 16
    Chapter 2 - In Love with Teaching "The Bible as Literature" (As a
    Pro-Womanist Black Man) *Gary L. Lemons* 37
    Chapter 3 - Jesus as a Pro-Woman(*ist*) Messenger of Hope
    Gary L. Lemons 58

Part II - Where Faith, Hope, and Love Reside 85

    Chapter 4 - Believing is Seeing: Visionary Perspectives
    Scott Neumeister 86
    Chapter 5 - Superstar: Retelling the Story of a Radical 112
    Chapter 6 - Jesus at the Intersection: Where Feminist Meets Womanist
    Gary L. Lemons 132

Part III - *Lean on Jesus* as a Passageway to *Jesus Feminist* 153

    Chapter 7 - Let Love Lead in Business *Susie Hoeller* 154
    Chapter 8 - Students Learn How to *Lean on Jesus Susie Hoeller* 166
    Chapter 9 - Jesus Christ: The Champion of All People—Regardless
    Susie Hoeller 188

Part IV - A Visionary Invitation: All Are Welcome 199

    Chapter 10 - Access Granted: Feminine Mystical and Mundane Pathways
    Scott Neumeister 200
    Chapter 11 - Where *Church* and *State* (University) Meet "Commissioned"
    for Community Service *Gary L. Lemons* 220
    Chapter 12 - Seated in the Circle of Love *Gary L. Lemons, Scott*
    Neumeister, and Susie Hoeller 245

Authors 259

So I am giving you a new commandment: that you love one another. Just as I have loved you, so too you should love one another. By this all people will know that you are my disciples, if you have love among yourselves.

Jesus, quoted in *The Single Gospel: Matthew, Mark, Luke and John Consolidated into a Single Narrative,* Neil Averitt

Preface

If Anyone Had Ever Told Me...
"A Litany for Survival"

Gary L. Lemons

For those of us
who were imprinted with fear
like a faint line in the center of our foreheads . . .

this instant and this triumph
We were never meant to survive.

"A Litany for Survival," Audre Lorde

We have this hope as an anchor for the soul, firm and secure.
It enters the inner sanctuary . . .

Hebrews 6:19 (New International Version)

Taped on my office door at the university where I teach is a copy of Audre Lorde's poem "A Litany for Survival." For years—even before I was hired as a "professor of English" at this institution of higher education—it has been my testament to having survived what I never thought I would—as a student and teacher of "English" in majority white colleges and universities. For all intents and purposes, though "[I was] never meant to survive," I have. While it has taken most of my life as a teacher in the college classroom to comprehend what this has meant, in this present moment, I have a clear sense that it has never been about my academic training in relation to what I have been *called* to do.

Since the publication of *Black Male Outsider, a Memoir: Teaching as a Pro-Feminist Man* in 2008 to the release of *Caught Up in the Spirit: Teaching for Womanist Liberation* in 2017, I have written about my professional path in institutions of higher learning.

As I share in each of these books (and in essays in a number of other edited books), this has been a thought-provoking intellectual *and* spiritual journey. While, on the one hand, acquiring academic credentials in majority white colleges and universities, my "specialization" in literary studies was *all* about the canonical traditions of British and American *white* male and female authors. What did this have to do with spirituality? In truth, had it not been for my experience growing up with certain teachings in "the" *black* church—even as complicated as this experience proved to be—I would not have acquired faith in a higher calling that led me to believe that my academic knowledge was not the sum-total of the meaning of *higher education*.

For nearly half a decade, as a professor in the English department at the University of South Florida, I have taught a course called "The Bible as Literature." When I first agreed to teach it in 2014, I had no idea that my pro-feminist and womanist pedagogical approach to African American literature and culture would eventually resonate with such liberating authority in the writings of students in the course. Moreover, my employment of "autocritography"—a writing style merging the personal reflection with one's professional concerns and critiques of social issues—as I utilized it in this course would also have such a transformative impact on the lives of my students. As conceptualized by Henry Louis Gates, Jr. and concretely defined by Michael Awkward in *Scenes of Instruction, a Memoir* (1999), this ground-breaking form of writing as a strategic tool in the class would further support my concept of the course. Having been caught up in the liberatory writings of such noted feminists as bell hooks, Alice Walker, *and* Audre Lorde (among a number of other feminist and womanist writers of color), I discovered a radical path to teach healing and self-transformation in the college classroom—as I have written about time and time again. Lorde's poetic rendering of love in her "A Litany for Survival" is not only thought-provoking but compelling in its critical indictment of fear as the agent of loneliness:

>when we are loved we are afraid
>love will vanish
>when we are alone we are afraid

>   love will never return (33-36)
>
> Fear as represented in the poem is also a perpetrator of silence against the will to speak:
>
>   and when we speak we are afraid
>   our words will not be heard
>   nor welcomed
>   but when we are silent
>   we are still afraid (37-41)
>
> Against the ideology of imperialist colonization, Lorde ends her poem by inscribing the integral relationship between love and the life-sustaining power of voice as a crucial tool of survival:
>
>   So it is better to speak
>   remembering
>   we were never meant to survive. (42-44)

Opening My Office Door to Survive Remembering That "it is better to speak"

Every time I approach my office door, before opening it, I stare at the words "we were never meant to survive." In the moment, I remember growing up hearing old black church folk saying, "What you meant for evil, God intended for good" (a version of the biblical scripture found in Genesis 50:20). When I first taped Lorde's words on my door, I never had this thought in mind. Yet in the context of writing this preface to *Let Love Lead on a Course to Freedom: A Study of "The Bible as Literature,"* I am continually provoked to a deep place of self-reflection by the poem's title—particularly concerning the meaning of the term "litany." In the *Merriam-Webster Dictionary*, it is defined as "a prayer consisting of a series of invocations and supplications by the leader with alternate responses by the congregation." Needless to say, ironically having been reared in the black church and having read Lorde's poem a number of times, I had never associated it with biblical scripture. Rather I focused only on the political and artistic factuality of her being a radical black feminist poet advocating the need for black folk to speak out against white supremacist, heterosexist patriarchy.

Yet in co-authorship of *Let Love Lead* with Scott Neumeister and Susie Hoeller, I am intellectually, pedagogically, *and* spiritually intrigued by the interconnected representation of spirituality and love in the writings of Lorde, bell hooks, and Alice Walker. The three of them radically "speak" love and its transgressive, healing agency in resistance to systemic and institutionalized forms of oppression. Now when I read "A Litany for Survival" on my office door—in a spiritual context—I know that it is a prayer. I was "meant to survive" in spite of…as Walker would declare in defining a "womanist"— "*regardless.*" hooks says in *Talking Back: Thinking Feminist, Thinking Black*:

> It is necessary for us to remember, as we think critically about domination, that we all have the capacity to act in ways that oppress, dominate, wound (whether or not that power is institutionalized). It is necessary to remember that it is first the potential oppressor within that we must resist—the potential victim within that we must rescue—otherwise we cannot hope for an end to domination, for liberation. (21)

At the same time, hooks specifically addresses the issue of love and black male identity politics in *Salvation: Black People and Love* (2001). Reading it, I have become aware that we—black folk—must address the "oppressor within" as we speak out for social justice. In our struggle for survival, we need to pray for deliverance against the ways fear of the loss of our power as black men keeps us bound *and* enslaved to the constrictions and shackles of patriarchal manhood. Moreover, in the context of what I will refer to as hooks' love trilogy—along with *Salvation*—she radically connects the "salvation" of blacks with the redemptive power of love in *All About Love: New Visions* (2000) and *Rock My Soul: Black People and Self-Esteem* (2003).

Once again, in line with the imperative of vocality against oppression that Lorde so poetically calls out in her "Litany," hooks confronts the history of our not having the right to survive our legalized enslavement in this nation—known as "the land of the free." To black men in particular, hooks says that we must attend to feelings of silence about "self-love":

Within white supremacist capitalist patriarchy, black male who embrace the values of these ideologies have enormous difficulty with the issue of self-love. Patriarchal thinking certainly does not encourage men to be self-loving. Instead it encourages [us] to believe that power is more important than love, particularly the power to dominate and control others. (145)

Now as a new congregant in the body of love, in touch with the supernatural in the vision of hope embodied in the womanist thought of Lorde, hooks, and Walker—I release myself from internalized fear that as a black man I will not survive. Free from the dictates of patriarchy, white supremacist, and masculinist notions of manhood—along with Scott, Susie, and students whose voices we include in this book—we speak in loving words as we *Let Love Lead*. With our hearts and arms wide open in our journey toward completing this book, we embrace the principles of salvation created for healing the mind, body, and spirit of all people in this nation and in this world today.

Collectively in composing *Let Love Lead*—across differences of race, ethnicity, gender, class, sexuality, culture, religion, generation, and abilities (among other variances not mentioned here)—our aim is neither to condemn nor hurt anyone who chooses to read this book. Instead we invite every reader to embark upon a course to freedom as we have conceptualized it. Rather than propagate walls of separation and exclusion, we have labored to create a vision of hope toward a destination of wholeness rooted in love—for all people *"Regardless,"* in the womanist word of Alice Walker.

Works Cited

Awkward, Michael. *Scenes of Instruction, a Memoir*. Duke University Press, 1999.

The Bible. New International Version, Biblica, 2011.

hooks, bell. *Talking Back: Thinking Feminist, Thinking Black*. South End Press, 1989.

---. *Salvation: Black People and Love*. HarperCollins Publishers Inc., 2001.

Lemons, Gary L. *Black Male Outsider, a Memoir: Teaching as a Pro-Feminist Man*. State University of New York Press, 2008.

---. *Caught Up in the Spirit: Teaching for Womanist Liberation*. Nova Science Publisher Inc., 2017.

"litany." *Merriam-Webster.com*. Merriam-Webster, 2019, www.merriam-webster.com/dictionary/litany.

Lorde, Audre. "A Litany for Survival." *The Black Unicorn*. W.W. Norton Co., 1978.

Walker, Alice. *In Search of Our Mothers' Gardens: Womanist Prose*. Harcourt Brace and Co., 1983.

Introduction

At the Pedagogical Intersection of Faith, Hope and Love

Gary L. Lemons

>And now these three remain: faith, hope, and love. But the greatest of these is love.
>
>1 Corinthians 13:13 (New International Version)

>[A womanist is committed] to survival and wholeness of entire people, male *and* female...Not a separatist... Traditionally universal, as in: "Mama, why are we brown, pink, and yellow, and our cousins are white, beige, and black?" Ans.: "Well, you know the colored race is just like a flower garden, with every color flower represented." Traditionally capable, as in: "Mama, I'm walking to Canada and I'm taking you and a bunch of other slaves with me." Reply: "It wouldn't be the first time"...[She] Loves music. Loves dance. Loves the moon. *Loves* the Spirit. Loves love and food and roundness. Loves struggle. *Loves* the Folk. Loves herself. *Regardless.*
>
>Alice Walker, *In Search of Our Mothers Gardens, Womanist Prose*

Believing that I have been led to teach "The Bible as Literature" as a literary studies course in a secular university context, I reflect upon this assignment as a spiritual "calling"— particularly related concepts of "faith, hope, and love." In an academic context they have compelled me to *recall* their meanings in the evolution of my teaching profession in the college classroom.

Many years before it ever even occurred to me that I could one day teach a college course on the Bible (particular in a secular educational setting), I had already—as a pro-feminist and womanist identified, black male professor—determined to reject an allegiance to religious, patriarchal dogmatism. I sought to begin a new path of spiritual enlightenment. In the process (outside my academic status as a literary studies professor), I had begun a personal search for liberatory ways to read, study, and to teach the Bible (in a "church" setting). As *Let Love Lead on a Course to Freedom,* not only would this search materialize in the framework of a college course, it would manifest itself in a book-form documenting my journey to teaching "The Bible as Literature." Moreover, the documentation of this venture would be formalized in a conceptualized, co-authored format with Scott Neumeister and Susie Hoeller. They would provide even more significant evidence of my calling to perform the task of writing about teaching this course. As pro-feminist and womanist allies—particularly linked to their own critiques of patriarchal domination and oppression—in writings they have published, these two biblical scholars joined me to validate the student-teacher, life-transforming reality of *Let Love Lead.*

Holistically, the three of us offer our own personal stories of social, political, and spiritual activism to support my pedagogical aims. Every semester when I have taught this class, they remained committed guest-speakers, sharing their spiritual visions of social justice and human rights with my students. Co-authoring of *Let Love Lead*, I join Scott and Susie to illustrate the transformational power of love thematically illustrated in my students' autocritographical writings. By integrating our interpretive analyses of them, we examine ways they represent how students translate biblical narratives and messages focused on the theme of love into their own life stories. I tactically employ autocritography from this perspective to work as a rhetorical strategy to create a community of writers—uniting differences of race, gender, sexuality, culture, ability, and ideas of religion *and* spirituality.

Together we transport our interpretive analyses across bridges for holistic narrative connection. We thus envision the college classroom setting as a critical space for border-crossing. In this communal setting for bridge-building, I experience the restorative labor of love. Over time, in the process of moving this book project from imaginative concept to narrative reality—Scott, Susie, and I sat many times at the dining table in my home dialoguing about the power of love union as writers, storytellers, and *inspirited* teachers. I have imagined our activist labor in the study of the Bible as an expression of feminist-womanist soul-work right from the beginning of our collaborative efforts over the course of three years to bring this project to fruition.

In Part I of *Let Love Lead* (Chapters 1-3), I recount the evolution of my soulful journey from childhood to adulthood. I provide a personal history of my religious upbringing, detailing ways it would over time begin to interconnect with coming to know the autobiographical writings of black feminists. As I show throughout the chapters I have written in this book, bell hooks, Alice Walker, and Audre Lorde instilled in my academic and spiritual development an unyielding love for social justice and human rights.

Scott and I articulate with compelling evidence in Part II, as "brothers of the soul," the transformative possibilities of feminist thought in the lives of men. In *Feminist Solidarity at the Crossroads: Intersectional Women's Studies for Transracial Alliance* (2012), we cowrote an essay about what it means to be "'Brothers of the Soul': Men Learning About and Teaching the Spirit of Feminist Solidarity." I cite our academic and spiritual work here to provide a preface to our longstanding relationship, having first met Scott as a student in a graduate "Feminist Theory" course I taught in 2010. Remembering a significant moment during the semester he remarks,

> I think that my relationship with males, females, and even myself has changed in one fundamental aspect during this course. I am much more in touch with what I would call my authentic self, what I am at the core that is spiritual. I have had a direct realization that, in my soul, I am not raced, gendered, sexually "preferenced," classed, or labeled with any other signification that the world of the physical can attribute. In fact, just recently…I have started calling you "brother of the Soul" (or B.O.S.), partly as a light wordplay on "Soul Brother" and a nod to the black culture of the 1960s, but really as a reference to the fact that at the soul level, you are not bald

and I do not have hair; you are not a professor and I am not a master's student; you are not a "black male outsider" and I am not a "white male insider"; and so on. Although the word *brother* really does a disservice by ascribing a gender that our souls don't have, it does describe a kinship that the physical world would deny to us. This kinship feeling, this opening of the "table" to be truly inclusive, has revolutionized my worldview. (115-116)

Having served as Scott's major professor for his M.A. thesis and his PhD. (which he awarded in 2018), over the course of many years our kinship as "brothers of the soul" has spiritually deepened in ways I never imagined. I absolutely concur with his "reference to the fact that at the soul level...[a]lthough the word *brother* really does a disservice by ascribing a gender that our souls don't have, it does describe a kinship that the physical world would deny to us." Clearly devoted to community building through the self-transforming agency of love, Scott did not surprise me when he offered the phrase "let love lead" as the main title of this book. He knows well that I spend much time in word-play when it comes to creating titles in my writings. However, it was not given me the task to conjure up this one. I call it his "shamanic gift" to me and Susie. In our essay in *Feminist Solidarity at the Crossroads*, within the closing section that we titled—"Through a Power that made and Loveth All: Beyond the Phallus(y) of Manhood at the Intersection of Our Differences"—we conclude that:

[b]y the end of the course, we had come to understand that what had connected us during the semester, indeed, existed at a level deeper than the intellect alone...The [lessons in the Bible] about the preeminence of love as a guiding force for social justice and freedom for the dispossessed we brought to "Feminist Theory"...The "brotherly soul connection" we made in one course in feminist literary studies not only had to do with a willingness to question our privilege as men but the will to contest sexist ideas of manhood and masculinity...[We concluded] that a power greater than ourselves had brought us together to experience as men an ethical, loving, and soul

connection to each other through feminist visions of social justice. In the process we became "brothers of the soul." (117-118)

In Chapter 4, Scott represents varying "ways of seeing" in his dialogical interaction with students toward "a higher vision [of] liberatory consciousness." He examines concepts of faith, hope, and love through this lens. In his chapter that follows, he opens with personal thoughts about his childhood upbringing Episcopal and Presbyterian churches. Scott recalls his experience as a thirteen-year-old eight-grader seeing a production of the musical *Jesus Christ Superstar* by Andrew Lloyd Webber and Tim Rice. Centering the chapter on a discussion of "Student Responses" written during the 2014 semester of "The Bible as Literature," he explores their thematic interpretations associated with Passion Week. Interestingly, while analyzing the students' writings (in April 2018), Scott notes that he is watching a televised version of *Jesus Christ Superstar* in which John Legend plays the role of Jesus. Considering the importance of self-reflection in students' interpretations of biblical narratives about the life of Jesus, in this chapter Scott once again emphasizes the critical significance of autocritography—not only in his childhood memory of the musical but its relevance to writings produced by student responses to events during Passion Week.

In Chapter 6, I further promote the concept of autocritography as a transformative writing technique in the college classroom. I simultaneously discuss how it functions to provide credence to the interconnection between the fundamental meanings of feminism and womanism. Moreover, as stated in the chapter's introduction, I contextualize Jesus' message for human salvation in the soulful agency of faith and hope. Ultimately, my aim is to show how students in "The Bible as Literature" articulate these virtues in their written responses in the course. I format this chapter as a "Class Discussion" based on a comparative exploration of the 2015 and 2018 course offerings.

Part III of *Let Love Lead* contains three chapters composed by Susie, who is a prolific writer. Her published articles have discussed corporate social responsibility, entrepreneurship, international trade and food safety. She has written books about Christian ethics in the workplace, immigration policy, food and product safety and a memoir about growing up in Montreal, Canada. In Chapters 8 and 9, she writes about her experiences as self-identified, white feminist-womanist activist lawyer. Like Scott, she has been an ongoing guest-speaker in "The Bible as Literature." To my surprise, after her talk during her first class visit (toward the beginning of my 2014 semester offering of the course), she gave me and every student in the class (composed of at least twenty-five students) a free copy of her book *Lean on Jesus: Christian Women in the Workplace*. I was so impressed by her talk about women's rights in the workplace and the book's aim that I decided to assign the text as a secondary source for students to read during the remainder of the semester. Thus, in Chapters 8 and 9, Susie responds to selected students' analyses of her book—over the course of two semesters (2014 and 2015). When she returned to speak toward the beginning of the term in the 2015 session of the class, she once more gave students copies of *Lean on Jesus*. I again required to students to read and write about the book, especially related to its purpose. Susie clearly states (on its back cover),

> *Lean on Jesus* is not just another self-help book for the busy working woman. Read it and discover how to transform yourself and your workplace using the power of Christian love. This book combines spiritual wisdom and practical advice for all women regardless of where they work or in what positions.

Coming to know Susie and her commitment to labor equality for all women—in and outside the U.S.—enabled me to experience the transformative agency of feminism and womanism in "The Bible as Literature." As I continued to teach it over semesters, when Susie gave me a copy of Sarah Bessey's *Jesus Feminist: An Invitation to Revisit the Bible's View of Women*, I knew her labor as a messenger of faith, hope, and love would lead me to reconceptualize the course. In Chapter 9, she dialogues with my students having written responses to their study of *Jesus Feminist* when I chose to revise the course.

While making Susie's acquaintance in a completely different environment some years ago associated with my work as a visual artist, I knew—once we began to share our backgrounds in profeminist activism—that there was a visionary, political, and spiritual alliance that would emerge between the two of us. Early on, as we continued to connect with each other through mutual close friends, I came to know that Susie's commitment to social justice was integrally tied to her profession as an international attorney and law professor. I also discovered that she practices law and lived for years with her husband (Ted) in my home state, Arkansas. Her vision of human rights is globally linked to her stand against sexist, racist, and cultural objectification and exploitation of women.

Susie Hoeller's longstanding devotion to human rights, purposely aligned with her international legal work, not only connects to her vision of labor rights for the disenfranchised, but also intertwines with her commitment to healthcare *and* spiritual enlightenment. Literally crossing territorial borders of separation in a global context, she works to enable marginalized people to believe they possess rights for social justice. Susie has written about her family's journey as immigrants to the U.S. to Quebec, Canada in *Building Womanist Coalitions: Writing and Teaching in the Spirit of Love* (2019), describing her "[commitment] to [the] survival and wholeness of entire people." Embracing the liberatory thinking of womanism, she daringly titles her essay "From Exile to Healing: I 'too' am a Womanist." She introduces herself,

> I am an American woman seen to be white in the 21st century. Why am I included in a book about womanism? It is not because I have suffered like Black women and women of color have under slavery, Jim Crow and continuing institutional and personal racism. It is because I wish to share my unusual experience of white privilege shattered by exile and how it leads me to a place not of bitterness but of healing. It is because I have embraced Alice Walker's definition of a womanist especially "Not [being] a separatist…[but] [t]raditionally universalist…" (123)

As a black man who neither experienced the history of black women's enslavement in the U.S., I, too, have been drawn to the Spirit of Walker's definition of a womanist as one who is "Not a separatist." It is her "Traditionally universalist…"point of view that opens up space(s) for difference. Like Susie, I see myself—literally and figurative—as a member of "the colored race [which] is just like a flower garden, with every color flower represented. Traditionally capable, as in: 'Mama, I'm walking to Canada and I'm taking you and a bunch of other slaves with me.'" At one point early in her life, Susie and her family immigrated from the U.S. to Quebec, Canada. Ironically, however—because English was their language of origin—they would ultimately be "exile[d]" from Quebec, thus returning to the U.S. She writes candidly about this experience beginning in a section of her essay titled: "I Was a Minority Growing Up in Quebec, Canada": "In 1960, when I was six years old, my father went to work for a Canadian company. Our family moved to a small town on the west island of Montreal in Quebec. I grew up as a minority . . . " (124). However, ending her essay she claims a status ripe with the fruit of sacrificial love for other "folk":

> I had a unique experience for a white American girl/woman. I grew up as a minority. Not a financially impoverished minority but still a minority. As a result, I believe that I have a unique insight into problems minorities experience that many whites do not have. This is what attracted me to the universalist values taught by Alice Walker and the womanist movement. In addition, losing a material foundation to our lives when we were forced out of Quebec led me to seek a spiritual foundation. What does this mean? It means that I am called always from self love to love God and my neighbor as myself. It means that I must put doing what is right over what is profitable or expedient. It means not only taking up my cross daily but helping others to carry their crosses. (134)

Scott and I follow Susie's lead in Part III, strategically employing autocritography in Part IV to explore this project's groundbreaking implications in the writings students produced in the class, as well as how working on this book has impacted us. In "Seated in the Circle of Love," the closing chapter of *Let Love Lead*, Susie, Scott, and I reflect upon the *course* and direction of our journey toward the completion of this book. We always sat around a dining table during times we met at my home and conversed about its concept, contents, and our interpretations of students' writings. Each time we sat in a circle at the table, reading and editing each other's chapters that we prepared to include in the book, we learned much about the depth of faith, hope, and love this work required, just as students in "The Bible as Literature" did. Sharing our personal stories—weaved together with those of students—moved us to deepen our commitment to bearing the weight of each other's crosses, transforming love into action.

"Love Your Neighbor": Becoming Cross-Bearers for Each Other

Susie, Scott, and I are witnesses to what "it means [individually] not only taking up [each of our crosses] daily but helping others to carry their crosses" in the longstanding writing and pedagogical soul-work that we—as pro-feminist-womanist, inspired allies—share with each other and our students. Metaphorically, without being reductive, this is essence of the labor we seek to carry in our aim to enable students in the study of "The Bible as Literature." As I have stated from the beginning of this introduction to *Let Love Lead*, in writing and sharing our life-stories in the classroom, we strive to integrate them thematically into the biblical stories are assigned to read and interpret—autocritographically. In fact, in Susie's conclusion above, her belief in carrying the weight of someone else's cross is the tough groundwork that I, too, desire for my students to take up in the classroom. This is precisely why I invited Susie and Scott to help me teach the transforming and self-liberating power of love for one's neighbor—both inside and outside the college classroom.

Setting into place the interpretive foundation for this study—Susie, Scott, and I agreed to write about our experiences engaging this work, together and individually. We would come to know the transformative analytical and self-reflective viewpoints students employed in their autocritographies. In paging through their papers, we would become witnesses to the inspiring thematics of the principles of love. We became convinced by the students' interpretive insightfulness that pedagogy for self-actualization was both about "student-centered learning" as much as its liberating impact upon the teacher. Weaving together each of our stories of spiritual enrichment through studying biblical literature, as authors of *Let Love Lead*—Susie, Scott, and I experience the radical notion of pedagogical reciprocity. In this idea, students partake in what bell hooks calls in *Teaching to Transgress: Education as the Practice of Freedom* "engaged pedagogy." Her idea of it as transgressive teaching is one I have held onto as long as I have taught in the college classroom. hooks views this way of teaching—merging the mind, body, and soul—as not only holistic but "sacred." She says,

> [t]o teach the practice of freedom is a way of teaching that anyone can learn. That learning process comes easiest to those of us who teach who also believe that there is an aspect of our vocation that is sacred; who believe that our work is not merely to share information but to share in the intellectual and spiritual growth of our students. To teach in a manner that respects and cares for the souls of our students is essential if we are to provide the necessary conditions where learning can most deeply and intimately begin. (13; emphasis added)

In my teaching practice, "engaged pedagogy" is the root of that which I have been *called* to perform—soul-work for student-teacher healing in the classroom. This is sacred. *Let Love Lead* personifies this acclamation as affirmed in my collaborative labor with Scott and Susie, and this fact is clear confirmation that I am not alone in my commitment to teaching love for freedom. We three—while offering differing interpretations of biblical narratives in the light of students' reflections upon them—speak in one voice guided by the Spirit of love as the core principle foundation uniting all movements for human rights and social justice. Thus—once again, as I stated in the opening of this introduction—as its co-authors, we represent the directives of our coursework together as a provocatively compelling demonstration of pedagogical comradeship.

"So it is better to speak"—"My Soul Looks Back in Wonder"

Moreover, in *re*-citing the aim of this book in closing this introduction, I set into place feminism and womanism as the transformational cornerstones upon which *Let Love Lead* is built. It stands for radical community building in the name of Love. Thus, as we—co-authors and students—share the coursework of "The Bible of Literature," we *all* remain "[c]ommitted to survival and wholeness of entire people . . ."

Here in closing, I repeat: if anyone had ever told me that one day I would teach a college course (in a secular university setting) called "The Bible as Literature," I would not have believed it. Yet, I have learned to trust this is precisely what I was *called* to do. I have deeply embraced this fact: as a professed "black male outsider . . . teaching as a pro-feminist man," I must hold onto my faith and hope. Even in moments of self-doubt "standing upon the constant edges of decision" (a line in Audre Lorde's "A Litany for Survival")—as to whether what *and* how I teach makes a difference in the lives of my students—that profession cannot always be about a traditional "religious" demonstration of my academic expertise. I have learned, as a student and teacher of "The Bible as Literature," that openly professing a commitment to letting love lead in the classroom is, indeed, the path to freedom. When I follow the revolutionary *One* who instituted it, I know we are free to be(ing)—though "we were never meant to survive."

I still remember some of the lyrics to the black gospel song "How I Got Over" (by Clara Ward, composed in 1951):

> How I got over
> How did I make it over
> You know my soul look back and wonder
> How did I make it over...
> Going on over all these years
> You know my soul look back and wonder
> How did I make it over...

Looking back "[g]oing on over all these years"—mapping the course of my teaching path—"You know my soul look[s] back and wonder[s] [h]ow did I make it over." Throughout *Let Love Lead*, Scott, Susie and I situate our biblical interpretations in a personal context where autocritography acts simultaneously as a self-reflective *and* critical analytic writing strategy. Students in "The Bible as Literature" course must interpret biblical texts both analytically and self-reflectively through autocritography. In this discursive framework, students study the Bible—as human beings—grappling with life issues represented in it, enabling them to move toward a deeper comprehension of selfhood. Their critical analyses and personal interpretations of the Bible bring them closer to the realities of their everyday lives. This writing strategy compels students to engage the complexities of life from a biblical standpoint—related to human challenges, joys, heart-felt moments, close calls, sadness, failures, and triumphs.

By employing autocritography as a pedagogical method, I call for students to read "The Bible as Literature" as a mirror for self-reflection—attending to our intellectual, emotional, physical, social, political, and spiritual needs. We, together as students and teacher, study biblical narratives focused on ethical principles of love not only to enrich our literary interpretive skills, but to enhance our critical awareness of insightful ways to think about issues of humanity and social justice in our daily lives. The inspirational lessons we learn from narratives in the Bible become a pivotal pathway toward enabling everyone in the classroom to become potential messengers of hope for all people denied it. In this emancipatory teacher-student connection, we can actively become allies (across our differences) more in touch with sharing personal stories of inner-healing and ultimately serving as promoters of human rights in the outer world.

Works Cited

The Bible. New International Version, Biblica, 2011.

Hoeller, Susie. *Lean on Jesus: Christian Women in the Workplace.* West Bow Press, 2014.

hooks, bell. *Teaching to Transgress: Education as the Practice of Freedom.* Routledge, 1994.

Lemons, Gary, editor. *Building Womanist Coalitions: Writing and Teaching in the Spirit of Love*. University of Illinois Press, 2019.

Lemons, Gary L., and Scott Neumeister. "'Brothers of the Soul': Men Learning About and Teaching the Spirit of Feminist Solidarity." *Feminist Solidarity at the Crossroads: Intersectional Women's Studies for Transracial Alliance*, edited by Kim Marie Vaz and Gary L. Lemons, Routledge. 2012, pp. 104-118.

Walker, Alice. *In Search of Our Mothers' Gardens: Womanist Prose*. Harcourt Brace and Co., 1983.

Ward, Clara. "How I Got Over," 1951.

Part I

Where the Personal, Pedagogical, and the Biblical Merge

Many professors remain unwilling to be involved with any pedagogical practices that emphasize mutual participation between teacher and student because more time and effort are required to do this work. Yet some version of engaged pedagogy is really the only type of teaching that truly generates excitement in the classroom, that enables students and professors to feel the joy of learning.

bell hooks, Teaching to Transgress:
Education as the Practice of Freedom

Chapter 1

A (His)Story of Love: Autocritography as a Writing Sanctuary

Gary L. Lemons

Writing was the healing place where I could collect the bits and pieces, where I could put them together again. It was the sanctuary, the safe place. Yet I could not make that writing part of an overall process of self-recovery. I was able to use it constructively only as an outlet for suppressed feeling. I was ashamed that I needed this sanctuary in words. Confronting parts of my self there was humiliating. To me that confession was a process of unmasking, stripping the soul. It made me naked and vulnerable . . . When I left home to attend college I carried with me the longing to write. I knew then that I would need to work through these feelings of shame.

bell hooks, *Remembered Rapture: The Writer at Work*

Telling stories is one of the ways that we can begin the process of building community, whether inside or outside the classroom. We can share both true accounts and fictional stories in a class [or outside it] that help us understand one another. For years, I was hesitant to share personal stories. *I had been trained to believe that anyone who relied on a personal story as evidence upholding or affirming an idea could never really be a scholar and/or an intellectual, according to dominator thinking via schools of higher learning. Telling a personal story to document or frame an argument was a sign that one was not dealing in hard facts, that one was not scientific enough.* (Emphasis added)
bell hooks, *Teaching Critical Thinking: Practical Wisdom*

Write it Out…in *Print*—Ending the Silence of Fear and Shame

In my most recent writing projects—*Caught Up in the Spirit! Teaching for Womanist Liberation* and *Hooked on the Art of Love: bell hooks and My Calling for Soul-Work*—I reflect on the transformative theory and practice of black feminism and womanism. Black feminism as conceptualized in the writings of bell hooks radically changed my life. Womanism envisioned by Alice Walker would give name to my search for the history of black men who defended women's rights. This project led to my discovering writings by Frederick Douglass and W.E.B. Du Bois on this subject. I claimed these two black men as my "womanist forefathers." Without their activist legacy and that of hooks and Walker—as well as that of other black/women and men of color—I would not possess the power or will to write about the deadening ill-effects of patriarchal oppression and domination. The (her)stories of black feminist and womanist activism laid the pathway for my journey toward becoming who I am today—a "brother" in solidarity against racism, sexism, classism, *and* homophobia, in and outside black communities.

I am not ashamed to identify as a pro-feminist and *womanist* black man, outside the dictates of masculinist ideas of manhood. As a long-time student and teacher of the writings of bell hooks, I gained the discursive and vocal tools to "talk back" to patriarchy. This chapter lays the groundwork for how I employ autocritography as a strategy to teach "The Bible as Literature," and I situate its authorial, liberatory agency in relation to hooks' validation of vocality in resistance to oppression. Her book *Talking Back: Thinking Feminist, Thinking Black* gave me the emancipatory language to expose ways I had internalized male supremacy. In *Talking Back*, hooks passionately speaks out about her pathway to self-actualization as a black female in resistance to years of silence connected to punishment for speaking out about the "personal." Sharing thoughts about the difficulty that writing this text entailed, hooks says,

> [I]n this book I was doing things differently—and what was slowing me down had to do with disclosure, with what it means to reveal personal stuff. In the very construction of this

> book, *talking back...* is the explanation for my uneasiness, my reluctance. It has to do with revealing the personal... *It has to do with punishment—with all those years in childhood and on, where I was hurt for speaking truths, speaking the outrageous, speaking in my wild and witty way.* (1; emphasis added)

In hooks' autocritographical voice, with its unyielding honesty and candor, I found my sanctuary to articulate freely my struggle for self-empowerment. Through it, I started "talking back" to masculinist ideas of manhood. Because of the boldness of *Talking Back*, I gained the strength to tell my own story of pain and anger repressed for years in fear of "disclosure, with what it means to reveal personal stuff." As I illustrate in the spoken-word piece that follows, when the personal is linked to the social, political, and spiritual—not only does one possess word-power to set oneself free from internalized oppression, but also to connect to the lives of people in need liberation. I title this work—"I'm a *Pro*-Womanist Brotha [from the 'hood] with a PhD."[1]:

> So you think you somebody 'cause you *think* you know it all?
> Man, your hike up that white ("ivory") tower set you up to fall.
> Why you bein' so hard on me?
> It took me a long time to get this prestigious degree.
> Yeah, I know you about tryin' to make a high-strung impression.
> You know studyin' all that white canon-stuff led you to a state of depression.
> Brotha, why you puttin' all my inner problems out on the line?
> 'Cause you ain't neva' gon' talk about how much it hurt—so just keep lyin'.
> That what's wrong you black folk who left us for them white folk.
> What you know about our history as a people in them white books?
> You keep citin' one white author after the next 'cause of their smart looks.
> You made yo' own self disappear. The truth is you wanted to be white.
> That's the reason why you never wanted to join the black struggle fight.

Fight—man you know I don't like violence.
Yeah, I know that's exactly why you keep yo' mouth closed in silence.

I'm a *Pro*-Womanist brotha [from the 'hood] with a PhD.

You don't tell nobody white that you grew up the 'hood.
You keep that info' hidden 'cause you believe they will think you ain't no good.
You right, but why you keep tryin' to expose all that I don't want them to know.
I ain't tryin' to hurt you. I just want to help you recova from your fall.
Man, I reached the top to white academic power. I accepted the call.
The call from who? You mean when the white man who said you got in?
Yes, I didn't think I could make it, but with God's help I climbed that ladder to win.
Every step up I took I understan' that my silence was the key to gettin' that prize.
But you do kno' that yo' "A" papers were filled with lies?
Yes, I would say to him over and over again that I love readings by them.
Who the "him" you talkin' about—God in the Bible "Him?"
No, I'm talkin' about the white Man them white artists painted as the Creator.
You know that ain't right! The white slave master was known to be a real "black" hater.
I'm *Pro*-Womanist brotha [from the 'hood] with a PhD.

You bought into the idea that everything white was recorded to be right.
Yeah man, that's why I became devoted to whiteness so I wouldn't have to fight.

Brotha, that's why you had to fall 'cause you realized you was really sick.
Once again, why you got to make my stuff public? Is this a trick?
That's what they taught you to think: "black" folk the ones that take each other down.
You know there's a name for that—"internalized oppression." It will cause you to drown.
You tryin' to tell me I should put my doctoral degree in the trash?
Man, that's you talkin'—that would be self-destructive and far too rash.
I'm just tryin' to help you to recover all that you've lost.
Bein' black ain't yo' problem; it was yo' claim to *whiteness* that became the cost.
You right. I knew I had to pass the white test to get that "A".
Brotha, you kno' you had to kneel down yo' butt and pray.

I'm a *Pro*-Womanist brotha [from the 'hood] with a PhD.

What I came to realize is that I could no longa think the Divine (Wo)Man is white.
That was the root of your depression. The Spirit of Love is the Way and the Light.
Give praise to the One who picked you up and carried all you lack.
The Word never said that it is a white supremacist sin to be black.
Embracing yo' black self in all the art you create, you name it this day.
You helped me to see my blackness in a soul-filled, light way.
Right, I was tryin' to build you up to achieve another form of greatness.
Now you kno' it couldn't be done through black self-hateness.
Now you undertan' it ain't yo' college knowledge that will save you.
You got to own the beauty-*fulness* of yo' undeniable dark-skin hue.

I'm a *Pro*-Womanist brotha [from the 'hood] with a PhD.

S/he knew what s/he was doin' when s/he created black; that's a fact.
Now you got yo' stuff together; you made that lastin' womanist pact.
It prepared you to get up a take a new, life-transformin' direction.
Joinin' the struggle for social justice, you all 'bout activist self-reflection.
This betta' way of thinkin' will make yo' "higher" education a new thang.
Recoverin' the black new you helped you find a liberatin' home-place to hang.
Now you make yo' PhD. work for you and not for that slave masta's plot.
Studying blackness from as a womanist, you found a radical self you can hold onto.
In the Spirit love, I claimed a radical way of bein' for the good of all.
I was led to *TALK BACK* to patriarchal power. I received it as my Divine *call*.

What's Love Got to Do with It?

Caught up in the heartfelt energy of autocritography—as exemplified in the writings of bell hooks—I found that composing the above "spoken-word" piece provided me an artistic means to voice my experience of colonized self-erasure linked to climbing the ladder of white validation associated with the "ivory tower." At the same time, in teaching "The Bible as Literature" I have reflected upon my employment of a captivating form of writing that is pedagogically liberating—personally, politically, *and* spiritually.

In *We Real Cool: Black Men and Masculinity*, bell hooks compels black males to look within ourselves to reflect upon ways we perpetuate sexist and masculinist ideologies of manhood (in the absence of "self-love"). She clearly points out that our path to self-recovery beyond the bonds of patriarchy is to pay attention to the "visionary [soul] work of black women." Listening to their (her)stories as "teachers and comrades" offer us lessons about different ways of survival that are not about domination as a means of control:

> *Individual black males searching for new life strategies utilize in a productive way the visionary work of black women. They embrace enlightened black women as teachers and comrades. Listening to healthy emotionally mature black females is essential to black male self-recovery.* (140-141; emphasis added)

Having grown up in a home scarred with domestic violence, for so many years, I held onto the fear of writing about my mother's experience of it. Eventually, freeing myself from the fear and shame associated with it, I would write about it in *Black Male Outsider, a Memoir: Teaching as a Pro-Feminist Man*. Once it was published—as documented evidence of my struggle for self-recovery—I could not take back my words. In spite of my mother's possible rejection of my work toward self-healing, I transgressed the boundary of silence. I came to voice. I continue to write about having grown up under the cultural rule that revealing the "dirty laundry" of family secrets was heresy—particularly outside the racial confines of "the black community."

In writing about my experience of domestic violence, I not only broke the code of black censorship related to family matters, I broke the law of the (black) patriarchal father telling me that I had no right to speak about it. My mind continued to struggle against the notion that I had betrayed my father, even though he had passed away (in 1997), over ten years before *Black Male Outsider* was released. Like hooks, I remembered "all those years in childhood and on, where I was hurt for speaking truths, speaking the outrageous." Every time I have read the chapter in *Feminist Theory: From Margin to Center* "Men: Comrades in Struggle," since my father's passing, I have felt a deep sense of black feminist solidarity with hooks. I feel wholeheartedly that my voice-work in and outside the college classroom counts in black feminist struggle for social justice. Having grown up under the dominating rules of patriarchy, sexism, and misogynistic ideas of manhood—if someone had told me that as an adult black man I would become a pro-feminist/womanist "brotha' from the 'hood with a PhD."—I would have laughed it off as a bad joke. I thought feminism had nothing to do with black folks. I had bought into the masculinist stereotype that it was about white women who hated men. I have nevertheless embraced my new-found identity with love for the soul-work of Alice Walker's concept of a womanist, and I have accepted myself as an activist black male professor laboring to break my students free from internalized, oppressive myths of race, gender, class, sexuality, culture, *and* religion.

As I have expressed many times, beginning with my education in black feminist thinking as professed by bell hooks when I was a doctoral student at NYU, my writings have focused on the inspirited craft of autocritography. This creative genre, moreover, not only became a radical self-reflective meditation and life-transforming tool to free myself from the dehumanizing effects of patriarchal oppression, but also a strategic pedagogical instrument for liberating my students from its depressing illnesses. My students' autocritographical writings in "The Bible as Literature" demonstrate the self-empowering strength of biblical analysis and interpretation integrally linked to personal reflection. They exemplify healing, but I also have begun to utilize it as a revolutionary path to self-recovery.

In Love with bell hooks and Dr. Martin Luther King, Jr. Imagining an In(Spirit)ed Dialogue Between to Two of Them[2]

In highlighting the creative liveliness, rhetorical expansiveness, and spiritual enrichment associated with autocritography, I imagine an insightful visionary dialogue between hooks and Dr. Martin Luther King, Jr.—an outspoken black male, religious leader, whose calling for equal rights and social justice continues to enliven the liberatory belief that oppression will not end until the unwavering practice of love begins. As hooks proclaims in *Writing Beyond Race: Living Theory and Practice* (2013), King's radical, life-changing words still radiate with hope for social justice and human rights for *all* people.

Acting as the imaginary interviewer, having arranged this hope-full dialogue with insightful spoken-words from both Dr. King and hooks, I showcase these two as visionary advocates for *higher* education rooted in love. In memory of his life-saving message for global healing, on April 4, 2018 (fifty years after he was assassinated in 1968), I actually shared a small version of this imaginary interview/dialogue as a guest speaker at a "Black-Out" open-mike, outdoor evening event sponsored by a black student USF organization.

Gary: To begin this "make-believe" conversation, as the interviewer, I begin by asking you, bell, to share with Dr. King your thoughts you write about him in your book *Writing Beyond Race*. In the chapter "A Path Away from Race: On Spiritual Conversion"—in which you focus on Dr. King, you speak about what you believe lies at the core of Dr. King's "divine calling...to preach."

bell: "[Dr. King, you preach] with an artistry, a divinely inspired creativity, that [is] wondrous to behold. [You can] call masses of people to hear the word of God: the holy, holy, holy spirit emanating from [you is] awesome. [You are] a prophetic witness. Able to convert listeners, [you] not only [make] it possible for them to hear sacred teachings, [you invite] them to open their hearts and be transformed. [I know] one of [your] favorite scriptures, taken from the book of Romans, admonished believers, telling them: "Be not conformed to this world but be ye transformed by the renewal of your mind that you may know what the will of [G]od is" [Rom. 12.2]." (92)

Gary: bell, would you mind summarizing for the audience what you have just said to Dr. King?

bell: "[Dr. King, you, are] a [p]rophet, preacher, man of God, seeker on the path of righteousness and right action. [I think you meditate] often this scripture because [you seek] direct connection with the divine. [You know you are constantly] in need of divine guidance. Willing to critically reflect, grow, and change, [you want] only to do God's will." (92-93)

Dr. King: "The function of education is to teach one to think intensively and to think critically. Intelligence plus character—that is the goal of true education."

Gary: Dr. King, you and bell hooks, who is a noted black feminist teacher, share similar ideas about education for critical consciousness.

bell: "In my classrooms, I do not expect students to take any risks that I would not take, to share in any way that I would not share. When professors bring narratives of their experiences into classroom discussions it eliminates the possibility that we can function as all-knowing, silent interrogators. It is often productive if professors take the first risk, linking confessional narratives to academic discourses so as to show how experience can illuminate and enhance our understanding of academic material. But most professors must practice being vulnerable in the classroom, being wholly present in mind, body, and spirit." (*Teaching to Transgress* 21)

Gary: Dr. King, you and bell agree on the idea of self-reflection as an important tool that "[functions for teachers to enable students] to think intensively and to think critically." What I hear you both saying is that "true education" for students is about connecting who they want to become—inside and outside the classroom—with the power of "self-actualization." Students need "to think critically" about issues of human rights and social justice that our black ancestors began to fight for in this land for before you were born.

Dr. King: "Nothing in all the world is more dangerous than sincere ignorance and conscientious stupidity...Darkness cannot drive out darkness; only light can do that. Hate cannot drive out hate; only love can do that."

Gary: It seems like you and bell are saying that we are all living in the darkness of this day. It's driving all colored folks out of this original, skin-color-filled land? We all need to see the light of our African-rooted selves? The answer to "making this country great again" is not about hating folks of color? I believe you both are right: "Hate cannot drive out hate; only love can do that." But when racist folk at the top are in love with white-light only, won't that lead us all into the darkness of white supremacist hatred?

Dr. King: "In the End, we will remember not the words of our enemies, but the silence of our friends...The time is always right to do what is right...Faith is taking the first step even when you don't see the whole staircase."

Gary: Would the two of you agree that many black folks high up in the "ivory tower" believe intellectual power continues to be our single path to liberation as a people, while we still struggle to climb every step up its slipp'ry staircase? We have a lot of brothers and sisters with Ph.D.'s. But what does that really mean? That we passed the test of white racial assimilation? Many black folks in institutions of higher learning still wear what Paul Lawrence Dunbar called the "mask that grins and lies." Dr. King, I am not trying to be disrespectful, but what does "faith" have to do with anybody moving up on the "staircase" of success? Are you both saying that "faith" is about embracing radical ideas of education for self-transformation in order to be liberated? That not only black folk—but all folk—must take one self-reflective step at a time up that visionary staircase for *higher* education? One thing I do know is that blacks in the U.S. must remember the African mother-land where we came from and where all life was first created. Dr. King, what do you think about bell saying that education for liberation should lead us on a journey of self-actualization that is about obtaining wholeness through love—in mind, body, and Spirit?

Dr. King: We must not stop with the cultivation of a tough mind. The gospel also demands a tender heart. Toughmindedness without tenderheartedness is cold and detached...What is more tragic than to see a person who has risen to the disciplined heights of toughmindedness but has at the same time sunk to the passionless depths of hardheartedness?

> The hardhearted person never truly loves...No outpouring of love links [this person] with the mainland of humanity... We as [African Americans] must bring together toughmindedness and tenderheartedness if we are to move creatively toward the goal of freedom and justice. (*A Gift of Love*, 5, 7)

Gary: Once again, bell, in your book *Writing Beyond Race* you not only say that Dr. King's "vision of living our lives based on a love ethic is the philosophy of being and becoming that could heal our world today"—you also say that he is "[a] prophetic witness for peace, an apostle of love [that you have] given us the map...that [his] spirit lights the way, leading to the truth that love in action is the spiritual path that liberates" (97).

Dr. King, in response to bell's compelling thoughts about you being an "apostle of love...leading [us] to the truth that love in action is the spiritual path that liberates," I must say she prompts me to reflect upon the biblical mission of Jesus when he says in the book of John 8:12: "I am the light of the world. If you follow me, you won't have to walk in darkness, because you will have the light that leads to life" (*New Living Translation*). bell, your inspirational *words* about Dr. King's supernatural giftedness also reminds me of Jesus' statement about a prophet, an apostle, a teacher, a performer of miracles, and healing —related to the superlative value of love. Jesus says,

> Is everyone an apostle? Of course not. Is everyone a prophet? No. Are all teachers? Does everyone have the gift of healing? Of course not...[Let] me tell you about something else that is better than any of them! If I could speak in any language in heaven or on earth but didn't love others, I would only be making meaningless noise like a loud gong or a clanging cymbal. If I had the gift of prophecy, and if I knew all the mysteries of the future and knew everything about everything, but didn't love others, what good would I be? And if I had the gift of faith so that I could speak to a mountain and make it move, without love I would be no good to anybody. If I gave everything I have to the poor and even sacrificed my body, I could boast about it, but if I didn't love other, I would be of no value whatsoever. (*New Living Translation*, 1 Cor. 12.29-13.3)

Actually, Dr. King, I believe bell's image of you as "an apostle of love" is a contemporary model of at the activist representation of love Jesus embodied. Do you think your vision of love as spiritually healing could lead us toward a new Civil Rights Movement—particularly when you hold onto the notion that "[l]ove is the only force capable of transforming an enemy into a friend?" This is exactly what From Jesus said in the biblical book of Matthew. I repeat his statement here:

> You have heard that the law of Moses says, "Love your neighbor" and hate your enemy. But I say, love your enemies! Pray for those who persecute you! In that way, you will be acting as true children of your Father in heaven. For he gives his sunlight to both the evil and the good, and he sends rain on the just and on the unjust, too. If you love only those who love you, what good is that? Even corrupt tax collectors do that much. If you are kind only to your friends, how are you different from anyone else? (Matt. 5.43-47)

To be honest with you, Dr. King, and bell, I find it very difficult to love someone who I know quite well hates me—especially related to the ideology of white supremacy. So, Dr. King, share more with us how you believe love figures into becoming friends with someone who is publicly known for the hatred of black/people of color—for example a KKK member. Do you mean that as black/folk of color we have to be friends with white people who hate us for the color of our skin and where we come from? Before you answer, bell has something she would like to say.

bell: Like many Americans [Dr. King,] I read your slim volume of sermons *Strength to Love* [when it was] first published in 1963, to give me hope. By then it was evident that [your] vision that love was the most constructive way to create positive social change benefiting everyone was changing our culture. Motivated by our belief in a love ethic, masses of Americans worked in the late sixties and early seventies to unlearn the logic of domination and dominate culture. While militant black power struggle certainly helped bring about important social reform it also produced a culture of despair because the support for violence and imperialism was a central component of that agenda. [Your] insistence on love had provided folk an enduring message of hope. (*Writing Beyond Race* 96)

Gary: Interestingly enough, as bell points out, it was not until "the late sixties and early seventies [that Americans really began] to unlearn the logic of domination and dominate culture." As I have written, it was not until the late sixties in my hometown (Hot Springs,

Arkansas) that segregated schooling came to an end—a decade after federal troops in 1959 literally had to escort nine black students into Central High School in Little Rock, Arkansas. The troops had to protect them against the racist protest of angry white segregationists, including Orval Faubus (the state's governor at the time). My experience attending an integrated school with white students was, indeed, an eye-opening lesson in unlearn[ing] the logic of [racist] domination and [white] dominate culture." Schooling with white students and teachers—even though it did involve for me personal moments of "despair"—I learned not to give power to white supremacist racial hatred by viewing all white folk as the *enemy*. bell believes, Dr. King, that you "[understand] that many unenlightened white folks feared that if black people gained greater power [we] would violently retaliate against those who had oppressed [us], hence [your] constant insistence that black people love our enemies" (95). I absolutely agree with the two of you that "[an] insistence on love [provides all] folk an enduring message of hope."

Dr. King, you have said that, "Life's most persistent and urgent question is, 'What are you doing for others?'" Related to bell's idea that your "message of hope" is grounded in your "insistence on love" as a way to bring folk together, you have said before that "[t]he ultimate measure of a man [or woman] is not where he [or she] stands in moments of comfort and convenience, but where he [or she] stands at times of challenge and controversy." So what I hear you telling us is exactly what Jesus told the people: loving one's enemy is not about personal ease. Are you and bell saying that right now—considering the separatist and wall-building ideology that is dominating the mindset of the current U.S. white male leader—this is not a time just for folk to sit in "comfort and convenience" and that in this "[time] of challenge and controversy," all of us should move and act out our stand for social justice and human rights for all people? bell, please respond first as you have commented in *Writing Beyond Race*:

bell: Just as I turned to [your] writing [Dr. King] in my early twenties to renew my spirit, more than twenty years later I returned to this work as I experience renewed spiritual awakening, an ever-growing awareness of the transformative power of love. Like [you], I had been undergoing a conversion, not in the conventional sense of a defining moment of change, but rather conversion as a process, an ongoing project. As I studied and wrote about ending domination in all its forms it became clearer and clearer that politics rooted in a love ethic could produce lasting meaningful social change. When I traveled the nation asking folk what enabled them to be courageous in struggling for freedom—whether working to end domination of race, gender, sexuality, class, or religion—the response was love. (97)

Dr. King: Once again, I will repeat my life-changing words (as I spoke them on Aug. 28, 1963, in my "I Have a Dream" speech on the steps of the Lincoln Memorial in Washington, D.C.)—

> We must accept finite disappointment, but never lose infinite hope...I have a dream that one day [as you all may recall in] the state of Alabama, whose governor's lips [were] dripping with the words of interposition and nullification, [that the time you are living in] will be transformed into a situation where little black boys and black girls [and children of all colors] will be able to join hands with little white boys and white girls and walk together as sisters and brothers...I say to you today, my friends, that in spite of the difficulties and frustrations of the moment, I still have a dream.

Gary: Dr. King, is there anything else you would like to add to these words of hope-filled inspiration?

Dr. King: On May 5, 1966—upon accepting the Planned Parenthood Federation of America's Margaret Sanger Award—I spoke these words: "Together we can and should unite our strength for the wise preservation, not of races in general, but of the one race we all constitute—the human race."

Gary: You and bell think so much alike in your call to *let love lead* us in the spiritual path toward healing and human(e) solidarity. Dr. King, I believe bell echoes exactly your vision of struggle for unity and wholeness—eradicating ideas of separatism as she restates your call for global alliance against domination:

bell: Aware of the need to end domination globally [in the past, Dr. King, you] cautioned: "In an effort to achieve freedom in America, Asia, and Africa we must not try to leap from a position of disadvantage to one of advantage, thus subverting justice. We must seek democracy and not the substitution of one tyranny for another...God is not interested merely in the freedom of black men, and brown men, and yellow men; God is interested in the freedom of the whole human race." [Your] vision of redemptive love [holds] the promise that both oppressor and oppressed could recover from the wounds of dehumanization. (*Writing Beyond Race* 96)

Gary: Dr. King, while I find your expression of God's vision of "freedom of the whole human race" inspiring, I have always been drawn to bell's ideas of "redemptive love" based on her inspirited viewpoint as black feminist. bell, your critique of patriarchal oppression and domination as always brought to our attention the intersecting relationship between race, gender, class, and sexuality. While you have spoken repeatedly about the power of alliance-building across differences, you have specifically stated that the promise of a radical movement for black political solidarity will only come when black men begin to imagine ourselves free from "male"-centered thinking. In *We Real Cool: Black Men and Masculinity* you say, "Black men who stand against sexism, who choose to be feminist in their thinking and action model a healing masculinity for all black men" (132). I think this is true for all men—white and of color—who support God's inclusive vision of love for social justice embracing *all* folk. As you say, Dr. King, "we must not try to leap from a position of disadvantage to one of advantage, thus subverting justice [and that we] must seek democracy and not the substitution of one tyranny for another."

    bell, just for a moment I want to return to a comment about "despair" you made earlier connected to the continuation of black folk's protests for social justice in the 1960s and '70s that reaffirms Dr. King's point here. You state in *Writing Beyond Race* that— "While militant black power struggle certainly helped bring about important social reforms it also produced a culture of despair because the support for violence and imperialism was a central component of that agenda" (96). While it was important for blacks to speak and act out against the perpetuation of white supremacy, as you have stated Dr. King that it was not in our best interest to promote violence

against violence. In this regard, I want to underscore the message, bell, that you speak to black men in *We Real Cool,* particularly related to issues of black male power.
bell: Visions of black men as healers, able to nurture life, are the representations of black masculinity that "keep it real" for they offer the vision of what is possible, a hint of the spirit that is alive and well in the black male collective being, ready to be reborn. They take our minds and hearts away from images of black males who have known soul murder and speak to us of resurrection, of a word in the making where all is well with black men's souls, where they are free and made whole. (132)
Gary: bell, your words to black men—like those, Dr. King, you speak to all humankind—are indeed messages of hope, healing, and restoration. It is so true that "images of black males who have known soul murder" continue to confront our communities daily in the physical (mis)treatment of our bodies—inextricably linked the life-execution of our souls under murdering of white supremacy. Yet, bell, you say that our souls in the "visions of black men as healers, able to nurture life [that which] is possible, a hint of the spirit that is alive and well in the black male collective being, ready to be reborn." In the Spirit of love we "are [set] free and male whole."

bell, I say to you and Dr. King this conversation with the two of you is personally life-transforming. Thinking about that "soul murder" as it relates to masculinist notions of black male power is a form of black phallic enslavement that keeps us bound to patriarchal ideas of manhood. Phallic authority will never be a loving representation of black manhood, especially when black males desire it as the only viable expression of our manhood in a culture of white supremacist heterosexism. Having embraced your loved-based, spiritual visions of black/human liberation, I can boldly say that I am a black man committed to speaking out in coalitional struggles for social justice in support of all men *and* women—especially in the U.S.—who are "x'd-out" of the "American dream". bell, you write in your book *Talking Back: Thinking, Thinking Black* that "[s]peaking becomes both a way to engage in active self-transformation and a rite of passage where one moves from object to being subject. Only as subjects can we speak. As objects, we remain voiceless-our beings defined and interpreted by others" (12).

I must say, Dr. King, that your continued boldness in actively voicing resistance to oppressive power is liberatory. In *Writing Beyond Race,* bell pointedly writes about your decision to speak against the U.S. in war with Vietnam. With surety, she says, "It took many days and nights of prayer and soul searching, [asking yourself] 'how can I say I worship a god of love and support war' to transform [your] consciousness and [your] actions" (94). bell, you further reference Dr. King's speech "A Time to Break Silence" delivered in 1967 stating that "[c]onfessing that it [could not have been an] easy decision to stand against the nation and oppose war" (94). As I read these words, Dr. King, I found your courage to speak out amazingly inspiring. You said, as bell quotes: "Some of us who have already begun to break the silence of the night have found that the calling to speak is often a vocation of agony, but we must speak" (94). Moreover, underscoring your belief in the life-saving power of love, she cites words from another one of your speeches titled "Where Do We Go from Here?"

Dr. King: I have decided to love. If you are seeking the highest good, I think you can find it through love. And the beautiful thing is that we are moving against wrong when we do it, because John was right, God is love. [S/he] who hates does not know God, but [s/]he who has love has the key that unlocks the door to the meaning of ultimate reality. (95)

Gary: Dr. King, as we conclude this inspirational dialogue between you and bell, I want to re-emphasize how clearly her message of black male soul-resurrection is integrally connected to your vision of love devoted to the liberation of the entire human race. In fact, in *Teaching Community: A Pedagogy of Hope,* bell talks about your having "imagined a 'beloved community,' conceptualizing a world where people would bond on the basis of shared humanness." bell says that "[your] vision remains...[that] you "taught that the simple act of coming together would strengthen community...that unlearning racism would require a change in both thinking and action . . . " (35-36). Would you repeat once again your thought about this?

Dr. King: "Together we can and should unite our strength for the wise preservation, not of races in general, but of the one race we all constitute—the human race."[1]

Gary: In closing, I thank you and bell hooks for this dialogue. In this day and time of trouble, we need to hear your voice continuing to "talk back" against the fatal ills of domination and separatism in the U.S.

Love Beyond Race

In hindsight, every time I drive on the street in Tampa, Florida, named after Dr. King, I think about the deep impression he made on the life and writings of bell hooks related to her vision of art and love. She invites readers of *Writing Beyond Race* to contemplate the power of love as the critical motivating force in struggles for social justice, remarking,

> Contemplating the factors that lead people to struggle for justice and strive to build community has led me to think critically about the place of love. Whether the issue is ending racism, sexism, homophobia, or class elitism, when I interview folks about what leads them to overcome dominator thinking and action they invariably speak about love, about learning acceptance of difference from someone they care about. (1)

However, for me, her comments about Dr. King's impact upon her keeps his voice alive in my mind, body, *and* soul. It is not by chance or luck that I would imagine speaking to Dr. King—in light of hooks' heartfelt thoughts about his messages of hope. Concluding her chapter "A Path Away from Race: On Spiritual Conversation," her last words about him are inspirationally healing and radically liberatory:

> King's insistence on love ha[s] provided folk an enduring message of hope...Just as I turned to King's writing in my early twenties to renew my spirit, more than twenty years later I returned to this work as I experienced renewed spiritual awakening, an ever-growing awareness of the transformative power of love. Like King, I had been undergoing a conversion,

not in the conventional sense of a defining moment of change, but rather conversion as a process, an ongoing project. As I studied and wrote about ending domination in all its forms it became clearer and clearer that politics rooted in a love ethic could produce lasting meaningful social change. When I traveled the nation asking folk what enable them to be courageous in struggling for freedom—whether working to end domination of race, gender, sexuality, class, or religion—the response was love…A prophetic witness for peace, an apostle of love, Martin Luther King has given us the map. His spirit lights the way, leading to the truth that love in action is the spiritual path that liberates. (97)

Note
[1] This work also appears in *Hooked on the Art of Love: bell hooks and My Calling for Soul-Work,* Ed. Gary L. Lemons.

[2] In this "imagined dialogue," I selected quotes by Dr. King from KEEPINSPIRING.ME, "123 of the Most Powerful Martin Luther King Jr. Quotes Ever."

Works Cited

The Bible. New Living Translation, Tyndale House, 2016.
hooks, bell. *Feminist Theory: From Margin to Center.* South End Press, 1984.
---. *Talking Back: Thinking Feminist, Thinking Black.* South End Press, 1989.
---. *Teaching Community: A Pedagogy of Hope.* Routledge, 2003.
---. *We Real Cool: Black Men and Masculinity.* Routledge, 2004.
---. *Writing Beyond Race: Living Theory and Practice.* Routledge, 2013.
King, Martin Luther, Jr. *A Gift of Love: Sermons from Strength to Love and Other Preachings.* Beacon Press, 1963.
---. *Strength to Love.* William Collins Sons and Co, 1963.
Lemons, Gary L. *Caught Up in the Spirit! Teaching for Womanist Liberation.* Nova Science Publishers Inc., 2017.

---. *Womanist Forefathers: Frederick Douglass and W.E.B. Du Bois.* State University of New York Press, 2009.

Chapter 2

In Love with Teaching "The Bible as Literature" (As a Pro-Womanist Black Man)

Gary L. Lemons

> THERE IS A QUIET REVOLUTION GOING ON in the study of the Bible. At its center is a growing awareness that the Bible is a work of literature and that the methods of literary scholarship are a necessary part of any complete study of the Bible. There are two sides to the movement: literary scholars are showing increasing interest in applying their methods to the Bible, and Bible scholars are calling for a literary approach. (11)
>
> <div align="right">Leland Ryken, <i>To Read the Bible as Literature . . . and get more out of it</i></div>

> Sometimes students mistakenly associate literature more with school than with life. Accustomed to reading it in order to write a paper or pass an examination, students may perceive such reading as a chore instead of a pleasurable opportunity, something considerably less important than studying for the 'practical' that prepare them for a career. *The study of literature, however, is also practical because it engages you in the kinds of problem solving important in a variety of fields, from philosophy to science and technology. The interpretation of literary texts requires you to deal with uncertainties, value judgments, and emotions; these are unavoidable in aspects of life* (emphasis added).
>
> <div align="right">Michael Meyer, <i>Literature to Go</i></div>

For years since finishing my coursework in literature—from undergraduate through graduate school—I have said to myself, "I am the black/teacher of color I never had." My study of literature in majority white institutions of higher learning never taught me to embrace myself as a black "English" major. In fact, if anything, I came to think of myself in the confines of the dominant cultural imperatives perpetuated in *whiteness*. From this point, for me, studying literature was not about what Michael Myers articulates as:

> [t]he study of literature [that is about the] practical [as] it engages you in the kinds of problem solving important in a variety of fields, from philosophy to science and technology. The interpretation of literary texts requires you to deal with uncertainties, value judgments, and emotions; these are unavoidable in aspects of life. (4)

Rather than thinking about how literature related to "problem-solving" in my everyday life, I was taught to focus on acquiring expertise in literary criticism—connected to wealth of my knowledge of "secondary sources" in my conceptual textual interpretation. Also, considering the fact that from my study of literature in courses from undergraduate through graduate school, I had not been required to read texts by any writers of color—black or otherwise—I simply believed that literary studies was the domain of the dominant culture.

As a person of color entering a canonical study of literature rooted in whiteness, I had to erase my cultural ties to "black" identity to be accepted as a legitimate literary scholar in the "ivory" tower. Michael Meyer's notion of literature related to real life problem-solving sounds, in theory, full of practical possibilities. However, before I could contemplate the idea of literary study as a critical location "[requiring me] to [personally] deal with uncertainties, value judgments, and emotions [as] unavoidable in aspects of life," I had to come to consciousness about ways I had been taught to erase a first-person ("I") approach to textual interpretation. What difference did my racial identity as a reader of color make in my interpretation of the lives of characters whose racial identity in texts I was assigned to read was hardly ever revealed? While whiteness was invisible in the literary texts I studied, I would come to understand through *self-*exposure to black feminist and womanist memoir-based writings I have read and researched (once again outside of any formal training in my literary studies) that the first person I needed to recognize in my study of literature was *myself.*

In Alice Walker's "Spirit" of love, I teach the Bible in a literary context that lends liberating strength to my pedagogical approach. I seek to heighten students' spiritual awareness through self-reflection by employing this perspective. As I discuss in the Introduction and the opening chapter to *Let Love Lead,* I intentionally teach autocritography to enable my students to personally reflect upon the biblical narratives they analytically engage. Students comprehend loving one's "neighbor" as a manifestation of activist soul-work by reading and writing about representations of love as unifying, redemptive, and literally life-saving in folks' lives recorded in the Bible.

Storytelling in a Biblical con(Text)
Community Building in Acts of Love

Telling stories is one of the ways that we can begin the process of building community, whether inside or outside the classroom. We can share both true accounts and fictional stories in a class [or outside it] that help us understand one another. For years, I was hesitant to share personal stories. *I had been trained to believe that anyone who relied on a personal story as evidence upholding or affirming an idea could never really be a scholar and/or an intellectual, according to dominator thinking via schools of higher learning. Telling a personal story to document or frame an argument was a sign that one was not dealing in hard facts, that one was not scientific enough.* (emphasis added)
bell hooks, *Teaching Critical Thinking: Practical Wisdom*

In my study of and teaching "The Bible as Literature," I must bring all the bits and pieces of my spiritual journey to its textual representation. I openly write in this chapter (as in the opening one, having been "caught up in the Spirit!—teaching for womanist liberation") to give voice to the complexities of the intersection between my profession as "professor of English" and my spiritual calling to teach biblical literature. Under the proto-"call" of this formal title, I teach the course in opposition to the deadening roots of white supremacist capitalist patriarchal colonization. I teach against religiosity that is rooted in racist, sexist, and homophobic ideas of human *being* and integrate into my instruction my own struggle in resistance to ways I internalized patriarchal religious dogma. Strategically, this point of view boldly allows me to cross borders of difference, deconstructing walls of separation to create bridges of personal, social, political, *and* spiritual solidarity for human rights and social justice.

While the concept of border-crossing was the center point of my pedagogical approach when first teaching the course in 2014, I must truthfully confess that I kept silent about the liberatory ways writings by black/feminists and womanists of color had impacted my pedagogical practice. I still required students to read two radically progressive texts to ground our study of the Bible. In one of them, *128 of the Greatest Stories from the Bible* (2005)—co-authors Daniel Elton Harmon, Colleen Reece, and Julie Reece-DeMarco state within their introduction:

> Fathers and mothers, husbands and wives, sons and daughters—the men and women of the Bible each have a story to tell. And between the covers of this book you'll find the intriguing stories of more than one hundred individuals, in order of their appearance in the Bible. From Adam and Eve to Lydia, Mark, Peter, and Paul, these stories will inspire and encourage you as you live out your own story. (11)

The other text I believed that would significantly complement students' analytical standpoint was *How to Read the Bible as Literature…and get more out of it* (1984) by Leland Ryken. In the book's first chapter title, he asks "Is the Bible Literature?" I quote Ryken's answer to his own question as he begins by saying, "THERE IS A QUIET REVOLUTION GOING ON in the study of the Bible." While this statement was published in his book more than three decades before I began teaching the course, it pointedly resonates in multiple ways with my approach to the course. At the same time, in fear that many of the students would drop it, I overtly resisted this moment as a critical opportunity to *politicize* its literary context—interconnected with the loving "Spirit" of a womanist. I address this fear of self-blind-sightedness in more detail in the next chapter as I stand with my focus on the life and work(s) of Jesus—at the intersection of feminism and womanism.

I agree foremost with Ryken's assertion that "the Bible is a work of literature and that the methods of literary scholarship are a necessary part of any complete study of the Bible," even in the face of my internalized fear of being too radical. Secondly, as an African American literary scholar, I remained interested in "applying my [autocritographical writing approach] to the Bible." I believe that this is a revolutionary methodology that would enhance students' literary interpretation of biblical narratives. Having shared this perspective in the Introduction to *Let Love Lead*, in my first time teaching the course, I would find the incorporation of personal interpretation linked to self-reflection as a writing tool to be significantly life-changing for my students *and* for me as their teacher.

Intrigued by how well Ryken's approach interconnects with my writing strategy for students' work in the course, I continue to reference his revolutionary standpoint. I read it as further affirmation of my literary perspective supporting students' self-reflective, "experiential, extra-intellectual" writing related to biblical studies. Ryken goes on to reveal,

> A number of ingredients make up this new approach to the Bible: a concern with the literary genres of the Bible; a new willingness to treat biblical texts as finished wholes instead of as a patchwork of fragments; a focus on the Bible as it now stands instead of conducting excavations in the redaction (editing) process behind the text; *an inclination to use literary instead of traditional theological terms to discuss the stories and poems of the Bible; an appreciation for the artistry of the Bible; a sensitivity to the experiential, extra-intellectual (more-than-ideational) dimension of the Bible.* (11; emphasis added)

I include what Ryken calls the "ingredients [that] make up this new approach to the Bible" by my method of teaching the course. I compel students to examine the poetics of texts composed in the Bible ultimately to help us understand ourselves as human beings, grappling with life issues in our journey toward a deeper comprehension of selfhood. In this manner, our critical analyses and interpretations of the Bible brings us closer to the realities of life—its challenges, joys, heart-felt moments, close calls, sadness, beauty, ugliness, failures, and triumphs. In this way, we read the Bible as literature as a mirror to life—attending to our intellectual, emotional, physical, social, and spiritual needs. Together we interpret the Bible as a pivotal pathway to critical engagement in and beyond the classroom—to our daily lives. Writers of the Bible become, in this way, messengers of hope and freedom, inspiring us to be more in touch with our inner selves in the outer world.

One of the continual themes my co-authors/editors and I have repeatedly observed surfacing in students' writings documented in this case-study is the evidential, biblical power of love as a mode of intervention toward the resolution of conflict—between individuals, families, cultures, and/or nations. Here is precisely where I believe teaching "The Bible as Literature" in an academic context grounded in an inspirational writing strategy such as autocritography enables students to move between the boundaries between the intellectual and the spiritual. Interestingly enough, when I began to examine the vision of global citizenship at the university where I teach, I could see a possible connection between the two frames of reference. The possibility for a perspective of education centered on a politics of human consideration based on love resonates between these two frameworks.

As an overarching framework for the *Let Love Lead* student writing case-study, I take a closer look at the University of South Florida's "Global Citizens Project" (initiated in 2016). The Project centers on three areas of skill-related competencies, as the university "envisions itself as a global research university . . . to prepare 'well-educated and highly skilled global citizens through [its] continuing commitment to student success'...." The areas are globally connected to one's "awareness," "responsibility," and "participation." As the only black male professor in the English department at the university for nearly a decade, I perceive a significant link between these competencies and my approach to teaching "The Bible as Literature." I teach students in the course transnational *awareness*, *responsibility*, and active *participation* related to struggles for social justice—motivated by the biblical texts they read. Based on the skill-related competencies above, I believe the university's Global Citizens Project articulates a clear set of learning outcomes which complement my motivation for teaching the course. I reference the Project's "learning outcomes" (quoted directly as they appear on the university's website[1]):

Affective/Cognitive [i.e. emotional]
- Self-Awareness in regard to values, beliefs, attitudes, and behaviors
- Willingness to make choices that reflect concerns for others
- Practice based on professed values, beliefs, and attitudes that express concerns for others

Cognitive [knowledge acquired through thought process]
- Knowledge of global/cultural systems and issues
- Analysis of global/cultural interrelationships and interdependences across place and time
- Synthesis of context-appropriate actions to address complex issues and/or unfamiliar situations

The learning outcomes above not only characterize the interweaving of the affective and the cognitive that we attempt to show in *Let Love Lead*, they help identify the healing and life-transforming work students collectively produced in their autocritographical writings.

Toward a Transformative Course of Action

In my longstanding commitment to ways of teaching aimed to end all forms of systemic and institutionalized oppression and domination, I understood that a demonstration of academic excellence is simply not enough to create a vision of "global citizenship." My vision of higher education in college courses I teach is grounded in pro-feminist and womanist thought. As such, in teaching this course, I impress upon my students the value of human life situated across differences of race/ethnicity, gender, class, and sexuality. What I mean here is that we all must be critically aware of ways we have been particularly colonized religiously in the West to think of ourselves as superior, judging "Other" cultures/peoples as less than. My co-authors and I agree that students, being guided by a compassionate love and care for all humanity in biblical literature, must be challenged to measure their intellectual growth in the course by an inner drive to demonstrate outwardly the compelling nature of soul-work for global human rights.

The movement from theory to practice, from the university classroom to the "living" rooms of our everyday lives, actively illustrates the empowering aspects of studying the Bible in a context of human compassion—celebrating the divinity of our differences, rather than reducing them to legalistic notions of acceptance. Representing a collective vision of global citizenship that is inclusive, autocritography in this book advances the cause of human bridge-building for a world-wide community founded upon principals and rooted in the Spirit of love. I call this *soul-work*. Integrating spiritual insight into the study of biblical poetic narration requires that students merge the skill of analytical interpretation with that of introspective self-analysis. It provides students an intellectual pathway to reflect upon ways the Bible offers invaluable and life-sustaining lessons for illustrating the power of love as a critical means to justify activism against global systems of injustice. In this way, the course actively serves to transport what students learn in the classroom (from simply obtaining an "A" final grade)—to a higher/deeper place of self-fulfillment calling them to act out lessons of love in their daily lives. Students therefore hold themselves personally accountable for giving thought-provoking credence to the New Testament calling us to "love our neighbors as ourselves" (Mark 12.31).

The texts students have written in the course, as I have taught it, clearly demonstrate that *loving* is about a complex human endeavor that begins with the self. I call for students to engage its complexity to become critically aware of struggles for social justice. In a womanist study of "The Bible as Literature," there is "A QUIET REVOLUTION GOING ON." Moving on from simply theorizing love into a transformative practice of it through lessons about resistance to oppression and domination that bridge concepts of feminism and womanism is, indeed, revolutionary. In the practice of letting love lead, teacher and students are transported to a visionary site of liberation. It is the home of the supernatural. The move away from the preeminence of "theological terms to discuss the stories and poems of the Bible" to "an appreciation for the artistry of the Bible" radically positions autocritography as an innovative pedagogical approach. It artistically resonates with a much deeper comprehension of the creativity of a love-centered learning environment. Moreover, in its restorative reliance on the art of storytelling, it emanates with "a sensitivity to the experiential, extra-intellectual (more-than-ideational) dimensions of the Bible."

I chose Ryken's *How to Read the Bible as Literature* the first time I taught "The Bible as Literature" as a clear affirmation of that which I had been called to do—even though a year later the university bookstore informed me that it was out of print. Nevertheless, I would always remember his saying that "…above all, the new attitude toward the Bible involves a growing awareness that literature expresses truth in its own way, different from ordinary propositional discourse" (11). Rather than proposing to my students a way of studying the Bible that inscribed a *discourse* of patriarchal, white supremacist, religious, fundamentalist dogmatism—one that I had spent most of my life in bondage under its enslavement—I have labored to set them free. Under the far-seeing tutelage of womanism—even though I did not conceptually foreground its "universal(ist)" appeal when first teaching the course, I have come to believe that its guidance has led me to remember my ancestral folklore to comprehend its liberatory legacy in my approach to teaching the Bible.

With knowledge of the historical narratives of black liberation in the U.S., my pedagogy grounded in a politics of love-centered freedom carries forward Walker's notion of a womanist as being

"Traditionally capable, as in: 'Mama, I'm walking to Canada and I'm taking you and a bunch of other slaves with me.' Reply: 'It wouldn't be the first time.'" My pedagogical approach—as collaboratively articulated with Scott and Susie—is that advocacy for social justice is integrally linked to "love your neighbor as yourself." I have read twenty-eight English Bible translations of this spiritual imperative. With insignificant variation in all of them, the message is clearly the same. As "brothers" and "sister" determined to "let love lead," our soulful, collaborative labor would enrich in this book. As I have written in its Preface, when Scott (who refers to me as "BOS," short for "brother of the soul") first suggested this phrase to me as the title of our book project, I immediately knew it was to be. When Susie (a well-published author) came as a guest-speaker in two semester offerings of my course, she gave each student (a total of thirty) in each class a (free of charge) copy of her book *Lean on Jesus: Christian Women in the Workplace* (2014). Before the end of each course, after Susie's talk(s), during the semester I not only assigned students to read her book, I also asked them write about at least three chapters from it that spoke personally to address their thoughts about female job-related treatment. In alignment with Scott's suggestion for our book title and my suggestion that our pedagogical course study focus on the theme of love as represented in students' self-reflective writings, Susie put forth the idea of the biblical/ethical principal of love for one's "neighbor" as a compelling source for a literary, interpretive perspective.

   We three authors are committed to this scriptural line of thinking as communal and liberating, and so there is a crucial question that we must address—how can you love someone when you possess no love for yourself? Every single time I have taught "The Bible as Literature," this is a question my students pose. I respond to it by suggesting that openly engaging issues of self-lovelessness is—first and foremost—key to comprehending the transformative agency in studying the thematic representation of love in biblical narratives. This is why I offer autocritography as a discursive form of self-expression for restorative healing. In other words, I tell my students to study Bible stories by "writing about them from the inside out." It is a process that interprets factuality from a standpoint of critical consciousness, interconnected to self-reflection.

Teaching Writing as Soul-Work

I maintained in the Introduction to *Let Love Lead* that this book demonstrates autocritography as a life-transforming writing tool for the student and teacher. Not only does it enhance the intellectual capacity to engage biblical texts, it simultaneously deepens the level of interpretative analysis intertwined with critical self-reflection. I teach this writing mode as a healing pathway for soul-work. Through this approach, students explore the study of "The Bible as Literature" to become more consciously aware of ways not only to comprehend more fully the interrelationship between personal and the spiritual. I also make it well known to my students that their differences (of culture, gender, racial/ethnic, sexuality, generation, abilities, disciplinary studies, *and* ideas of religion) occupy a defining place in autocritography. The challenge in teaching biblical literature in this discursive format is quite compelling when students have been traditionally taught to write textual analysis in "third-person" formality.

Quite often in the beginning of the semester, most of my students resist incorporating their individual experiences into their analytical interpretation of the Bible—especially related to issues of love. I completely understand this from a cultural standpoint, as I was always told particularly as member of the working-class "black community"—"Don't put your dirty laundry out on the line." In *All About Love: New Visions*, bell hooks says,

> I have given and heard testimony about the mounting lovelessness in our culture and the fear it strikes in everyone's heart. This despair about love is coupled with a callous cynicism that frowns upon any suggestion that love is as important as work, as crucial to our survival as a nation as the drive to succeed. Awesomely, our nation, like no other in the world, is a culture driven by the quest to love (it's the theme of our movies, music, literature) even as it offers so little

opportunity for us to understand love's meaning or to know how to realize love in word and deed...However, this love often eludes us. And we spend a lifetime undoing the damage caused by cruelty, neglect, and all manner of lovelessness experienced in our families of origin and in relationships where we simply did not know what to do. *Only love can heal the wounds of the past.* (xxviii; emphasis added)

What I have learned in my life as a black man and what I teach students in "The Bible as Literature" is that repression of feelings related to "damage caused by cruelty, neglect, and all manner of lovelessness" is deadening in body, mind, and soul. Not dealing with one's feelings and/or experiences of lovelessness, while sowing an infestation of inner "dis-ease", will ultimately manifest itself outside in the infectious *disease* of hatred. As hooks continues to say in *All About Love*, "...the intensity of our woundedness often leads to a closing of the heart, making it impossible for us to give or receive the love that is given to us" (xxviii-xxix). Do I want to share with my students the woundedness of my past that I continue to struggle with emotionally? My initial answer—"No!" Yet I now comprehend in bell hooks' ideas of "engaged pedagogy" this concept of resisting traditional academic notions of separation between the intellectual and the spiritual. Recounting her college experience in *Teaching to Transgress: Education as the Practice of Freedom*, she notes,

> It was the actual experience of college that . . . there I was made to feel as though I was terribly naïve about "the profession." I learned that far from being self-actualized, the university was seen more as a haven for those who are smart in book knowledge but who might be otherwise unfit for social interaction. Luckily, during my undergraduate years I began to make a distinction between the practice of being an intellectual/teacher and one's role as a member of the academic profession.
>
> It was difficult to maintain fidelity to the idea of the intellectual as someone who sought to be whole—well-grounded in a context where there was little emphasis on spiritual well-being, on care of the soul. Indeed, the

objectification of the teacher within bourgeois educational structures seemed to denigrate notions of wholeness and uphold the idea of a mind/body split, one that promotes and supports compartmentalization. (16)

hooks goes on to underscore the limitations of "bourgeois educational structures" that reinforce "the idea of a mind/body split" through "compartmentalization." In merging pedagogical practice(s) with attention to crossing boundaries between the intellectual and the spiritual, I facilitate community building in the classroom. I labor to make it a place of comfort. In it, writing self-reflectively is an open discursive form for personal storytelling, shamelessly composed of "ups and downs". How exactly is one to share life experiences in a public classroom setting, where doing so may cause one to be judged by classmates *and* professor? It most often has to do with fear of being seen as incapable, powerless, unqualified, helpless, weak, low-grade, too vulnerable (especially if male-identified), dependent, mediocre, unknowledgeable, ineffective, defenseless, inferior, low-class, imperfect, shoddy, too hoody…and the list goes on and on.

I spend most of the semester, each time I teach "The Bible as Literature," challenging my students to share openly the writings they produce weekly based on the biblical readings assigned. A central question for many of them is—what impact will candidly reading their autocritographies in class have on each other? Professing my own reservations about sharing personal experiences that expose feelings of self-doubt, I challenge myself to lead the way for students to embrace an attitude of shamelessness. Especially in the context of possibly generating self-negating feelings related to narratives of human failure as portrayed in the Bible, I tell my students that "we have nothing to be ashamed about" that which we choose to tell each other about life-challenging events we (never desired to) experience. Writing *and* publicly telling my life-stories as a "black male outsider" and "survivor"—confronting varying forms of adversity—I have found "The Bible as Literature" a life-saving source for my will to teach and live in active alliance with the Spirit of love.

I find that as my students become more confident in telling their own stories of survival, the critical analysis and interpretive depth of the biblical writings they engage becomes stronger but, even more importantly, life-changing. In studying and writing about the lives of biblical figures, not only do my students explore the healing effects of love, but they come to realize it as an emancipatory force—for those who embrace it as the writers of the Bible documented it. I tell my students that in a global context while contemporary narratives of human experience may appear to be more complex and complicated than those recorded in biblical times, many issues—particularly those connected to conflicts rooted in nation-state affiliations, territorial borders, and immigration status—have not changed. Many of my students studying "The Bible as Literature" have written about how today's issues surrounding racism, sexism, homophobia, and ableism mirror ways folk in biblical narratives were perpetually (*mis*)treated. Yet I make the case that love remained a unifying element of possible bridge-building connection in their stories.

One of the continual themes my co-authors and I have repeatedly observed surfacing in students' writings documented in this study is the evidential, biblical power of love as a mode of intervention toward to resolution of conflict—between individuals, families, cultures, and/or nations. Here is precisely where I believe teaching the biblical narratives in an academic context grounded in critical self-reflection helps students to move between the boundaries of the intellectual and the spiritual. Interestingly enough, when I began to examine USF's vision of "global citizenship," I could see a possible connection between the two frames of reference.

Activating Soul-Work: A Liberating Path to Hope

My longstanding commitment to ways of teaching aimed to end all forms of systemic and institutionalized oppression and domination has allowed me to understand that a demonstration of academic excellence is simply not enough to create a vision of global citizenship. As citizens of this world, we all must be critically aware of ways we have been particularly colonized religiously in the West to think of ourselves as superior, judging "Other" cultures/peoples as less than. Being guided by a compassionate love and care for all humanity, students and teacher in the study of the Bible should be challenged to measure their intellectual growth by an inner drive to show outwardly the compelling nature of soul-work for human rights globally.

The movement from theory to practice, from the university classroom to the "living" rooms of our everyday lives, actively illustrates the power of studying the Bible from a politicized context of human compassion—celebrating the divinity of our differences, rather than reducing them to legalistic notions of acceptance. This form of course study represents a collective vision of global citizenry that is inclusive, advancing the cause of human bridge-building for world-wide community healing. I believe this is the essential principle of soul-work.

Incorporating soul-work into "The Bible as Literature," as I teach it, guides me and students onto a course of action requiring us to "let love lead." This principle course objective requires that students and teacher hold each other personally accountable for giving credence to the Bible calling us to "love [our] neighbors as [ourselves]" (Mark 12.31). I understand clearly in continuing to teach this course that there is a profound interconnection between the personal, political, pedagogical, *and* spiritual. As the course teacher, I continue to be inspired by biblical *her*stories and *his*tories of women and men in their struggle to overcome systemic and institutionalized forms oppression and domination. Jesus in particular was a revolutionary embodiment of love in resistance to misguided practices of religion and government, and he showed the way for universal healing from them. Laboring in the college classroom to foreground themes of survival—through love as exemplified in his words and actions—I teach about his life and work(s) to illustrate how our lives can be transformed in mind, body, and soul.

Committed to teaching the Bible in a "revolutionary" context, I am no longer blind-sided by the fear that students will refuse to join me on a path of hope to *higher* education. I must continue to boldly express my radical take on the visionary healing power of love. In *All About Love: New Visions*, bell hooks says, "[W]e want to live in a culture where love can flourish. We yearn to end the lovelessness that is so pervasive in our society" (xxix). Having instructed in a university setting for more than two decades, I love teaching literature to change the lives of my students. I profess time and time again that my purpose in the college classroom is to compel students to take what they learn in it into to the *living* rooms of their everyday lives. As Leland Ryken suggests in the idea that there is a "movement" taking place in what he perceives as a joining of literary scholars who see the Bible as literature and those biblical scholars who have begun to agree with them—this border-crossing represents "a quiet revolution going on in the study of the Bible."

When Jesus Enters the Conversation, Love Reigns

I share in Chapter 1 that, having grown up as a "church boy," I am still captivated by biblical stories. With this in mind, when I began teaching "The Bible as Literature"—rather than choosing a traditional version of the Bible to study—I chose *128 of the Greatest Stories from the Bible* (as retold/interpreted by its editors) as the primary course text because it is quite conducive to a revolutionary study of biblical narratives. While the book's co-editors conceptualized a title for each "short story" included in the collection, at the end of each one, they list a scriptural citation. Of all the 128 stories I assigned for students to read during the semester, the ones that most drew my interest were focused on Jesus and his relationship with women, men, children, the disabled, and his resistance to religious dogmatism and governmental legalism. In the next chapter, I *re*-create an autocritographic student-teacher dialogue to illustrate the transformative, life-saving power of love enacted by Jesus.

Moreover, this conversation functions to show the unwavering commitment to love that Jesus embodied in his teachings and actions against systemic and institutionalized notions of religion. Exemplified in the supernatural ways he healed folk in his word *and* deed, this dialogue dramatically foregrounds the radical nature of Jesus' liberating "good news" of human salvation. The students and I, conversing about Jesus' life story as it unfolds in the Bible, bear witness to his revolutionary activity. We combine our stories of survival with his story-telling methodology, and together we become living testaments. In sum, we enact a dialogue engaging the mind, body, and soul to exhibit Jesus as the life-transforming *messenger* of hope spoken *and* acted out in love for wholeness, unity, and inclusion of all the people. When Jesus enters the conversation, love reigns.

In my mission to teach the life and works of Jesus in a biblical narrative context, I foreground the stories of his deliverance of folk from varying forms of dis-abilities (in mind, body and spirit)—against institutionalized patriarchal, religious, social, and political systems of legalized injustices. When I first began teaching "The Bible as Literature" in 2014, after choosing *128 of the Greatest Stories from the Bible*, I discovered Ryken's *How to Read the Bible as Literature* in my research for an incisive secondary source to this book. Joined together, both texts served to fulfill my initial course objectives and learning outcomes I included in the syllabus. Originally, my objectives for the course encompassed the following:

- To foreground the literary genres of the Bible;
- To examine the genres as complete works in themselves;
- To employ literary terminology rather than theological terms to interpret biblical texts;
- To feature an artistic representation of the stories and poetry we read;
- To offer a critical link between an interpretive, experiential, and personal engagement in the study of "the Bible as literature."

My desire was for students to finish the class having obtained the following, as I stated in the syllabus: "At the end of this course, [students] should possess a clear understanding of the foundational elements of literary study related to genres in the Bible. Moreover, [students'] ability to read, think, and write about biblical literature should reflect—

- A critical knowledge of terminology associated with literary study;
- A broad knowledge of different literary genres represented in the Bible;

- An ability to employ critical reading and writing strategies to literary interpretation of biblical texts."

As I now reflect upon the evolution of journey in the theory and practice of a feminist-womanist pedagogical approach to this course, it is quite obvious that I chose not to include language in the syllabus that intentionally situated my scholarly background in gender studies. Why did I not overtly address issues of culture, gender, class, sexuality, *and* spirituality in the course concept, its objective, and learning outcomes? Quite frankly, I think it had much to do with my religious background. In my mind, openly discussing issues of oppression and domination in a feminist-womanist context would undermine the literary centrality of a secular reading of the Bible—even when I *required* students "to offer a critical link between an interpretive, experiential, and personal engagement in the study of the Bible as literature." Once again in reflection, I now consider the extent to which I had internalized white supremacist patriarchal ideas of literary studies. Since this is a "literary"-based course, I had thought that to teach it from a pro-feminist-womanist viewpoint of biblical narratives would be heretical, transgressing the boundaries of my formal training in literary studies.

Moreover, as someone new to teaching such a course, I had no desire intentionally to complicate class discussions outside a literary conventional context. Regardless as to whether "I" believed it necessary to question biblical representations of "Christianity" in contemporary U.S. society perpetuating patriarchy, racism, sexism, classism, and homophobia—I kept it unabashedly simplistic. Even though in the syllabi from 2014-2016 I quote Leland Ryken as saying—"THERE IS A QUIET REVOLUTION GOING ON in the study of the Bible" (11), I had kept silent about the really radical possibilities of this statement connected to feminist and womanist pedagogical practice. Certainly, as I openly shared in the title of Chapter 2, I am "in love with teaching 'The Bible as Literature' as a *pro*-womanist black man."

Let the Circle Be Unbroken
Bringing Students Together Across Disciplinary *and* Racial Boundaries

During the years I have taught "The Bible as Literature," the majority of the students who enrolled in the course were not English majors or minors. Rather they came from varying disciplines across the University—including the arts, humanities, business, communication, social, political, engineering, and medical sciences. Frequently, these students' nationalities were not U.S.-based; many of them were also *trans*-national. Moreover, they often came with a varying cultural differences and ideas of religion not rooted in biblical studies. More often than not, my course enrollment maxed out at thirty students. The room in which I was assigned to teach the class was usually configured with student desks arranged in a traditional row-to-row setting. In my idea of a student-centered learning space, I have always envisioned the classroom as an interactive space for student-teacher dialogue.

Invested in a pedagogical style in which conversational exchange guides the learning experience, I insist that the desks be re-arranged in a circle formation. I sit with my students in the circle in every class session during the semester. This seating arrangement means that I or students in the class come before class time begins to create the circle formation. In this vision of the classroom, no one sits outside the circle—including myself. This allows me to be a part of the group as a facilitating member rather than literally positioning myself and my literary, "professorial expertise" at the *front* of the classroom. This is my idea of a student-centered learning space which visually supports an open atmosphere of dialogic interaction—where everyone in the room is able not only to hear each other's voice, but *to see* the speaker in person. This is exactly how my incorporation of the "personal" interacts with my figurative employment of autocritography as a critical, self-reflective writing strategy works in complement with the physical *re*-organization of the classroom. Sitting in a circle together with my students, I promote our coming together in this format to study "The Bible as Literature" as a metaphoric gesture for global community building—where every human being in the room is equal to one another...Let the circle be unbroken.

From the time I began teaching the course five years ago, I have chosen to teach it once a week in the evening during a two-hour, forty-five-minute session—with a fifteen-minute break. The semester is composed of at least 15 class meetings. It is also important to mention here that as a "night class"—while most of the students in it are registered academically as "full-time"—there are those among them who hold full-time day jobs, and some have spouses and children. Even in this complex dynamic, to facilitate student-teacher dialogue (as stated in the syllabus), each student must write what I call a "discussion-starter paper" weekly. Rather than officially label it an "autocritography" in the syllabus, I chose to ground it in relation to a "down to earth" pragmatic purpose. Yet, an ongoing question many students ask at the beginning of each semester I have taught "The Bible as Literature" is: how in-depth are their self-reflections to be? As I explain my reasoning for valuing personal reflection in the "discussion-starter paper," students want to know to what degree sharing openly in class the complexities of their identities and life experiences will enhance their interpretive analysis of the reading(s) assigned. I suggest to them that although openly sharing life experiences—especially ones that are painful—is indeed troublesome, there are some life-altering, self-transforming benefits. They manifest themselves as unifying elements for human bridge-building connection. I believe that in my students openly sharing their life-stories they not only portray the self-transformative power of them, but they also characterize their unwavering strength for community building.

As I have stated earlier—while in the first semesters teaching this course, I chose not to connect issues of the "personal" to a feminist-womanist critique of identity politics—I remained committed to the power of storytelling as potentially self-liberating. Even though, when I first began teaching this course, I did not personally share with my students my allegiance to Alice Walker's womanist idea of love for all humanity—I knew from the beginning that my pedagogical approach reaffirmed Jesus' undeniable commitment to hope for all people vested in his visionary, (super)natural call for folk to love one another.

Works Cited

Harmon, Daniel Elton, Colleen Reece, and Julie Reece-DeMarco. *128 of the Greatest Stories from the Bible.* Barbour Publishing, Inc., 2005.

hooks, bell. *Teaching Critical Thinking: Practical Wisdom.* Routledge, 2010.

---. *Teaching to Transgress: Education as the Practice of Freedom.* Routledge, 1994.

---. *All About Love: New Visions.* HarperCollins Publisher, 2000.

Meyer, Michael. *Literature to Go.* Bedford/St. Martin's, 2011.

Ryken, Leland. *How to Read the Bible as Literature . . . and Get More Out of It.* Zondervan, 1984.

Chapter 3

Jesus as a Pro-Woman(*ist*) Messenger of Hope

Gary L. Lemons

> Then I heard the Lord asking, "Whom should I send as a messenger to my people? Who will go for us?" And I said, "Lord, I'll go! Send me."
>
> Isaiah 6:8 (New Living Translation)

A Prophetic Calling: from Love to Action

In *The Life Recovery Bible* (New Living Translation), the Old Testament book written by the prophet Isaiah, he records his vision in chapter six of a deeply profound interaction with the Lord. During it, Isaiah responds affirmatively to the Lord's question about his need for a "messenger." However, before the Lord reveals to Isaiah what he is to tell them (that which they definitely will not desire to hear), he agrees to "go!" Enter with me the conversation between the Lord and his called prophet. Surely what Isaiah would be commanded to tell the people must have astounded him, as it states in verse 10: "Harden the hearts of these people. Close their ears, and shut their eyes. That way, they will not see with their eyes, hear with their ears, understand with their hearts, and turn to me for healing." Because the people have utterly "close[d] their ears and shut their eyes...[and failed to] understand [the Lord] with their hearts," they will experience literal, horrific destruction in body, mind, and heart until they "turn [back] to [the Lord] for healing." In response, Isaiah asks, "Lord, how long must I do this?" After communicating to him the events that will lead the people to return for healing, the Lord's response is—"Do not stop until the Lord has sent everyone away to distant lands and the entire land of Israel lies deserted. Even if only a tenth—a remnant—survive, it will be invaded again and burned. Israel will remain a stump, like a tree that is cut down, but the stump will be a holy seed that will grow again" (verses 11-13). Clearly at the center of this visionary dialogue lies the imaginative and figurative power of the Bible, as indicated in the symbolic representation of Israel having to "remain a stump," "like a tree that is cut down." The reader comprehends, in the intense visuality of this simile, the horrific suffering the people must experience for their willful rejection of the Lord. However, what is very clearly communicated is that the people will be restored (symbolically "the stump will be a holy seed that will grow again"). Once Israel comprehends the transformative agency of the Lord's loving power to restore, the people will hear, see, and feel *in their hearts* what this means, physically *and* spiritually.

I purposely reference this conversation between the Lord and Isaiah in the Old Testament to lay the narrative foundation for the coming of Jesus in the New Testament—particularly related to his acts of love, hope, and healing as represented in the books of Matthew, Mark, Luke, and John. In the Christian faith, Jesus would become the Lord's ultimate messenger of hope for humanity and recovery not only through his active embodiment of the Creator's mercy, but also by his gracious enactment of love personified in divine human flesh. In acceptance of himself as prophetic messenger of the Word(s) of Lord to Israel, Isaiah would in fact set the stage for the redemptive work of John the Baptist. In the Gospels ("good news") in the Bible, John—according to the ritual practice of the Jewish faith—baptizes Jesus. It not only illustrates John's calling to ministry, but it signifies his prophetic authority, in spite of it being questioned by the Jewish priests and Levites. To their dismay, not only does John defy their queries, he prophetically reveals that the baptism of Jesus was symbolic of his calling as the "Messiah" (Jesus Christ, deliverer of the Jews, as had been prophesied in the Old Testament). Metaphorically, Jesus would be the "holy seed" of the "stump" of Israel, regardless of the Jewish religious leaders (known as the Pharisees) refusing to believe it. John responds to their denial, "I am the voice of one crying out in the wilderness, 'Make straight the way of the Lord,' as the prophet Isaiah said" (*English Standard Version,* John 1.23). John knows that Jesus has come to him as the Messiah to be baptized, as is affirmed afterwards by the voice of God:

"You are my beloved Son; with you I am well pleased" (*English Standard Version*, Mark 1.11).

At the age of thirty—well over two thousand years ago—Jesus began his ministry of soul-work in teaching love and acted out in the healing the people's minds, bodies, and spirit. This is where my stories of inspired hope and healing began in 2014 teaching "The Bible as Literature." As stated in the Introduction to *Let Love Lead*, I focus on the life and teachings of Jesus. His impact in the lives of people across differences (of religion, culture, gender, class, generation, and abilities) is, indeed, revolutionary. Acting as the "beloved Son" of God, Jesus would accomplish all that his father had called him to perform as the "holy seed" to enable the stump of Israel (a fallen people) to grow again. Jesus began his missionary labor of loving liberation in the acceptance of his task as the messenger of good news for *all* people,.

Jesus' Mission to Set Free Humanity
Student-Teacher "Reader Response(s)"

I previously shared my pedagogical approach to "The Bible as Literature." The remaining sections of this chapter invite the reader into the classroom setting where students and I dialogue about Jesus' calling as a healer sent to the earth to set free humanity. Before beginning the dialogue, I provide more detail about the "reader response" papers (discussion starters) students produced based on *128 of the Greatest Stories from the Bible* to guide our interactive conversation. I assigned ten stories each week for students to read and write about in this collection (organized in narratives from the traditional Old to New Testament formation). While each narrative is written (in contemporary standard English) by the co-editors of the book, each is grounded by a scriptural reference at the end of it. Having read back over the autocritographies students composed in the first three semesters of teaching the course, in this chapter I have chosen to focus this student-teacher dialogue on the fall 2015 version of the course. I find the responses to stories in the book about the life of Jesus particularly compelling and deeply self-reflective.

Considering this, many of the twenty-two students in the class were clearly impressed by his revolutionary standpoint—as shown in his loving acts of healing.

As stated in the course syllabus I conceptualized in 2014, students were to bring to each class session during the semester their "reader response" paper to format our class discussion. I point out here again that in my description of the papers students were to write for the course, I did not formally reference them as "autocritography," even though the paper format embodied its concept. This is because I understand that students writing about "The Bible as Literature" purely analytically—absent of an integral connection to a personal, life experiential interpretation of it—made little if any space for an interpretative, spiritual engagement. Over time, in the evolution of my journey in teaching this course, I would eventually move toward a radical, pro-feminist-womanist interpretation of biblical narratives.

In offering the series of class discussions that follow about Jesus as a human model for revolutionary, inspired activism—I employ the "reader response" papers from the class of fall 2015 to guide the dialogue. While *re*-reading students' responses to narratives assigned about the life of Jesus, I found particularly interesting the ways the biblical dynamics of his relationships with females was a major concern—especially for female students in the class. Jesus continually called into question patriarchal social, cultural, and religious politics related to gender, and issues of female (*mis*)treatment became a topic of consistent engagement most predominately by female students in the class. Indeed, this suggests that the study of Jesus' relationships with females in the biblical narratives is, in and of itself, revolutionary. My representation of the class discussions that follow centering on Jesus' female relationships includes his acquaintances with the disabled/sick, family members, and the disenfranchised. As a teacher, I find most intriguing about students' responses to these relationships the way that Jesus employs them to confront the oppression and domination of women in and outside the legalistic boundaries of the "official religion." My students reveal in their discussions that Jesus' interactions with women are clearly founded upon the healing enactment of love. They show that what he performs in his encounters with them is a life-transforming gesture of hope and healing.

Class Discussion Part I: Who Does Jesus Think He Is?

> Jesus answered, "I am the way and the truth and the life."
> John 14:6 (New International Version)

First and foremost, as personified in the narratives of Jesus' relationships with women found in the *128 of the Greatest Stories from the Bible*, the theme of love is rooted in the hope of the restorative power of healing—in mind, body, and spirit. This is—as my students interpret—central to the mission of salvation Jesus actually embodies. To contextualize the series of class discussions illustrated here, I will not only cite passages from the stories interwoven with students' responses to them—but also include student citations from *How to Read the Bible as Literature* to provide contextual the figurative aspects of the stories.

As re-envisioned and written by the co-editors of the *128 Greatest Stories from the Bible*, these stories portray the straightforward, unabashedly loving way(s) how Jesus dealt with issues of human frailties and failings. He purposely sought to defy the boundaries of patriarchy, and how he dealt with issues of gender is profoundly filled with loving compassion—especially related to his interaction with women. I begin this opening discussion with students who responded to three stories in particular: "A Woman of the City" (197-98, ref., Luke 7), "The Woman at the Well" (204-05, ref., John 4) and "The Woman Accused" (207-209, ref., John 8).

"A Woman of the City" is a story about Jesus' encounter with a woman of ill-repute "known to be a sinner" who has heard about his esteemed reputation. She finds out that Jesus is to have dinner with a Pharisee named Simon. During his life, Jesus clearly contests the Pharisees and other Jewish religious folk regarding their false interpretation of what it means to follow the Holy Spirit. According to Matthew 23:1-3, he publicly calls them out—"Jesus said to the crowds and to his disciples: 'The teachers of the law and the Pharisees sit in Moses' seat. So you must be careful to do everything they tell you. But do not do what they do, for they do not practice what they preach" (*New International Version*). In "A Woman of the City," this un-named, uninvited woman shows up at Simon's house with plans to give "[t]he Master" a "deserved tribute" and "she had the means to give it to Him." This woman:

> entered Simon's house, carrying in both hands her most precious possession: an alabaster box of ointment. She stood at Jesus' feet and wept, then washed His feet with her tears. She used her long and lustrous hair to dry them, then kissed the Faster's feet and anointed them with ointment. (*128 Stories* 197)

Seeing this, Simon is completely insulted—that "she dare[d] to enter his home and minster to Jesus was beyond decency." According to Simon, if Jesus is the "prophet" that he had told the folk he is, he should have known that this woman was "a sinner" and not allowed her "to touch Him." However, Jesus does not refuse this woman's gift. Widely known as a storyteller, Jesus responds to Simon in a parable about a "creditor": "There was a certain creditor who had two debtors: The one owed five hundred pence, and the other fifty. And when they had nothing to pay, he frankly forgave them both. Tell me, therefore, which of them will love him most?" Simon's response was "he who was forgiven most" (197). In that moment, even as Jesus faces the woman, he tells Simon that his accusation of this woman is groundless. If anything, it is Simon who has been disrespectful toward him (having offered Jesus "no water for [his] feet.") It is this woman who has graciously "washed [his] feet with her tears and wiped them with her hair." Jesus goes, on telling Simon,

> You gave Me no kiss, but this woman since the time I came in has not ceased to kiss My feet. My head with oil you did not anoint, but this woman has anointed My feet with ointment.
>
> Therefore I say to you, her sins, which are many, are forgiven; for she loved much. But to whom little is forgiven, the same loves little. (198)

Telling the woman that her sins are forgiven, Jesus boldly speaks his mission into being through this woman's illustrative praise toward him. This provokes a deep moment of self-reflection within this unnamed woman who metaphorically "felt as though she had stepped under a fall of clear water, cleansing and pure." Interestingly enough, those whom Simon has invited to dinner are utterly amazed at the fact that Jesus possesses the power to forgive the woman's sins. Despite this, Jesus tells her: "Your faith has saved you; go in peace." She is so astounded by his words that she can hardly stand up to leave Simon's home. Yet upon stepping outside, she notices that her vision has been changed. She no longer sees herself as the "sinner" she had been. Who she has become in the encounter with Jesus has totally transformed her life. This woman now experiences a form of "peace" she has never imagined: "Now, in twinkling, it had come. The alabaster box was empty, but the woman's heart filled to bursting. A new life beckoned. She raised her face to the sky and ran to greet her vastly changed future" (198). This story characterizes Jesus' prophetic mission for human freedom through his calling to forgive; it also represents his stand against the legalism of the Pharisees, who misrepresented the mercy, grace, *and* love of the One (his Father) who sent him to this earth.

In the "reader response" papers four women in the class wrote on this story, they clearly comprehended the theme of forgiveness as the main point. One of them states that it is connected to "faith involving humility, gratitude, and service." Leland Ryken points out that, since this story is based on the New Testament book of Luke, it "included a number of distinctive incidents and teachings of Jesus that involve the poor, women and non-Jewish people..." (64). He also states, "We might also note in passing that one of the most distinctive traits of biblical writing, especially biblical stories, is the prevalence of direct speech and dialogue" (20). Of the student's responses to "A Woman of the City," one stands out for me in its "application" of its theme to her personal life experience. This student, Laura (Escamilla), states,

> [This] story reminded me of my mother's wisdom. She has always reminded my sister and me that actions speak much louder than words, which obviously is true in almost every circumstance imaginable. Some, however, don't seem to realize that the statement also applies to faith...Luckily, there

are still individual in the world that like the woman in the story; they will do everything possible to show God that they are truly deserving of forgiveness of their sins. These types of people pray unto the Lord for forgiveness and then continue by actually taking action...These people also show praise to the Lord by attempting to help others in whatever needs they have—[t]hings raging from helping someone pick up a book they dropped, to ensuring that the orphans in Haiti have a better living environment by building them houses. What I'm trying to say is that things might look good on paper, but they look even better in action.

Another female student, Cynthia (Leets), remarked how she understood what the woman in the story might have felt and what she experienced before meeting Jesus,

This woman reminded me very much of myself—the way she was willing to give everything she owned in order to be loved, accepted, and forgiven by Jesus...After going through a long, long grieving process for believing I was not good enough, I began to look back and reflect on [certain] decisions I made [in life] and I realized how foolish I had been. It really is so sad to think of the things you allow someone to do to you when you don't know how to value yourself for what you truly are. I have always let people take advantage of my kind nature and use me for what they need in order [for me] to feel love and accepted.

Defending "A Woman in the City" as an impactful piece of biblical literature, a black male student, Tromonte (Relford), quoted Ryken as saying: "God is always concerned with the acts of people" (184). He states that the story's resolution "came when Jesus told the un-named woman that she was saved by 'faith' and to go in peace." He further remarks,

[This story] brought up two obvious but essential questions: Why was the woman saved by Jesus for doing something [I consider] so simple? Why is her name not mentioned? [I will respond to the second question first.] Her name probably is not mentioned because it is not important what her name is rather

her action, her service that superseded that. People [may not] remember us by name, but they mostly remember what we did or did not do, or say...When we are doing something out of the ordinary like the woman washing the feet of Jesus, we will have others like Simon who watches us in anger or wonder [or jealousy]...Christianity especially in modern times has so many denominations and divisions that we complicate [the meaning of] faith. This unnamed woman was saved by her faith [in service to] someone else...This woman had a [clear] motive according to the story, but she did not go into Simon's house asking to be save or begging Jesus for anything. She provided a service that most people would not [have attempted]. She did not even know [what] the results of her actions [would be], but Jesus ended up blessing her in the end. *We should approach others this way having no desire for reward but for assisting them and allowing them to feel that we care about them and their needs.* (emphasis added)

As it is clear in "A Woman of the City," the Pharisees not only believe that women of ill-repute should not have any relationship with devout, holy folk, they also believe that Jews should not befriend anyone of another culture.

In the story of "The Woman at the Well" (204-205), we find Jesus once again crossing boundaries. He has a life-altering conversation with a Samaritan woman at a well-location only for Jews—"She hated going there," but she needs water "to live." Also, she is scorned by her neighbors because of her reputation as an adulterer: "Her neighbors pulled their skirts aside when she passed by and murmured against her." She goes there during a time of day (early in the morning) when she thinks few, if anybody, will be at the well. However, she notices there is a man near the well whose clothing shows that he is a Jew. This scares her. As the narrator of the story reveals: "It was bad enough being the object of scorn among her own kind, but the smug, self-righteous Jews who came to the well as they passed through Samaria made her feel less than the dirt beneath their sandal." Yet before she draws water from the well, she hears "a pleasant voice" say, "Give Me to drink." Startled and afraid, her response is, "How is it that Thou, being a Jew, askest drink of me, which am a woman of Samaria? For the Jews have no dealings with the Samaritans" (204). Exposing her feelings of low self-esteem as a Samaritan woman in the presence a Jewish man, quite frankly she is amazed that this man would even be speaking to her.

In this moment, Jesus who knew beforehand what the outcome would be in his dialogue with this woman, says to her: "If thou knewest the gift of God, and who is that saith to thee, 'Give Me to drink,' thou wouldest have asked of Him, and He would have given thee living water." Of course, the woman does not understand what he says, as she came to the well literally to get some water to live. She wants Jesus to explain what he means, given that he has nothing to draw water from the well, and it is deep. She does, however, question him about his knowledge of the well having been given to the people by the people's "father Jacob." In her mind, does Jesus think he is "greater" than him? Patiently, Jesus tells her that the water that comes from this well would supply the people's earthly need for survival, but "those who drank of the water He [Jesus' father] gave would never thirst [again]." Adding yet more detail to help this woman understand who he is, Jesus says, "The water that I give [you] shall be in [you] a well of water springing up into everlasting life" (205). Surely, this imaginative re-configuration of water metaphorically connected to Jesus' vision of living eternally must have been revelatory for "the woman at the well."

Interestingly, the story's narrator references Jesus as a "magician"—stating in the form of a question why would he not be able to "give [this woman] water so she never again had to thirst or come to the well and draw?" She, in fact, loves this idea. However, Jesus has a plan to take their conversation to a deeper level—telling her to go and bring her husband "back to the well." This becomes another moment in which the woman feels ashamed of her identity: "Shame reddened her face, and she cast her gaze downward to escape His piercing look." She remarks, "I have no husband." Jesus already knows all about her life of adultery, "[t]o her amazement." The narrator notes that Jesus compliments her for telling the truth that she, indeed, "had five husbands [and] the man she now had was not her husband." At this point, she knows something is very different about this man she has been talking to; he knows all about her adulterous life. Thus, she says to Jesus that he must be "a prophet." In line with her perception, he "expounded many things to her." Clearly, "with each truth" he reveals to her, she knows she is right in her perception of his *calling*. She boldly states, "I know that Messiah cometh, which is called Christ. When He is come, He will tell us all things." Jesus directly confirms her comprehension as to his identity: "I that speak unto thee am He" (205).

Like the woman in "A Woman of the City," *the woman at the well* leaves Jesus transformed (leaving her "water jar" behind). From that moment, "[s]he raced to the city and said unto the people, 'Come, see a man which told me all things ever I did. Is not this the Christ?" Moreover, as the narrator further reveals, "She ran to others, proclaiming what had come to pass that day to all who would listen." Apparently, this new path of vocal freedom about her non-condemning encounter with Jesus leads others to go "out of the city and come to Him. Many believed on Him by reason of the woman's testimony...He was indeed the Christ, the Savior of the world. The Samaritan woman found a niche in history because she listened, believed, and shouted the truth of Jesus, the Christ, through the streets of her city" (205). One student, Danica (Tinsley), wrote about the story of the Samaritan woman,

> The resolution [of this story] occurs when Jesus defies man-made rules. Imagine the woman's surprise and awe when she finds out she is speaking to the Messiah! This woman, because she has heard and given testimony, brings many other Samaritans to Jesus. Essentially, she is a disciple herself...Jesus, the most holy man to ever walk the earth,...continually meets...with the lowest of society...I am comforted by this in a way I hadn't noticed before. My feminist views make me anti-Christian in the eyes of some who believe feminists have ruined the nuclear American family. I am afraid to say the "F"-word in conservative circles. *So, yes, I'm comforted that Jesus saw value in women. He*

ministered to them; he revealed himself to them, and he loved them. (emphasis added)

As Danica states, "Jesus saw value in women." I absolutely agree with her that a critical aspect of his missionary work on earth, specifically related to women, was three-fold. He was to minister to them, make known his identity, *and* love them.

In "The Woman Accused," once again Jesus fulfills his mission setting women free from the (man)dated laws of religious patriarchy. This story opens with an un-named woman having been brought by a group of scribes and Pharisees to a temple where Jesus is teaching—"The wretched woman...dared not raise her head" (207). Ironically, however, "she felt a certain sense of release. Today would end her miserable life" (208). It was customary for a woman with her despicable reputation to be stoned to death by holy leaders in the Jewish community. Feeling the weight of their accusations, "[i]f it weren't for the agony to come with the sharp stones hurled by men no better than she, she wouldn't care." One could say that she has fully given up that the case against her would be dismissed.

Suspiciously, the accusing scribes and Pharisees, recognizing Jesus as "Master," say, "[T]his woman was taken in adultery, in the very act. Now Moses in the law commanded us that such should be stoned. But what sayest Thou?" (208). Apparently, given their knowledge of Jesus' pro-liberating treatment of women, this question is simply rhetorical, for they know how the "Master" would respond. A long silence prevails, to the extent that "the accused woman risked a quick glance at the teacher [Jesus]." What she perceives about his demeanor is much different than that of the men who have brought her into the temple; "[h]e looked kinder..." But does this make any difference? According to the narrator, "A law was a law, not to be broken." In the long moment of silence, the woman wonders to herself why the man she had committed adultery with was not brought to be judge as well. She asks herself, "Had those who took [me] conveniently allow him to escape?" She knows the answer to her question. In a religious culture of male supremacy, men most often get excused from any penalties connected to adultery.

The long silence in the temple ends when Jesus "stooped down" to the ground to address the question the scribes and Pharisees pose to him—"[W]ith His finger [he] wrote on the ground as though He heard them not." Why would Jesus act in this unexplained manner, rather than speak directly to these men in response to their question? Whatever he writes on the ground, he acts as if he did not hear anything they spoke. Like the men, the woman "prisoner" has no idea what Jesus is attempting communicate. Even so, the scribes and Pharisees "continued railing against her, demanding that Jesus answer" (208). When he does respond, they all must have been completely surprised. He simply says, "He that is without sin among you, let him first cast a stone at her." Surely, this is not the answer to their question they expect. While the men contemplate his statement, once again, Jesus "stooped down again and wrote upon the ground." While the men remain silent, "[t]he woman's mouth fell upon." Here the narrator explains,

> Little as she knew about Jewish law, she realized Jesus had challenged those who brought her to be judged with the sharpest challenge imaginable. Not that it would benefit her. Some of these self-righteous men considered themselves so holy they wouldn't recognize sin in their hearts if it stung like the desert scorpions.

Not one of the men respond to Jesus' statement as he "still stooped down, busy writing." We are never told in the story what Jesus is writing on the ground, but what we do know is that, while he is writing, the scribes and Pharisees respond by walking away. Jesus stands up and looks the woman in her face, saying, "Woman, where are those thine accusers? Hath no man condemned thee?" Utterly amazed—"[t]rembling, unable to believe she alone remain before Jesus, she stammered, 'No man, Lord'" (208-209). Just like "the woman at the well," Jesus looks at this woman in a way that she knows "He knew everything about her, more than anyone on earth could know." Just as Jesus allows "a woman of the city" to go in peace, so he does with the "accused woman." His final words to her are transformative and liberating with no condemnation—"Neither do I condemn thee. Go and sin no more" (209). Surely, this is a breathtaking moment for this woman, for she knows had it not been for Jesus' power of loving salvation, she would have been stoned to death by those men. At the end of the story, when Jesus departs, this woman is "dazed from the strange encounter with even stranger results." The narrator closes by asking, "What lay ahead [for this woman]? New life, surely. For once she looked into Jesus' face and beheld His majesty, the past meant nothing; the future, everything" (209).

All three of these biblical narratives are well-known to many who study the Bible. However, emphasis on Jesus as a revolutionary pro-womanist must continue to be discussed. Monica (Goyeneche), the one student in the class who wrote about Jesus' unwavering defense of "the accused woman," says,

> The men [in the story] have a shallow righteousness that shows no concern for the soul of this woman, but rather they just want to condemn her for what she has done…When Jesus calls for the one without sin to cast the first stone, he accomplishes some [life-changing] things: first, it relieves him from the charge of having to instigate the woman's stoning, since none of the accusers want to take responsibility for it. Secondly, it causes them to reflect on their own sinfulness before God…Jesus could have easily condemned her, but he forgave her…Jesus teaches [the scribes and Pharisees] that instead of looking at other people's sins, they should look at their own first…Pointing fingers at others has always been an easy way of shifting blame…As I was reading this story, I couldn't help but think how easy it is for us to judge other people for what we think is right…We don't know what that person is going through or what made her or him take that path.

Considering this student's insightful perspective on "The Accused Woman" and as a closure to Class Discussion Part I, am reminded of the New Testament scripture in Matthew 7:1-3: "Do not judge, or you too will be judged. For in the same way you judge others, you will be judged, and with the measure you use, it will be measured to you. Why do you look at the speck of sawdust in your brother's eye and pay no attention to the plank in your own eye?" (*New International Version*).

Class Discussion Part II: Jesus and Women of Faith

> Now faith is confidence in what we hope for and assurance about what we do not see.
> Hebrews 11:1 (New International Version)

Jesus' acts of love in biblical narratives demonstrate the power of their thematic coherence centered on life-transformation—rooted in faith and hope. As the plot of these stories develops, Jesus is clearly not interested in any individual's high standing—whether it be associated with culture, gender, class, or religious affiliation. As I sought to illustrate in the first teacher-student Class Discussion, Jesus radically employs loving actions to liberate the hearts, minds, and souls of human beings—especially those of women under the dictation of patriarchy and religious legalism. He purposely reaches out to help save the lives of women to make a critical point about the emancipatory agency of his missionary labor for salvation for *all* folk—even for those whose gender identity positions them at the bottom of humanity.

In Part II of our Class Discussion, we invite the reader to observe ways in which we portray Jesus as pro-womanist related to women and the representation of their faith. There are three stories in *128 of the Greatest Stories from the Bible* about Jesus and the faith of women. "A Woman of Faith" (159-161, ref. Matthew 8), "The Canaanite Woman, Mother of Faith" (171-172, ref. Matthew 15; Mark 7), and "The Poor Widow's Mites" (190-191, ref. Mark 12; Luke 12) all feature the self-empowering evidence of faith.

In the first of these well-known narratives, an un-named woman who has suffered with a "rare blood disease that had plagued her for twelve endless years" (159) finds herself compelled to seek out Jesus. Doctor after doctor have told her this is a terminal illness; she will never recover from it. However, based on rumors, she has heard about Jesus, "the new prophet," even though he is "the son of a Nazarite carpenter." At this desperate time in her life, she has basically given up hope of surviving this disease. She thinks to herself, "Does [his economic status really] matter?" Considering this,

> One evening when she lay sleepless [and] decided, "I will arise in the morning and seek this Jesus. I will cast myself at His feet. If He is all people say, He will have mercy on me. If not, I die and the pain will be no more." She knew it would require her last measure of strength to travel the short distance to Jesus. (159-160)

At the same time, she struggles with her thoughts about him—"She felt weakness wash through her as waves wash against the shore during a storm" (160). Yet she begins her trip to find him. There he is, standing among a huge crowd; "[i]t was enough to renew her." She begins to experience a deep feeling of faith that causes her to think: "*If I may but touch his garment, I shall be whole*." According to the narrative she said these words "in her heart." The woman begins to put her thought into action: "She stretched forth her hand. The edge of Jesus' cloak felt rough against her searching fingers. Strength flowed into her. She opened her mouth to cry out she had been healed, but no words came."

Indeed, the activation of her faith is the source of her healing. At that moment, Jesus knows something has happened—"that virtue had gone out of Him" (160). He asks his disciples, "Who touched Me?" They have no idea, considering the large number of people who surround Jesus. Even so, he sees the woman. Kneeling down "in fear and trembling" before Jesus, she admits that she is the one who touched him and further reveals her faith in his healing power. She speaks these humble words to him: "Lord, it was I. I know if I could but touch the hem of Your garment, I would be healed." After she says these words to Jesus, she has no idea how he will respond. The narrator of the story indicates, "Jesus spoke [to her] in a voice like none she had ever heard before. 'Daughter, be of good comfort; your faith has made the whole.'" Like the stories shared in Class Discussion Part I, this story ends with breath-taking revelation. This woman thinks the little faith that she has when she touches the hem of Jesus' garment is mostly done out of complete desperation. But for

Jesus, just the little bit of faith she acts upon is enough to activate her healing—"She looked into Jesus' face, filled with compassion and understanding that swept away any need for explanations" (160-161). His act of healing is done. The people move on—having no knowledge of what has happened— but the woman "stood, praised God, and ran, rejoicing with each breath of air that filled her lungs, every long stride that carried her on her way" (161). Indeed, her the encounter with Jesus is physically *and* spiritually life-transforming.

Two female students in the class responded to this story. Interpreting "A Woman of Faith" through Ryken's idea in *How to Read the Bible as Literature* that "[one] of the commonest of all the strategies that storytellers use is to put the protagonist into situations that test him or her," the first student, Jacqueline (Gardner), lists these tests in her discussion: "1. Tests of Physical Strength or Courage; 2. Tests of Resourcefulness; 3. Mental or Psychological Tests; 4. Moral or Spiritual Tests" (50-51). She goes on to say,

> The story of the woman with the issue of blood is one of my favorite stories in the Bible. I can relate to her story in so many ways. My issue is personal freedom. It always seems as if I have never been able to be free. I love this story so much because everyone can relate to wanting so badly to be free from sadness, depression, financial setbacks, heartache, dead-end jobs, and health scares…The lady in the story visited so many doctors [in search of healing]. Today, [looking for healing] we visit so many doctors, our friends, and families. We shop, eat, travel only to end up often even more hurt and discouraged [than when we started out]…The lady in this story is a true representation of the flaws we humans carry, waiting until we get to our last but of hope before [many of us as Christians] end up crawling to Jesus saying, "If I [too] could touch the hem of His garment I would be made free."

The second student, Raquel (Gebre St. Fort), opens her discussion of the story sharing the scripture: "for with God nothing shall be impossible" (*New King James Version*, Luke 1.37). Transitioning to her personal story, she then recalls,

When I first read the title of this story, it was my mother who came to mind...Every decision she made was taken in faith. My mother grew up in Haiti, coming the U.S. when she was only nine years old. She grew up with family friends [committed to attending church]. She was reared strong in the word of God...[To this day], I look at my mom in awe [as to] how she turns to God [in faith].

The second story in Class Discussion Part II continues the theme of faith characterized in a mother's journey for Jesus as popularized prophet and healer. In "The Canaanite Woman, Mother of Faith," the protagonist (un-named) mourns the fact that her daughter is (in contemporary terminology) psychologically disabled. As the narrator recounts, she is "vexed with a devil" (171). Rather that recount at length the history of this biblical term, I will state here that in the New Testament (specifically as documented in the Gospels) Jesus encountered many individuals who were possessed by "a devil." This figure is most likely related to the one who tempted Jesus during his forty days of fasting in the wilderness after he had been baptized, as documented in Matthew 4:1—"Then Jesus was led up by the Spirit into the wilderness to be tempted by the devil" (*New King James Version*). Experiencing the traumatizing depth of her daughter's deadening state of mind, the mother often feels that "[d]eath could surely be no worse than life as the maiden lived it."

Like many other people, this mother has heard stories about Jesus' healing power. However, as a member of the Canaanites (considered an idolatrous people by the Jews), she still wonders, "Why [had her people] had been so cursed?" As the narrator notes, these people are "shunned" by folk who lived around them. The mother nevertheless listens to positive things said about Jesus. In a conversation with a neighbor, she quietly remarks, "It is said He heals those who come to Him" (172). Yet she can hardly believe that, as a Jew, Jesus would heal a person from the land of Canaan. With bitterness, she smirks— "Such a thing could not be!" However, her desperation for help prompts her to "pursue every rumor on behalf of her daughter." In the face of hopelessness, she decides anyway to go in search of Jesus.

As in the stories shared in Part I and thus far in Part II of the Class Discussion, when these women speak in the presence of Jesus, they always do so in great fear of possible rejection. Yet, as we have witnessed, they speak out anyway. This mother, upon finding Jesus, approaches him "in a loud voice" saying, "Have mercy on me, O Lord, Son of David, my daughter is grievously vexed with a devil" (172). While the narrator does not share how she came to know Jesus' heritage, obviously, she knows of his lineage. Fearfully, she waits to hear what his response will be. Unlike in the other women-centered stories, Jesus says nothing back to this woman. Perhaps she thinks he did not hear her, so "[s]he cried again." The narrator reveals that Jesus' disciples are present, and they insist that the woman's plea be ignored. They tell Jesus to "[s]end her away, for she cries after us." Ironically, one would think that given that they had witness on a number of occasions his attention to other women's pleas for help, they would be more patient with her. Even more surprisingly, Jesus' response seems to *re*-inscribe a separatist perspective. He says to her: "I am sent to the lost sheep of the house of Israel." This sounds exactly like what a scribe or Pharisee would have said.

What is Jesus up to here? Surely Jesus is not going against his bridge-building work through love to save all people across religious walls of separation? In response to what appears as Jesus' rejection of her request, she feels hurt. However, she does not give up. Figuratively, the narrator describes her feeling and action:

> The woman's hope flickered like a lamp with only a few drops of oil. Should she leave off beseeching Him? Nay. Better to risk the wrath of the One she implored than go away heavy-hearted. She fell at Jesus' feet and worshiped Him, saying, "Lord, help me." (172)

Like the other wounded women Jesus encounters and heals, this mother is willing to humble herself—even if it means falling down and worshipping him at his feet. I admire the humility of these women, for in their hearts they sense the One who can transform their hopeless situations. Jesus' response to her clearly indicates that he is testing her faith, telling her, "It is not right to take the children's bread and cast it to dogs." This again resembles what a Jewish religious authority would have said to this woman, for the "children" represent the Jews (as the "chosen" ones) and "dogs" are the down-cast, metaphoric image of the unworthy Canaanites. Even these words do not silence the mother, considering "her great need." She keeps on pleading for Jesus to help: "She refused to let [him] walk away, for if He did, all hope must go with Him." So she speaks out in agreement with what could have been taken as an overt insult to her people—"True, Lord. Yet even the dogs eat the crumbs that fall from their masters' table." While saying these words, she does not look at Jesus. Continuing to listen to the exchange between her and Jesus, the disciples remain scornful of her insistence—"that she should speak so to the Master." In contemporary terms, the invocation of "Master" as the disciples' authoritative title for Jesus reminds me of the U.S. history of the dominating, oppressive relationship between the black slave and the white "master"...Back to the story.

As the biblical narrative draws to a close, there is an amazing turn in the conversation between the mother and Jesus. Despite the disciples' move to disregard her and urge their "Master" to do the same, once again Jesus breaks the law of separation in(scribe)d and enforced by the Pharisees. After having tested her faith, he says to the mother: "O woman, great is your faith; your request is granted" (172). The narrator records, "And her daughter was made whole from that very hour." It is interesting to note that Jesus never has any contact with this mother's daughter to verify her illness, yet he comprehends the extent to which her mother would yield in worship to him as a sign of her unrelenting faith in his supernatural power to transform her daughter's life. The narrator ends the story, "The woman of Canaan is a permanent reminder of how love and concern for others and faith born of despair can prevail even when circumstances appear hopeless." As I read these words, I am compelled to question my own faith as a believer in the healing power Jesus demonstrated in human beings—especially women. My own mother is a living testament to the liberating agency of faith. As I stated in my opening chapter to *Let Love Lead*, in spite of years of experiencing domestic violence, she persevered—never giving up hope in the belief that Jesus would answer her prayers of deliverance *and* survival. I will say here, as my autocritographies have stated numerous times, that my mother is the reason why I have not given up on my belief that Jesus was sent to the earth on a single mission—to set free human beings from the deadening thought that "we were never meant to survive" ("Litany for Survival," Audre Lorde).

I turn now to students responding to this story. As was the case in the last story, only two of them wrote about it—again both female. Of the two written responses, one clearly stands out. In it, the student, Mariah (Silva), incisively interprets the narrative through the lens of Ryken's understanding of satire. In *How to Read the Bible as Literature,* he states,

> There is more satire in the Bible than one would guess from standard discussions. Many a passage in the Bible would make a great deal more sense to us if we simply added satire to our lexicon of literary terms.
>
> Satire is the exposure, through ridicule or rebuke of human vice or folly...[It] may appear in any literary genre (such as narrative, lyric, or parable), and it may be either a minor part of a work or the main content of an entire work. (159)

This student points out, "This story, although short, is as impactful as any moral teaching can be." I certainly agree with her. Continuing her reading of it, she further draws upon the four elements of satire Ryken says "that require the reader's attention"—they are: "the object(s) of attack...[t]he satiric vehicle...a prevailing tone...[and finally, it] always has a stated or implied satiric norm—a standard by which the object of attach is being criticized." What stands out in this student's narrative interpretation is her employment of his idea that "[t]he satiric norm is the positive model that is offered to the read as an alternative to the negative picture that always dominates a satiric work" (161). I think this student is right on point with how she applies this perspective to her analysis in which the negative is transformed into the positive. She states,

> The uncomplimentary metaphor Jesus [uses] to reply to the woman's cries, calling her a dog [because she a Canaanite, seems as if] the Lord is directly insulting the woman but without the intent of being a brute. In actuality, he is

comparing her to [an inhuman] creature in order to heighten her own worth. If she is a believer in him [as the Lord], she will not cast herself as being the "dog" the Lord speaks of. [I believe the] purpose of this [story as a satire is what Ryken refers to as "prophetic writing"].

Ryken states that it is "[t]he largest category…in the Bible." Moreover, he says that "[t]he two major types of prophetic oracle (pronouncement) are the oracle of judgment and the oracle of salvation. The best literary approach to the oracle of judgment is satire" (162). I agree both with Ryken and this student's interpretation. However, I would add that by the end of the story the "oracle of judgment" has been transformed in the "oracle of salvation"—as Jesus saves the lives of both the mother and her daughter, mentally *and* spiritually.

A particular aspect of this one student's "personal" experience reading this story stood out for me, as she sought in her research to get a clearer understanding of Jesus' seemingly insulting words to the mother in the story—related exactly to who were the "children" and who were the "dogs" he spoke about. She writes,

> Jesus' response to the woman threw me a curveball. Well aware that the story, like many [biblical narratives,] consists of metaphors, similes, and allusions—I knew that there was a meaning beyond [the insulting words Jesus spoke to the woman]…I turned to everyone's friend for knowledge—Google. I typed in the quote from Matthew 15:26, thinking that there would be a plethora of sermons to choose from [explaining why Jesus said what he spoke to her]; however, I was wrong. Instead there were a plethora of sites with the scripture posted without explanations…I altered my search to be more specific by adding the word "meaning" into the engine. This time a few more things popped up, yet none of them offered the explanation that I was looking for. As a matter of fact, they all either disregarded the scriptural quote and went on about the situation that Jesus and his disciples were in at the moment of the encounter, or they read it at face value simply as an insult to the Philistines.

> Frustrated, I decided to continue the readings assigned and began to skim through Leland Ryken's chapter in his book on satire. It was after reading the elements that Ryken claims to be the components of satire that Jesus' [seemingly insulting statement to the mother] began to make more sense...With this interpretation of the story as satiric...[I believe] we are all looking for the [life-transforming effects of] faith [as Jesus affirmed it in the of healing of the mother's daughter].

Like this student, I also found Ryken's discussion of satire as critically important to my interpretation of this biblical narrative, demonstrating how Jesus employed figurative language to test human faith in his revolutionary abilities to liberate the wounded soul.

In the final story to be engaged in this two-part restaging of our class discussion, out of the three stories included in Part II, "The Poor Widow's Mites" provoked a number of reactions by female *and* male student in the class. In the analysis and personal reflection of the story's theme, these students demonstrate its transformative impact as applied to their everyday lives. Most compellingly, together they reveal some complex issues related what it means to live in a capitalist-driven society. To open the discussion about the theme of this story, I begin by citing certain significant details in its plot. First and foremost, the opening sentence is quite thought-provoking related to Jesus' positionality as the story unfolds. The narrator opens it stating: "Jesus loved to watch people" (189). In this context, how Jesus determines to enter peoples' minds, bodies, and hearts is guided by his observation of them. This is key to his mission of salvation as he "[y]earned over them and longed for them to break the bondage formed by sin and be free" (190). Over and over again, Jesus' most heartfelt desire—as personified in his calling as God's *messenger*—is to act as revolutionary liberator. As a (super)natural being, like the folk who often surrounded him, he too felt hurt when they did not "[listen] to Him and [lay] aside their burdens, prejudices, and hypocrisy. He wept." Yet "He watched."

One day while in a temple, Jesus watches as worshippers come to give their "money" offerings—placing them in the "treasury" (a set of storage chests). The narrator describes what Jesus sees: "He noticed the careless way the rich flung in much, then went away with heads held high, proud to have done their duty so magnificently. Perhaps He sadly smiled, knowing they had their reward by being seen and noted for their generosity" (190). In this moment of observation, it is clear that Jesus is not just displeased with how the "rich" desire to be seen giving, he is saddened (though hiding his dismay behind a "smile"). Yes, Jesus (in human form) experiences feelings of (inner) hurt toward the ways religious folk with money tout (with outward arrogance) their allegiance to capitalism.

However, Jesus continues his watch, as if waiting to see if anyone will defy this classist, money-based parade. The narrator then notes: "A poor widow hung back until the more worthy finished making their offerings, then she timidly came forward. Evidence of poverty showed in her clothing and in the work-worn hands that had obviously known great toil" (190). What a sight this must have been—especially in the ways her conspicuous low-class standing appears among the wealthy temple-goers. Nevertheless, she proceeds to give: "Her tired fingers fumbled in her cloak and drew for two mites, which make a farthing" (a very small copper coin). Translated into modern, U.S. monetary terms—this amounts to only half of a penny. As humble as she represents herself, she boldly gives what she possesses, as a woman without a living husband to support her financially. After giving, she simply "disappeared into the crowd," having no idea that what she has done would make a difference to anyone.

At this moment, having *carefully* watched this little-noticed scene, Jesus interprets the value of her giving to his disciples, and he speaks these words to them: "Verily I say unto you that this poor widow hath cast more in than all they which have cast into the treasury" (190). How could this be true, when obviously the rich folk had given so much of their money—clearly as they desired to be publicly recognized and exalted? The disciples are completed baffled by Jesus' remark, "look[ing] at one another in amazement." I, like them, would have been puzzled as to why Jesus would think that "the poor widow" in giving less than the rich had given more. This is precisely where human reasoning fails. One must move from the rational to the spiritual to comprehend what Jesus sees represented in this woman's giving. Jesus explains to the disciples that "[a]ll they [the rich] did cast in of their abundance; but she of her want did cast in all that she had, even all her living." This is the point of Jesus' "watch[ing] people."

The narrator closes this story for contemporary readers by comparing this underclass woman to another un-named widow in the Old Testament who lives in a town called Zerephath (inhabited by people who did not believe in God). However, this widow—also materially poor—"gave the last of her meal and oil to the prophet Elijah" (190). She willingly gives him almost all the food she and her son have left to eat—even though she thinks she and her son would most likely later die of hunger. Though most of the people in her town do not believe in God, upon the prophet Elijah's desperate request for food, she with unabashed kindness gives him a meal to live (See 1 Kings 17.1-12). Is this, indeed, a measure of faith in the power of giving? In this act of inspired generosity, she and her son would be blessed to live on for many years—as survivors of a hunger plague. Jesus is, indeed, deeply impressed by the poor woman in his time having "[given] everything she had." This is the message Jesus had been called to communicate in this narrative. As it ends, the narrator proclaims, "If she [the poor widow] could speak to us down the path from the past, perhaps this devoted servant would tell of blessings great as those experienced by her giving counterpart [the widow from Zerephath] who lived hundreds of years earlier" (190-191). What a life-transforming pronouncement!

Collectively, the students who wrote in response to "The Poor Widow's Mites" agreed that the protagonist's action in giving all she had exemplified a moral foundation to contest the propagation of capitalist egotism. However, the response of one (male) student, Omar (Ali), stands among those the others (all female). Focusing on the widow's humble act of giving, he references Ryken's comment about the power of "single action" in biblical narratives. He further remarks,

> The message of the story about the widow is a powerful one, yet it is so simple...In actually [her small action] means so

much more...After reading the story, it brought back memories of my childhood. Personally, it made me think of my great-aunt. Ever since I was a young boy, she has always instilled in me the idea that I should always help those in need ...She came to the United States with a couple of hundred dollars and a determination to seek a better future. Since coming to this country, she has had many great opportunities, but recently she has experienced a great deal of misfortune and grief. The same people she helped over the years are nowhere to be found. She helped countless numbers of immigrants get the paperwork in order to obtain citizenship. She has provided housing for many friends and family members, and has even offered them assistance both financially and emotionally to get back on their feet. However, do you think she curses or blames any of them for not helping her in her time of need? She does not. Instead, she continues to help more people. Just like the poor and overworked widow, she still offers the little she does have to others. To me, the widow and my great-aunt are two powerful and rare women. In this day and age, they could be considered outsiders from our mainstream, money-based society. Regardless, I aspire to be just like the both of them.

I have engaged the reader in the two class discussions offered in this chapter by presenting some of the most thought-provoking responses my students and I participated in during our study of "The Bible as Literature" in my fall 2015 semester course. I shared some of the compelling student responses related to several of the most popular biblical narratives about Jesus' interactions with women, attempting to reveal the depth of their impact on each other *and* me. We hope to show in our collaborative analyses and reflections that the hope the female protagonists possessed—regarding the free-will agency Jesus embodied—lies at the core of their faith in his message of love and salvation for the human race. Teaching the life of Jesus as a pro-woman(ist) revolutionary, in the next chapter, I focus on the autocritography at the intersection of feminism and womanism for the liberation of all people, compelling them to return to healing power of his unwavering love.

Acknowledgements

I would like to thank the following students (from the fall 2015 semester of "The Bible as Literature") whose responses I included this chapter—Omar Ali, Laura Escamilla, Jacqueline Gardner, Racquel Gebre St. Fort, Monica Goyeneche, Cynthia Leets, Tromonte Relford, Maria Silva, Danica Tinsley.

Works Cited

The Bible. English Standard Version, Good News Publishers, 2016.
The Bible. New International Version, Biblica, 2011.
The Bible. New King James Version, Thomas Nelson, 1982.
Harmon, Daniel Elton, Colleen Reece, and Julie Reece-DeMarco. *128 of the Greatest Stories from the Bible*. Barbour Publishing, Inc., 2005.
The Life Recovery Bible. New Living Translation, Tyndale, 1992.
Lorde, Audre. "A Litany for Survival." *The Black Unicorn*. W.W. Norton Co., 1978.
Ryken, Leland. *How to Read the Bible as Literature . . . and Get More Out of It*. Zondervan, 1984.

Part II

Where Faith, Hope, and Love Reside

> And now abide faith, hope, love, these three; but the greatest of these *is* love.
> I Corinthians 13:13 (New King James Version)

Chapter 4

Believing is Seeing: Visionary Perspectives

Scott Neumeister

> When you change the way you look at things, the things you look at change.
>
> Wayne Dyer

I am sure the saying "I'll believe it when I see it" is familiar to most readers. Back in the early 2000s, however, I was shocked into a "double take" when I saw a book entitled *You'll See It When You Believe It* on my local bookstore shelf. I had already read one self-help book by its author and one of my early spiritual mentors, Dr. Wayne Dyer, and was searching for a new one. Dyer's premise is simple: when you change the way you look at things, the things you look at change. I would add to this maxim that changing the way one looks at things can also change oneself. In this manner, the alteration of perspective—or as I sometimes call it, the using of a new lens to look at life—represents a fundamental means of outer and inner transformation. In this first chapter of my dialogue with the writing of students in Gary's "The Bible as Literature" course, I will take an approach that discusses ways of seeing. His classroom is a locus where this view changing/lens fitting happens via reading and analyzing transformative biblical stories and texts in concert with self-reflective and -reflexive thought. The efficacy of reframing this literature in discourse with life brings students into a "higher vision" of liberatory consciousness. Aligning with the title of this book, *Let Love Lead*, I will begin by examining how the three theological virtues—faith, hope, and love—underpin Gary's instructional values that enable his students to obtain not only new ways of seeing but changed hearts.

I have heard one part of the Bible, besides the yearly-repeated Nativity and Easter narratives, read aloud more than any other over the course of my life—1 Corinthians 13, spoken from more pulpits and especially at more wedding ceremonies than I can count. If Christ's summarization of God's commandments, on which "the entire law and the prophets depend" (Moore *Book of Matthew* 143) has only one verb—*love*—then the "Love Chapter" of Corinthians is the most concentrated discourse on his core tenet in the entire Bible. The chapter ends in verse 13 with the compelling list of what are known as the theological virtues: "And now these three remain: faith, hope, and love. But the greatest of these is love" (*New International Version*). Paul has already mentioned the trio in 1 Thessalonians 1:3: "We remember before our God and Father your work produced by faith, your labor prompted by love, and your endurance inspired by hope in our Lord Jesus Christ" (*New International Version*). Nevertheless, Paul ends the Love Chapter with a provocative moment of value-setting for his audience; he gives love the preeminent position. In fact, Paul's valuing of love as the leading of the three virtues inspired one of the meanings of the title *Let Love Lead*. Not until I started researching and writing this chapter, however, did I realize that all the virtues were contained within the pedagogical techniques of Gary's approach to teaching "The Bible as Literature."

Theological Application: Faith, Hope, and Love in Pedagogical Practice

A literature class by nature requires tasks such as deconstructing conflict, interpreting figurative language, and other literary diagnostic techniques. Understanding the artistic craft that authors use greatly assists in appreciating them. Still, Gary's unique requirement of intentional *application*, as he calls it in "The Bible as Literature" course, allows his student readers to move beyond simply analyzing and appreciating the literary workings of any given biblical story or Psalm. The Latin root of *apply* means "to fold onto," an apt description of the joining or linking of the reader's story to a biblical one. Of all the interpretive techniques the students may use, finding a *theme* of a given reading is the key required for successful application. The beauty of literature as rich as the Bible is that its stories contain multiple, interlocking themes, and the one that any given reader chooses speaks deeply about the reader's soul as it encounters the text. The student scholar's work of theme choice then can advance into the application process.

Application requires "seeing" the resonance of biblical themes with lived experience. The encounter with the texts of literature is not very different from the encounter with life; in fact, the power of story to move the reader lies in how it unfolds much as our lives do. Nevertheless, unlike movies or plays, which have visual components, reading exclusively takes place in the imaginal realm, requiring an act of imagination for the reader to "get" or "see" the story. The imagining reader therefore intuitively attempts connections with the characters and events within the literature. The reader's mind, while taking in a story, subconsciously identifies similarities and differences with her or his lived experiences. In doing so, she or he seeks to correlate literal worlds with literary ones. Great authors facilitate this linkage through their artful constructions of character and plot, and the ease with which a reader slips into the realm of a story often relates proportionally to the skill of the writer. More than passively relying on authorial virtuosity, however, readers can mindfully set out to discover these connections that often happen unconsciously. This mindful approach is the foundation of Gary's application-based pedagogy.

Application writing requires an attention shift from a millennia-old biblical narrative into the students' personal, modern story. This perspective change necessitates seeing the Bible in a way different than many of them have been taught to view it, i.e. as an embodiment of dogma or as a dry historical account. In his *Power of Myth* interview with Bill Moyers, mythographer Joseph Campbell asserts this need for pulling the Bible into the present, "We have a tradition that comes from the first millennium B.C. somewhere else…It has not turned over and assimilated the qualities of our culture, and the new things that are possible, and the new vision of the universe." Students who perform the application process in Gary's class must foremost possess a perhaps-unacknowledged belief that biblical writing somehow—transhistorically, transculturally, and transpersonally—

resonates with their present-day experience. I characterize this shift as a leap of faith. As students descend into their memory to unearth personal resonance with what they are reading, they then *see* (themselves in the text) because they *believe*, to apply Dyer's precept. I use the terms *descend* and *unearth* here deliberately because I regard the process of memory exploration as a digging down into the soul. This view change into the subterranean is not simply a matter of recalling pieces of a life narrative. It also may require the re-membering of the particular story, an innovative re-configuration of the memory's text that allows it to be "read" like a text, with the student writer searching for their story's theme. When this memory work finds its connection of the personal to the literary, the application takes on deeper significance.

The depth of relating to literature depends on the experience cathexis—the investing of emotion and meaning. Gabriele Schwab claims that, in order to experience this cathexis, "The reader must find a productive and generative literary space for such an engagement" (53). The moment in the application process in which cathexis truly occurs springs from students writing about *characters* in stories they read that relate to a theme from their memory. Students most often identify themselves or someone close to them with a biblical character who either exhibits a strong positive quality or is hurt or oppressed in a given circumstance. In the first case, the readers find evocations of an inspirational attribute, such as forgiveness, compassion, or gratitude. Within the second instance, the students find solace in knowing not only that their suffering is part of the human condition, but also that the Bible provides examples of individuals meaningfully enduring adversity. In either case, cathexis with characters gives them what bell hooks describes as "the process of investment wherein [someone] becomes important to us" (*All About Love* 5). When readers "feel deeply drawn to someone, we cathect with them," hooks asserts. Application fosters this investment.

Following my concept of faith being present in the belief in seeing connection, I perceive this cathexis as a moment containing the second theological virtue: hope. In *Teaching Community: A Pedagogy of Hope*, hooks quotes from Mary Grey, "Hope stretches the limits of what is possible. It is linked with that basic trust in life without which we could not get from one day to the next" (xiv). Just as Grey connects *trust* (or *faith*) to *hope* in daily living, I see within the cathecting juncture that students' faith in the Bible as a relatable text then leads to "limit stretching," or in my words, view shifting. At the moment of cathectic investment, perspective widens, and hope enters. A *de facto* new mode of seeing now emerges, an ascension into a "higher vision" after delving into the depths of memory. I have labeled this the "50,000-foot view" and have most often applied it to Campbell's work. His own "higher vision" brought into focus the stunning thematic connections between the world's religions in books like *The Hero with a Thousand Faces*. For Gary's students, this perspective of wider possibility—not only in connecting with but also learning from biblical characters—can then facilitate the ultimate of the theological virtues.

Even though the application process fosters a cathectic juncture, neither cathexis nor hope by itself is the final product of application. In *All about Love: New Visions*, hooks distinguishes cathexis from love, which she defines as "the will to nurture one's own or another's spiritual growth" (4). Students who transform their cathectic investment into personal spiritual nurturance find that application is indeed "all about love." They must ask themselves, "If I ascend high enough, can I catch a new vision with this biblical perspective that allows me to grow in love for myself or others?" This is the juncture where love can lead. This transformative moment—where not only "the things you look at change," as Dyer posits, but the one doing the looking changes—embodies love in action. Not only does this galvanize Campbell's "new things that are possible," it fulfills hooks' admonition that "Profound changes in the way we think and act must take place if we are to create a loving culture" (*All About Love* xxii). Gary's biblical application methodology clearly uses the path of the three theological virtues to weekly provide a "productive and generative literary space" for love to lead his students into not only believing and seeing but also to, as he phrases it, moving love from "classroom to living room."

I now transition into dialoguing with various students' applications from the fall 2014 "The Bible as Literature" class, who used the text *128 Greatest Stories from the Bible* by Dan Harmon, Colleen L. Reece, and Julie Reece-DeMarco, as well as the Bible of their choice for their Psalm readings. In each case, I highlight the perspective-shifting that their application writing describes, and I explore those occurrences of students' applying their biblical readings to personal stories most often in the context of love, but also of faith and hope. I draw attention to the nuanced ways that the theological virtues bring about each student's new vision. How is hope also an act of love and love an act of hope? The same line of questioning applies to faith—how does it interplay with love? I would posit that both these virtues deal with the *mystery* of the Divine, the qualities of the universe that extend beyond our perception and, more importantly, our rational explanation. The fact of humanity's limited perspective on what is "out there," how things truly "work," and what meaning lies beneath life drives faith and hope to the core of human experience. Even beyond spiritual implications of these words, we hold these values moment by moment. We hold faith in human systems and social contracts to keep the civilized world running smoothly. We maintain a conception of hope that foresees our obtaining what we need and want in life by some combination of personal agency and factors beyond our control. The spiritual vision of these values simply extends their scope beyond the mechanistic, logical view of the world and into the great mystery of the Divine. Just as faith, hope, and love underpin the individual students' application process, so they also interweave in the applications themselves.

To Suffer Yet to Hope: Job's Love of the Great Mystery

Gary has asked me on occasion to speak to his students in "The Bible as Literature" and share my thoughts on their readings of the day or the application writing process. The first time I did so, the students had just read "Job, Man with an Upright Heart" in *128 Greatest Stories*. I was elated, because Job's story speaks to me like few others in the Scripture. No other book in the entire Bible, besides Psalms, uses the word *hope* more than Job. This fact allows it to become as much a meditation on hope as it is on suffering. Job's own words indicate that his circumstances have curtailed but not extinguished his expectations, what he defines as hope: "If the only home I hope for is the grave, if I spread out my bed in the realm of darkness...Where then is my hope? Who can see any hope for me?" (*New International Version*, Job 17.13-15). Here, though his "days have passed, [and his] plans are shattered" (*New International Version*, Job 17.11), having lost his vision of improvement, he has also released his attachment to a fixed idea about how his given condition will resolve. Here is where I find a connection between hope, faith, and love, enhanced by a portion of the Love Chapter. 1 Corinthians 13:7 asserts, "Love bears *all things*, believes *all things*, hopes *all things*, endures *all things*" (*English Standard Version*; emphasis added). Especially in times of trial, love is the great power of imagination, the ability to release the rational mind's need to know all the facts and what the outcome will be. When the disciples question Jesus about how anyone can be saved given what appears like draconian standards, Jesus replies, "With people, this is impossible, but with God *all things* are possible" (*New American Standard Bible*, Matthew 19.26; emphasis added). Jesus' clarity of "all things are possible" enhances the understanding of "all things" of the Love Chapter. When love leads, the consciousness that an ultimately unknowable mystery surrounds humans allows for potentialities beyond our limited imaginings.

Besides the facts and outcomes of human situations, the other aspect that faith and hope unlock in relying on the Great Mystery, as I sometimes call the Divine, is meaning. After "what" and "when," people seem to want to know "how" and "why" the most. In a mechanistic view, they want to look under the hood to see how the car works, so to speak. From the philosophical perspective, they wish to give significance and purpose to the events of their lives. This relates directly to the advice of Job's friends, who overwhelmingly think the "how" of Job's miserable circumstances is that God is punishing him for sin and the "why" is to drive him to repentance. Their understanding of the "how" and "why" cannot satisfy Job, because it seeks to limit the imagination. Therefore, their words are not ultimately acts of love. When God finally talks to Job, He only speaks about His unfathomable power to act and humanity's impotence even just in the face of nature, much less of the Divine itself. God shrouds the "how" and the "why" in mystery. Any attempt to truly fathom them will fall short and thus is prone to disappoint. Job's final realization embraces the love that is full of imagination: "I know that you can do *all things*" (*New International Version*, Job 42.2; emphasis added). Faith and hope spring from a love for the Divine that surrenders to the omnipotent Great Mystery and the unknowable what, when, how, and why.

    A female student responds to "Job, Man with an Upright Heart" with an application that investigates the human reaction to personal tragedy and suffering. Framed as a test-of-faith story, the book of Job also signifies how love underlies both hope and faith. After enumerating the afflictions Job experiences, the student posits, "It would be expected that a human would fall into a deep state of depression after all of these extreme, sequential losses." She tells the story of her friend MB, whom she praises as "the best woman that I know." MB had manifested her faith in God, the student reveals, by personal beliefs and by compassionate action for others. Nevertheless, MB experienced a major downturn in her health—worsened by a moldy apartment—which both caused her personal suffering and disrupted her plans for nursing school: "It seemed as though it could never get any worse for her, and somehow it always transpired to. During her distress, MB simply could not see what God was doing." Her faith unshaken by setback after setback, MB eventually began to recover her health, locate and move into a new apartment, and return to nursing school with top grades. She even found the blessing of a wonderful partner. This female student connects Job's faith to that of her friend during a dark night of the soul: "Like Job, she remained faithful, and she now can look back and safely say that she knows it took a series of tribulations in order for her to get to where she is in life presently."

Another female student applies the story of Job to her cousin Katy. A woman of Christian faith, this cousin had always been grateful for the many blessings of her life: a beautiful, spacious home that was always the center of communal get-togethers; a loving husband, whose air-conditioning business success allowed her to quit her well-paying job and remain full-time at that home and raise their son; and the financial means to allow her to purchase the neighboring house for her mother. "Katy was faithful to the Lord," the student asserts, "and God blessed her with wealth, health, and love." However, just as with Job, "Queen Katy," as the student lovingly refers to her, met with devastating loss—her husband, a Colombian by birth but an almost lifelong U.S. resident, was suddenly deported for reasons unknown to her. Colombia did not require his A/C trade skills nearly as much as the United States, and he found himself poor, nearly homeless, and unable to support his wife from another country: "Queen Katy started to lose everything; little by little it was all disappearing. She was eating away at her savings, because a mortgage on a house like that with no income was not cheap. She wasn't working and didn't have a car." Driven by both monetary lack and a devotion to being with her husband, Katy abdicated her "throne" in the beautiful house and moved to Colombia with her son.

In framing her cousin's story with the application of Job, this student takes the beginning of Job's troubles as a starting point. God permits Satan to attack, in her words, "a righteous man who has everything—money, land, family, and health" as an obstacle and a test of faith in order to mature and discipline it. She readily parallels her cousin Katy's worldly blessings with Job's. When devastating losses strike them, the lingering thought that God only blesses the righteous and only sends misfortune on the unrighteous persists in Job's, as well as perhaps her cousin's, mind. In one moment, Job, at a simplistic level, acknowledges God's sovereignty. Many of his own words about God's power echo what later issue from God's own voice: "He moves mountains without their knowing it...He alone stretches out the heavens" (*New International Version*, Job 9.5, 8). Still, he continues to view his conditions as sent punitively in some way: "Even if I were innocent...I am already found guilty" (*New

International Version, Job 9.20, 29). Only by faith beyond what his mind and his limited theology tell him can even suffering look like an act of love from the Great Mystery. The student cites the wisdom that Job speaks to his wife as the key to creating perspective-shifting meaning: "Shall we accept only good from God, and not trouble?" (*New International Version*, Job 2.10). For Job and "Queen Katy," their unrefined, superficial faith—arising amidst worldly success and circumstantial happiness—gets challenged and called to evolve into one that recognizes love in misery. Contemplating this unfinished work-in-progress at the time of her writing, this student herself has faith that Katy's "world falling apart...is not [because of] an act of sin but to test her faith in the Lord." Not knowing where love is leading is how faith works in tandem with it, believing that the same power that moves mountains only ever operates with love for humanity.

A male student uses the story of Job to activate his own imagination about the events in his life during the four years prior to his taking "The Bible as Literature" course, particularly in relation to his breakup with his girlfriend. This student recalls deeply questioning his belief in God during the heartbreak of that period: "I would get so angry at God that I would curse Him...I would ask myself, what's the point of being a devoted follower?" The student reveals that during his time of dating this fellow student, his goal was to provide her with enough money to allow her to just attend school and not need to hold a job. This required him to work over forty hours a week, limiting the amount of time he could devote to his own studies. With his being wrapped up in overtime and his studies, his girlfriend cheated on him. This student uses the lens of Job's story to reframe what could have been a victim narrative: "I could not see the big picture God had planned for me. I did not notice that my ex-girlfriend was pulling me off track from my goal in life...[but] God saw that [she] was taking advantage of me. He also knew that I was too in love to see it." The student thought, in the moment, that he was letting love lead, love for his girlfriend and the compassionate impulse to ease her life. However, the "big picture" of love that called him to a greater vision and purpose moved him higher, despite his attachment to the lesser one. Job, attached to his friends and their

"God must be punishing you" ideology, needed faith, hope, and love in his difficulties in order to transcend his small vision. This student required a similar experience "to realize that I was being distracted from my chosen path."

Whereas Job's experiences never drive him to lose faith, the story of Thomas from the Gospels clearly exemplifies a different kind of faith testing. A female student delves into doubt versus belief as she analyzes the story "Thomas, Doubting Apostle" and makes its application to her life. She describes the physical and mental abuse she experienced as a child from her father, who himself is a preacher. She had become acclimated to this maltreatment because "he raised me to believe that what he was doing wasn't abuse...I thought it was normal." Finally, in a moment of open conversation with her mother and brothers one day, she reports, "The realization hit me like a freight train chugging at 100 miles-per-hour": her father was an abuser. Her epiphany immediately drove her to suicidal thoughts and provoked night terrors filled with death and sorrow. Her faith in God immediately turned to doubt and even anger. Like Job, she asserts, "I needed Him to come down and explain the exact details of why this had to happen to me in order to forgive Him and believe in Him again." Again, like Job, the drive to make sense out of suffering always leads back to God and the Great Mystery—why?

For this student, as with Job, the question itself remained unanswered in the large sense. She realized in her struggle to create meaning that her earthly father, not her heavenly one, had chosen to behave in the ways that he did toward her. With an act of will, her father could have ceased from the abuse. This fact differs from Job's suffering in that Job underwent mostly natural events, e.g. the tornado that kills his children and the ulcers that cover his body. Still, his loss of animals to the Sabeans and the Chaldeans shows human free will in action, although not as intimately and personally as this student's experience of parental abuse. The question of how an all-powerful, all-loving God could permit either natural or human evil persists. But, as Jesus tells Thomas, faith that comes without understanding imparts a blessing far greater; I would assert that this blessing is the ongoing feeling that we humans can let go of our stress about being in control and having all knowledge about meaning. This is the "rest" that Jesus promises in Matthew 11:38, a freeing from the existential anxiety about every "why" we ask. In the student's case, her survival to tell the story has made her faith stronger, without the deep "why?" being answered: "He has pulled me to safer waters amidst the storm that was my life. Now it doesn't matter if I 'see' God or not—because I know He is there." And although, unlike Job, nothing can "replace" what was lost in any true sense, her statement "I also believe in the blessings that follow" indicates her faith in a restoration, and a peace "which transcends all understanding" (*New International Version*, Phil. 4:7).

Let the Children Come to Me: And a Little Love Will Lead Them

The majority of Gary's students are on the path of coming straight up through primary and secondary education and into college. Thus, most of their memory explorations consist of events that occurred as children or as young adults. Many have recently entered the work force, started living on their own, and in many other ways begun in earnest the individuation process. In the transitional years from childhood to adulthood, a paradox exists. Children have a dependency on adults for protection and education. Their relatively narrow experiences can only provide so much practical wisdom. Nevertheless, they are unburdened by the biases and prejudices of the world, the cynicism about humanity, and the dysfunctional adult ways of handling both rationality and emotion.

The Bible's stories and teachings often live in this paradoxical space where a child is both helpless and powerful, a know-nothing and a wisdom-bearer. Proverbs 22:15 states, "Folly is bound up in the heart of the child," yet David magnifies the Lord in Psalm 8:2, "Through the praise of children and infants you have established a stronghold against your enemies" (*New International Version*). Ephesians 5:1 exhorts, "Follow God's example, therefore, as dearly loved children," but in the prophetic words of Isaiah 11:6, God's vision for beings living peaceful co-existence includes that "A little child will lead them." Although instructed to "Honor your mother and father" in the Ten Commandments, children have a direct, divine connection that Jesus indicates in Matthew 18:10: "Their angels in heaven always see the face of my Father in heaven." Many stories that Gary's students recall in their application writing address this contradiction of being aware as non-adults of higher wisdom and calling and yet also appreciating the discerning, although at times restricting, guidance of grown folks. For these students, sometimes the love that leads comes from an intuitive or divine source, and sometimes it arrives via adults.

One female student, over two of her application writings, outlines the sometimes-rocky relationship with her parents that she reflects on through biblical lenses. In choosing the story "Walking Through Parted Waters" from *128 Greatest Stories*, she notes how the people of Israel both rely on Moses as a parental figure in their flight from Egypt yet also question and rebel against him. This student connects the Israelites' disobedient generation to the rebellious teen years and then makes the application to herself: "As a teenager, I always doubted my parents knew what was right for me and what was wrong. They were always re-convincing me…but not without me putting up a fight." With her retrospective application of the Israelites' story, she can see how she "continually lost faith" in her parents throughout her journey into adulthood. She can find two lessons from seeing the Moses/Israel story in parallel to the parental/child relationship. The first is that, despite her frequent inability to "see" the larger realities her parents could in her teen years, she ultimately could make sense of the right path she had to be "re-convinced" of during that time. Secondly, just as the pillars of cloud and fire represented the love of God leading the Israelites in the desert, so this student finds love, via her parents' unfailing intention, leading her in the right direction.

Later in the semester, this same student reads and responds to "Daughter of Jarius, Restored to Life." In this story, she sees her own father in Jarius himself. She recalls how she had been in a serious car accident a few years prior, in which her vehicle rolled three times off the highway. When her father rushed into her hospital room to see her, she immediately noticed his eyes appeared smaller, due to the puffiness of the surrounding skin. Her mother indicated later that he had been crying, something the student had never seen him do and which her mother had only seen in his tears of joy at their children's births. The student also saw that he repeatedly looked up at the ceiling as he spoke with her, although, due to an oppressive religious upbringing, her father was not a man of overt faith. "I often wonder," she muses, "was he thanking someone or something greater for my safety?" For her father to both break down his masculine stoicism and to acknowledge a hidden but deep reliance on the Divine clearly is another indicator of his love for his daughter. In the context of her prior application, I believe that this story embodies a very powerful "re-convincing" that parental love indeed is leading, and that somehow her father's spirit yearns to be led by it as well.

A female student writes compellingly of an incident in her life when the dependency of her youth was not met with love. She remembers a time when, having doubts in her own faith because of the negative influence of her atheist boyfriend, she approached her pastor. To her surprise, he employed a heavy-handed approach that shut down her questions as childish, using Bible verses as a bludgeon rather than a balm. Reading the story of "Jesus and the Children," this student resonates with "the Master" welcoming and blessing the children, despite the scorn of Jesus' disciples. Harmon, Reece-Demarco, and Reece conclude this story, "Long after [the little girl] forgot the words of Jesus' blessing, she remembered the [kind] look in the Master's eyes" (185). This student, unfortunately, remembered the "look" of derision in the pastor's eyes. Only in reading this story and re-membering what happened did she make the application that the one whom she *really* was seeking that day would never turn her away.

In a recollection of a time when the potentiality of youth was ignored, another female student connects the story "Jeremiah, Youthful Prophet" to her employment at a job with much older co-workers: "They hold the belief that any of the young team members are 'lesser than' in position, even if they continuously outperform the veterans." She recalls a man thirteen years her senior being in the running with her for a higher position. "Even though we were working in the exact same job and making the exact same wage, I was 'inferior' to him because of my age." This student's hard work eventually prospered, and she earned the position. In another scenario at her job, a twenty-six-year-old man who had only worked two months at the company began instructing her how to handle a situation: "He snapped that I was clearly doing it wrong...[and] went off on a rant how I wasn't old enough to understand the gravity of the situation . . . he would cut me off and tell me exactly what he believed I should do, while insulting my immaturity since I wasn't taking his advice." The student's memories of these work incidents arise in relation to Jeremiah's protestation about his own inadequacies for his call to ministry. In fact, she strongly resonates with God's reply to him from Jeremiah 1:7: "Do not say, 'I am too young'" (*New International Version*).

This same student, five weeks later in the semester, serendipitously read "Timothy, Youthful Pastor" in *128 Greatest Stories*, alongside Psalm 147. Here once again is a story speaking compellingly on the theme that ageism can run contrary to the divine calling in people's lives. Two facts become evident in her applications for these pieces. First, the student, though still stinging from the open hostility to her youth at her job, now feels empowered to stay true to her call, seeing in Timothy a New Testament exemplar of actions speaking loud against prejudice. As Paul exhorts him in 1 Timothy 4:12, "Let no one look down on your youthfulness, but rather in speech, conduct, love, faith, and purity, show yourself an example of those who believe" (*New American Standard Bible*). The student additionally connects the theme of Psalm 147—the omnipotent Father who nevertheless wields power with goodwill—to the way her earthly father interacts with her. She admits that she often approaches her parents with the same tenacity and determination she does her job, and at times this has meant rebellion. Nevertheless, unlike the domineering pastor in the previous student's application, this student's father has balanced forbearance with authority. "Throughout my life," she asserts, "my dad has acted like the powerful figure that extends mercy to me in the moments that I least deserve it." In her two-step introspection about age and authority, the student has let love nurture her spiritual growth into both confidence in her calling and appreciation for both her earthly and heavenly fathers who equipped her for that calling.

I find in this and other students' writing the power of gratitude in relation to parents as a vision-shifting technique, because it forces a perspective change from viewing only what one perceives as negative or even just neutral to what is positive. Paul closes his first letter to the Thessalonians with the brief but powerful exhortation "Give thanks in *all circumstances*" (*New International Version*, 1 Thess. 5:18; emphasis added). I find strong resonance of "all circumstances" with the "all things are possible" that I mentioned above. This admonition does not imply that we never *recognize* bad circumstances or that we paint over them as "all good." It simply suggests that challenging times, more so than good ones, call us to evoke the difficult imaginative task of meaning-making, and thankfulness (just like Gary's assigned application) obligates us to search for the faith/hope/love virtues that provide that meaning.

After recognizing the theme of grateful praise from Psalm 100, one female student connects the transformative potential of gratitude with a tradition her father has maintained since she was young. She reflects on the power of "entering His gates with thanksgiving" and narrates her father's ritual of appreciation for life's blessings: "Every year for Thanksgiving, my dad has a story he shares about a Thanksgiving years ago when each person was rationed five kernels of corn. Therefore, in a bag we have five pieces of candy corn, and everyone in my family goes around and lists five things that we are thankful for." The student's father, by enacting this ritual in a communal rather than just personal setting, powerfully evokes biblical remembrances such as the Passover feast and the Last Supper. In this case, however, the *contrast* of having little (five corn kernels) and having much (a full Thanksgiving meal) is an amplification of gratitude via perspective shifting. This student concludes her Psalm 100 application saying it "reminds me of how lucky I am for all the good things in my life and not to focus on the bad." Thanksgiving for all of her blessings, she realizes, can extend beyond a single day. Moreover, purposely entering into those "gates" of gratitude expands both her hope as "basic trust in life" and her understanding of love as evidenced by both divine and human providence. As Michael Bernard Beckwith affirms, "Gratitude is...a recognition that even before we ask, good has been given to us" (13).

    This motif of a psalm awakening memories of parents and gratitude also occurs for another female student. In her application of Psalm 104, she relates the admonition "forget not all [God's] benefits . . . who satisfies your desires with good things" (*New International Version*, Ps. 104.2,5) to her nightly childhood prayer ritual with her brother: "Mother would have the two of us say ten things that we were grateful for, our blessings from God. We would say...our family, friends, school, shelter, food, clothes, etc." The student then realizes that her gratitude in that very writing moment, resonating with the psalm, is allowing new appreciation of the long-forgotten practice, instilled by her mother. She proceeds to expand that childhood list with people and things from her current world, such as the opportunity to attend college, her computer, and the like. Moreover, the psalm's repeated exhortations of "Bless the Lord . . . bless the Lord" create the perspective shift and epiphanic moment the student needs: "People ask God to bless them...but hardly bless the Lord...This Psalm made me think that I rely on God to bless me and take care of me...but I need to off more praise to God, thanking Him for watching me day after day." All manner of perspective shifting is occurring here. The student dives into memory to appreciate her mother's wisdom in encouraging "giving thanks in all circumstances." That appreciation allows her to see she has been remiss in that practice. Finally, she mindfully moves beyond the view of the good things in her life as given or arising from natural and logical reasons to the perspective that sees blessings as a mystery and thus gratitude to the Great Mystery as imperative for those who wish to let love lead.

    While another female student can relate to gratefulness for love leading from her parents, she nevertheless—both in her life and in the story of a close friend—finds resonance with biblical stories of needing to separate from cruel and oppressive adults. Coming from a South Asian background, the normative scenario of her culture entails submitting to many male and parental-dominated traditions. This student relates to the tale of Michal, Saul's daughter, who becomes a mere tool for political manipulation by the males in the story. The student feels a retrospective gratitude for the empowering way that her own parents raised her:

> My parents always taught me to stand up for myself and not allow anyone to make my decisions for me. They taught me to be my own person and to develop my own sense of being. Traditionally, this goes against the culture of that I originate from. I chose my own husband, and I was not forced into any sort of ridiculous traditions. My mother-in-law, on the other hand, wanted me to abide by the old-fashioned rules. She wanted me to listen to her and to be available for her if I was needed. While I allowed her to take advantage of my kindness for seven years, I realized that I had to become my own person. Although she does not like the new me, I have made myself quite clear to her.

The student also relates the story of the escape of the Hebrews from Egyptian slavery to the harrowing experience her friend endured living with an abusive mother. "In some ways, she was a slave in her own home," the student recalls. "She was beaten by her mother on a regular basis, all because my friend would not conform to the way her mother wanted her to be. Flesh was pulled out from my friend's arm, and her blood streaked the walls." When her friend finally moved out to escape her torture, she had to endure a time of trial, just like the wandering Hebrews. The student's biblical framing of her friend's enslavement, liberation, and adversity on the road to independence represents not only the Hebrews' journey out of Egypt but embodies the words of Isaiah 61:1—later echoed by Jesus—that God purposes to "proclaim freedom for the captives and release from darkness for the prisoners" (*New International Version*). She also draws inspiration from her friend's self-love, the inner-directed spiritual nurturance, that provided strength to break free her bonds.

A similar application by another female student details a friend's escapes from an abusive parental situation. She recalls the painful story of a confidant opening up about her cruel father. This man challenged his then-five-year-old daughter to race him over a ledge and down an icy slope, with the prize for her winning being a puppy. The father sprinted toward the falloff, his daughter on his heels. He stopped suddenly as she went careening over the edge, tumbling face first down the hill and into a tree. He stood laughing at her suffering. The cruelty of her friend's father, whom she eventually emancipated herself from, stunned the student. Her negative reaction was met with a moment of perspective-changing wisdom:

> I said to her, "I don't even know him, and I want to kill that bastard."
>
> She said to me, "I used to want to also, but now I feel sorry for him because he will never know what it feels like to have his children respect him like my children love and respect me every day. In a way he taught me everything not to do, and because of him I did everything the right way.

In reading how the early Christians forgive Saul for his deadly persecutions, the student finds the application that within forgiveness lies inner freedom. That which a person hates becomes an entrapment. For the original followers of Christ, forgiving Saul allowed his conversion into Paul to exert a transformative influence on their own Christian walks. In her friend's case, pardoning and learning from her father's example gave her the freedom to let love lead in her new family.

A final story of youth and gratitude comes from a female student's application of the story of Boaz. She evokes the similarities between her position as an immigrant from East Asia to the U.S. and Ruth's situation as a stranger coming from Moab to Bethlehem. This student's unfamiliarity with the language, food, people, and environment were only the beginning of her troubles: "People discriminated against me because of my race. My classmates made fun of me because of my accent. I was the only 'different one' in the entire school. They all looked at me like I was a panda in the zoo. I was actually planning to commit suicide because it was just too hard for me to live." This student clearly understands, like Ruth, what being a stranger in a strange land entails, to the point where she had almost given up faith and hope in living because she felt no love.

Love enters the student's story via her version of Boaz, a young man named Leon, who is of Hispanic heritage. He is also a person on the margins, so he can empathize with those in a similar position. She remembers, "The only reason why I didn't kill myself is because of Leon [,]…the only person that understood me and accepted me as a friend. Leon didn't care [where I was from], and he told me he was different, too." Ruth's story provides a way to give this student new meaning and appreciation to Leon. In fact, Ruth's name possibly derives from $r^{e'}$ $ût$, meaning "view" or "seeing" (Hubbard 94), for indeed just as Ruth is truly seen by Boaz—an act of love itself—so Leon sees this student as a person of worth. Even more connected with vision, she is able to view Leon's act of kindness in a new way via her resonance with Ruth in the application moment. This young man restored her faith and hope via his loving act of seeing, and in closing her writing, her spiritual nurturance turns to gratitude: "If I ever had the chance to talk to Leon [again], I would tell him 'Thank you for being my friend.'"

Lighting the Shadow: Revisioning to Re-love

I mentioned earlier in the chapter that students most often see themselves in resonance with the protagonists of the Bible stories they read, either as the hero or the sufferer. Another case I find even more compelling is when students identify with the antagonist—the adversary or victimizer. Sometimes the realization of past wrongdoing via the mirror effect of the biblical application process brings about a change of heart, a new perspective gained via the illumination of one's shadow side. I would offer a more nuanced term about this than the word *repentance* and its connotations. Considering this book's theme, perhaps the word *re-love* might be more appropriate, for in all cases, the application path of theological virtues leads to re-visioning something through the lens of love.

I find compelling the fact that the Bible itself has a version of this process whereby story leads to shadow lighting and then re-love. After David impregnates Bathsheba and sends her husband, Uriah, into particularly hazardous battle conditions to kill him, the prophet Nathan tells the king a parable, as retold in *128 Greatest Stories*:

> A rich man owned many cows and sheep. In the same town a poor man lived who owned just one little lamb. The lamb meant a lot to the poor man and his family. In fact, it was their pet. One day the rich man began to prepare a banquet, but he did not want to kill any of his own animals for the meal. So he stole the poor man's lamb, cooked it, and served it to his guests. (113)

When David reacts in fury at the fictitious rich man, Nathan shifts the king's vision for him: "You are that rich man." While Nathan uses the parable to empower David to make the connection to the king's life and values, David himself must complete the application process by delving into his memories, cathecting with the poor man, and drawing his parallels to the story. By doing so, he derives new meaning about what has transpired and ultimately must re-love Uriah, whose wife he stole and whom he killed. At the moment of identification with whomever a reader perceives as misguided or erring, that new, loving perspective can open an opportunity for change of thought, and maybe of deed as well.

A female student writes of such a moment in her application of Psalm 141. Her particular focus is verse 5: "Let a righteous man strike me—that is a kindness; let him rebuke me—that is oil on my head. My head will not refuse it" (*New International Version*). She relates this wisdom to her friend of over a decade, Uma. The two met as coworkers and formed a bond of similar dedication to their jobs. Beyond her friend being industrious, this student describes Uma as "loyal, trustworthy, sincere, honest, a good listener, and empathetic," attributes she values in a friendship. However, despite all these qualities that would make her feel good, the student asserts, "She cares enough about me to rebuke me. I realize that a true friend who has my best interests at heart may have to periodically hurt me by correcting me. I accept and appreciate this from Uma because I understand she is protecting me from the consequences of wrong behavior." Although this student does not mention a specific instance of Uma's reprimand, this single verse reminds her of the nature of loving rebuke. Although scholars do not agree on whether David wrote Psalm 141 before or after Nathan's parabolic reproof, clearly David's attitude of openness to a re-loving view change is unquestionable in both his words and his deeds. More importantly, this student uses this verse as a springboard to realize her blindness to her imperfections and that, like David needs Nathan, she needs Uma to lovingly lead sometimes.

Another female student finds her moment of re-loving via reading Psalm 78. Here the psalmist focuses not on a single guilty party but on the rebellious people of Israel as a whole. This student feels struck by being "taught using a negative example," at first co-participating with the psalm writer in the censure of the Israelites unbelief and erring ways. In the contrast between the people's rebellion and God's love, she grasps the "wonderful example of God's good deed towards his chosen people." By not obscuring the people's shortcomings, the psalm provides a form of societal confession that also serves as a warning to future generations. The student quickly progresses from seeing Israel's faults as "Other" and into her own confessional moment: "I really should stop judging the Israelites so harshly . . . especially since I do not claim to be saved...I am a sinner. I know full well that I would go to hell if I died right now." In the student's shift of approach, I find a strong Gospel resonance with the story of the woman caught in adultery and the stunning words of Jesus: "Anyone here who has never made a serious mistake be the first one to throw a stone at her" (Moore *Book of John* 55). This statement highlights the recurring biblical principle of self-reflective application that underlies Gary's pedagogy of reader response. Jesus fundamentally asks, "Is the Other in you?", and by seeing her own deficiencies and easing up on her censure of the Israelites, this student drops the handy stone she might easily have hurled and enters a confessional mode. Her moment of "The Other needed to re-love God" morphed into "I, too, need to re-love God."

A male student also finds a re-loving moment in observing the strong parallels between himself and Lydia, a merchant from the city of Philippi. Although only mentioned in two verses in Acts 16, she receives a full narrative, "Lydia, Merchant of Purple," in *128 Stories*.

He notes that this woman distinctly represents a certain transgression against ancient Asia Minor's patriarchal notions of who could earn prestige in the market, especially selling purple with its scarcity and overtones of male-dominated royalty. The story describes her as one who "worshiped God" already; however, the portion that resonates with the student powerfully explains, "She felt her heart being opened to Paul's message. It burned within her" (217). From this single point of entry, this student begins his application reflecting on his struggle with intellectual and emotional change as a theme of his life: "The irony of this is that at a very young age, as an Army Ranger team leader, flexibility was not only one of the most important attributes for success, it was one of the very first lessons we learn." His twenty-seven-year business career after the Army, however, found him "as rigid and firm in my ways as a piece of lumber." Part of his inflexibility expressed itself in strict controls placed on both his corporate and home lives. He was not so much living life as managing it—scheduling everything, including dinners and social functions with his wife.

The student's application continues, finally describing his wife's complaint about the military precision and business-like handling of their family that had drained the warmth of love from it. "My response to her," he confesses frankly, "was a coldly-framed request that she send me an evite [electronic invitation] in order that I might schedule [a family meeting about] it in my BlackBerry." The student's wife presented him with an ultimatum—either change and set his priorities straight, or leave. Via the biblical lens of his application, he describes his epiphanic moment: "I *aspire* to become like [that young, flexible Army Ranger team leader] again. My wish is that by becoming more flexible and willing to change, my *heart* open as well. This is who I *hope* to become" (emphasis added). This student views the short story of Lydia as both something he resonates with—her business' prosperity—and as a cautionary tale for himself to keep his heart open to the warming influence of the Gospel. In noting Lydia's marketplace success, especially against the forces of patriarchy, this student finds empathy with a fellow businessperson, willing to devote effort to succeed. By embracing Lydia's openness to moving beyond simply worshipping God and into the closer relationship that Paul encouraged, the student parallels his desire to move from being a hard-working, efficient breadwinner and house manager into a deeper and more connected relationship to his family. His use of *aspire*, *hope*, and *heart* clearly indicate his application moving through all three theological virtues. In this student's case, the ultimate desire to nurture and re-love his family really is a signal of the deeper love which he has that matches Lydia's: a love for a more profound truth, a truth revealed by change of perspective.

Descending to Ascend: The Power of Perspective

All students in "The Bible as Literature" class undertake a weekly journey in the application writing process. I have framed this journey through the three theological virtues of faith, hope, and love as a descent into memory and then an ascent to "higher vision." However, this journey motif, while innovative in terms of pedagogical technique, is not new to the human experience or literature. In my background in classical literature, I have studied how both Odysseus and Aeneas descend to the underworld to gain a vision of how to reach home. This pattern, of course, is repeated in Dante's *Divine Comedy*. In the Bible itself, both the Hebrews and Jesus had desert experiences—forty years and forty days, respectively—in which they went through a "hell on earth" to reach their callings. Even the Jewish practice of Merkabah mysticism, according to theologian Bruno Borchert, relates both a "descent into the inner being of the individual" and "an ascent to God's throne" (141). In leveraging the dynamism of an archetypal pattern, Gary has constructed a "productive and generative space" where literary *investigation* can morph into personal *transformation*. I will close this chapter with the reflections of one last female student, from her final paper for the semester. She writes,

> I want to take this personal response to say how thankful I am for this class…[It] has forced me to venture out of my shell…to also expose some of my darkest moments…and when given the opportunity to share our stories with the world,

[to] have the ability to change the lives of others, like others have changed our lives...[I now realize] we must accept people for who they are.

I could offer no more fitting conclusion than this student's epiphany from the course. Not only did her weekly application journeys transform her by the leading of unconditional love, but she also now acknowledges her connectedness and commitment to both her small (classroom) and larger, human communities.

Acknowledgements

I would like to thank the following students (from the fall 2014 semester of "The Bible as Literature") whose responses I included in this chapter—Mary Lauro Bell, Lihui Cao, Arielle Cruz, Aasia Dastgir, Hillary Davis, Jose Flores, Carmi Jiménez, Hali Kudler, Elizabeth Lee, Jon C. Lee, Kaitlind Mendoza, Anslee Merchant, Jessica Pane, Vonabell Roocke-Sherman, and Jamie Sproat.

Works Cited

Beckwith, Michael Bernard. *Spiritual Liberation: Fulfilling Your Soul's Potential*. Atria Books/Beyond Words, 2008.

The Bible. English Standard Version, Crossway Bibles, 2001.

The Bible. New American Standard Bible, The Lockman Foundation, 1975.

The Bible. New International Version, Biblica, 2011.

Campbell, Joseph, and Bill Moyers. "Ep. 3—The First Storytellers." *The Power of Myth*. Billmoyers.com. 23 June 1988. https://billmoyers.com/content/ep-3-joseph-campbell-and-the-power-of-myth-the-first-storytellers-audio/. Accessed 29 Sep. 2018.

Dyer, Wayne. *You'll See It When You Believe It*. William Morrow, 1989.

Harmon, Dan, Colleen L. Reece, and Julie Reece-DeMarco. *128 Greatest Stories from the Bible*. Barbour, 2005.

hooks, bell. *All About Love: New Visions*. Perennial, 2000.

---. *Teaching Community: A Pedagogy of Hope*. Routledge, 2003.

Hubbard, Robert L., Jr. *The Book of Ruth*. William B. Eerdmans, 1988.

Moore, Thomas. *Gospel—The Book of Matthew: A New Translation with Commentary—Jesus Spirituality for Everyone*. SkyLight Paths, 2016.

---. *Gospel—The Book of John: A New Translation with Commentary—Jesus Spirituality for Everyone*. SkyLight Paths, 2018.

Schwab, Gabriele. *Imaginary Ethnographies: Literature, Culture, and Subjectivity*. Columbia University Press, 2012.

Chapter 5

Superstar: Retelling the Story of a Radical

Scott Neumeister

> I am frightened by the crowd, for we are getting much too loud.
> Judas in "Heaven on Their Minds"
> Andrew Lloyd Webber/Tim Rice, *Jesus Christ Superstar*

In 1980 when I was in eighth grade, my Episcopal parochial school arranged for my entire class to go see Andrew Lloyd Webber and Tim Rice's *Jesus Christ Superstar*. Even at thirteen-years-old, I knew that some controversy surrounded this musical, from the depiction of Mary Magdalene as having affection for Jesus beyond an agape-type of love to the omission of the Resurrection. Its most subversive quality for me at that age, though, was its use of rock music mixed with its biblical narrative. Since I had grown up in very traditional Episcopal and Presbyterian churches, this contemporary cultural relevance with my favorite music genre hooked my attention immediately. Preparing to write this chapter for *Let Love Lead* in early 2018, I was perusing the "Reader Responses" from Gary's fall of 2014 class that serve as material for this chapter. Synchronistically, NBC was set to broadcast a live performance of the revamped *Superstar* with John Legend in the role of Jesus and Brandon Victor Dixon as Judas. Gary asked me, "Have you seen that they are broadcasting the show live?" and on the evening of April 1, I was in front of my television. As I watched the musical, tears came to my eyes at the power of both the music and the story line. Many of the students in Gary's course wrote on subjects and themes from the Passion Week. Immediately put into autocritographical mode, I wanted to explore why I was reacting so strongly to this musical in relation both to my past and to the students' work.

One of the factors that my introspection afterwards about *Superstar* revealed to me was that the musical, in many ways more than the biblical account, highlights the events of Jesus' life in a political context. While the Gospels obviously emphasize Jesus' spiritual ministry with their focus, the workings of all the figures of political power in his story—the Pharisees, Pontius Pilate, and Herod—all come to the fore within the musical. Just as importantly, Judas gains an almost sympathetic voice, perhaps another reason for the controversy that *Superstar* roused upon its release. I see now that the musical wakened my first inklings that Jesus was a *radical* political figure, entangled in politics but not the revolutionist that Judas had perhaps envisioned he would be. Given the fact that I have now spent almost a decade both studying and living the tenets of feminism and womanism—the radical notion that the "personal is political" and that people of all identities deserve social justice—I now realize where one of the germinal seeds of my "radicalization" lie: *Jesus Christ Superstar*.

As I am writing this chapter in September of 2018, the season for the Emmy Awards is occurring. John Legend, Andrew Lloyd Webber, and Tim Rice have just won the Emmy for producing the best variety special, *Jesus Christ Superstar*. For Legend, his accomplishment is historical, in that he now has not only the distinction of the EGOT status—winning an Emmy, a Grammy, an Oscar, and a Tony award—but he is also the first black man to do so. Legend, speaking of his racial background in relation to Jesus, remarks, "Well, we've often seen Jesus look like he's probably from Oslo or something. The chances of Jesus being born and raised in the Middle East and looking like he's from Oslo are pretty slim. I think I probably look closer to him that a lot of people who have played him in the past" (Fallon). But even more than authenticity (some argue that Legend is merely "blackwashing" a Jewish figure), his portrayal counteracts the supposedly "unracial," and therefore white, representations that precede him in so many *Superstar* casting choices. NBC chairman Bob Greenblatt admits the positive response in the casting, "I got so many emails from [African American] people in our company…the day we announced the casting just saying thank you for doing this.

It's radical" (Fallon). By the vision shift allowing blacks to *see themselves in Christ*, Legend and NBC are further opening the radical relatability of Jesus to more people.

Another factor that moved me so much about the musical, in memory and in the contemporary moment, is the emotionality of the performances. Neither the Episcopal nor the Presbyterian churches in which I grew up contained much emotion—I was a member of the "frozen chosen," the term for a decorous, businesslike, and reserved congregation. Within these settings, not even the biblical readings would take on an undue amount of feeling or intensity. Having grown up in very unemotive church settings, I was accustomed to pastors, priests, and lay readers presenting the Gospels in very somber ways. The emotive qualities of *Superstar*'s performances, enhanced by the music, really *humanized* the characters in the biblical story for me. They opened up a perspective to me about the Gospels that enlivened them beyond just pieces of spiritual wisdom interspersed within a plot narrative. In a way, they brought the Bible down from the lofty, spiritual pedestal I had set it upon and grounded it in really human grit, feeling, and—as I mentioned above—politics. In the opening song "Heaven on Their Minds," Judas warns that he wants to "strip away the myth from the man." This aim provides a warning about the shadow side as one of the cruxes of *Superstar*: if we become too heavily invested in the spirituality and worship of Jesus, we also slide into elevating him to merely "superstar" status and thus disconnecting him—and the other people in the Gospels—from our lived experiences.

I will be using *Superstar* as both a means of reflection on aspects of Holy Week and as a way to dialogue with the students' work. My thematic from Chapter 4 runs into this one: the power of perspective shift in awakening to new vision. Jesus himself was a compelling view-rearranger, offering time and again new modes of seeing people, situations, and the Divine itself. Rice and Lloyd Weber, as well as the various actors of *Superstar*, also injected their own dynamic approaches to the biblical stories, walking the line between exact duplication of the biblical stories and creative license to reinterpret them—as Harmon, Reece-Demarco, and Reece do in *128 Greatest*

Stories from the Bible. Ultimately with the Gospel accounts, the reader is left with what Robert M. Price calls "the open-ended, open-textured character of literary texts [that] compels the reader/viewer/hearer to fill in certain 'zones of indeterminacy'," factors left under- or unaddressed in the text that ask for the recipient's collaboration ("Introduction"). We readers/viewers are active collaborators in filling in the blanks. Additionally, the work of autocritography/application itself enables this collaboration and empowers transformative shifts of mindset. By the process of Reader Response, "The Bible as Literature" provides a lens to students for new ways of seeing events in their lives in relation to the Bible and in doing so, as this book is titled, of letting love lead.

Temple Therapy: Healing the Inner Sanctum

I already mentioned the fact that *Jesus Christ Superstar* planted the seed for me to grasp how radical the ministry of Jesus is. One of the first radical acts he performs during Holy Week is his cleansing of the temple. This event is actually the second one recorded in the Gospels, the first occurring just after Jesus begins his ministry (John 2.13-17). From sitting in church and hearing flatly read scriptures, my image of Jesus as a human often came across as the "meek and mild" protagonist of these readings. This particular episode had never conveyed the affect of what was going on—*Superstar* completely changed that fact in its song "The Temple." The hedonistic intensity of the vendors' portrayal in the Temple and the almost-diabolical, entrancing musical riff juxtapose with the fierceness with which Jesus drives them out, screaming, "My temple should be a house of prayer, but you have made it a den of thieves!" In an interesting move, the musical then portrays the sick overwhelming Jesus with demands to be healed. This connection between the temple and the body makes for a linkage to the first of Gary's students I will engage in dialogue.

A male student performs a similar move in his application from the story of "Jesus Cleanses the Temple." Although he doesn't specifically cite the verse in his writing, this student extends the metaphor found in 1 Corinthians 6:19: "Do you not know that your bodies are temples of the Holy Spirit, who is in you, whom you have received from God?" (*New International Version*). Inspired by the resonance of the "temple" from both the figurative and literal standpoints, this student describes his personal story of the defiling of his own temple(s). When he was nine, his father hired a woman for the family restaurant and permitted her to stay at their house during the week. This arrangement precipitated an affair between the student's father and the female worker. The "temple" of the family household plummeted into chaos, with terrible fights between the parents. In a display of righteous indignation similar to Jesus' wrath at the money changers in the temple, this student tried to stand up for his mother. His father physically abused him in retaliation. Clearing the home/temple was beyond his capability as a child, although eventually his parents would reconcile.

Long after the student's physical wounds healed, however, the emotional ones remained. The theft of his home's sanctity parallels the degeneration of the Jerusalem temple into a "den of thieves." He divulges, "For a long time, even after my parents were able to reconcile, my temple, my soul, and my spirit were polluted with hate for that woman and bitterness toward my father. Even when I went away to college, thinking that would help me, those feelings still went along with me." Michael Bernard Beckwith has termed this misplaced notion of moving locations to bring inner peace a "geographical healing." He proposes, "Even if we succeed in improving an external situation and gaining some temporary relief, nothing has actually transformed. Eventually, we are forced to face what we sought to avoid in ourselves" (28). The student, only by relying on his faith, has begun to release his anger toward his father and the woman. Moreover, in reading the narrative of Jesus' temple-clearing, he now joins his own story into the biblical one: "I realize that the pollution inside of my temple needs to be cleansed...God is the only one who was able to help me get rid of such pollution. I am very grateful to Him for cleansing my temple." This young man's slow inner transformation, his driving out the inner thieves of his peace, has allowed a healing process to begin, and the mysterious connection between himself and Jesus honors the life-changing power of "The Bible as Literature's" application component.

In this Passion Week episode, I can see the working of both the political and the personal. The cleansing of sacred space of the Temple in Jerusalem embodies a social act of disrupting capitalism's greedy excesses in a location set aside for spiritual devotion. However, much more is occurring than disrupting commerce through protest. As Beckwith notes with his "geographic healing" concept, those moneychangers could easily go other places and be the same "thieves" they were in the sacred space. Their greed goes with them everywhere they go. The radical notion of Jesus is to have an *inner* revolution of values, not just external respect for any spiritual institution. Thomas Moore extends the clearing of the Temple to mean more than just a physical act, "Jesus brings to an end the notion of…the religious institution as a business…His message is a radical one. The kingdom is inside you and all around you" (*Book of Matthew* 132). The temple we all carry around must therefore be resanctified.

This student is describing something similar to what Jesus later calls out for the Pharisees in Matthew 23:27-28 concerning their externally "clean temples" without a changed (and healed) soul: "Watch out, you legalists and Pharisees! You're like painted mausoleums. Outside they look great, but inside they're full of the bones of the dead and all sorts of filth. In the same way, on the outside you look beatific, but inside you're full of hypocrisy and scheming" (*Book of Matthew* 147). Origen asserts the link between this story of the temple clearing and soul cleansing: "The temple is the soul equipped with reason. Jesus applies his discipline to it, when it has . . . dangerous qualities. It appears to be beautiful but isn't" (qtd. in Moore *Book of John* 14). So, just as Jesus' clearing of the Temple *physically* could only create a temporary fix, He calls people (this student included) to self-reflect, become authentic at the soul level, and begin to experience an inner wholeness that goes beyond any external circumstance or action.

Before leaving this scene of the musical/biblical story, I also wish to address the immediately subsequent healing described in Matthew 21:14. Jesus tends to the physically disabled after the temple cleansing. In *Superstar*, Rice adds another element to this scene: Jesus gets so crowded by the hoard seeking to touch Him that He ultimately yells, "Heal yourselves!" This moment was also quite stunning for me as an eighth-grader; wasn't Christ supposed to be this infinitely-patient, all-compassionate being that could refuse no one's request for restoration? How could he be so...*human*? I see two factors operating in this moment. The first is Rice's intention, as stated in Judas's opening song, to "strip away the myth from the man." Could Jesus "lose his cool" if overwhelmed by a mob? He had just done so with the moneychangers, so the potential in that moment exists. Secondly, and perhaps more importantly, the directive to "heal ourselves" matches squarely with the temple-cleansing move. All of the years of sitting passively in church (sometimes six days a week) saw me often "touching Jesus," but no active connection was occurring. Only personal intentionality, not mob mentality, could activate real divine connection. This is another aspect of autocritography: the active seeking of oneself within the text is an intentional, as well as intimate, act of "healing yourself." It does not discount divine presence—instead, it joins the personal to the Great Mystery that is part of all healing.

Judas: When Greed Leads

The next aspect of re-viewing *Jesus Christ Superstar* that prompted my introspection is the role of Judas Iscariot. My understanding of Judas from having grown up in the church was very one-dimensional. In literary terms, he is almost a "stock," flat character, with little depth to him. The musical expanded the role of Judas and gave him the prominent position of the opening song—as well as the penultimate one, delivered posthumously. The approach Tim Rice took in presenting Judas, especially in the opening "Heaven on Their Minds," highlights the radical nature of Jesus' ministry because it illuminates how different Jesus was than expected *logistically*. Judas, as Peter Malone describes him, "acts as a devil's advocate" (70), constantly opposing Jesus' methods and motives, just as the devil does in the Gospels' accounts of Jesus' desert temptation.

Judas questions Jesus' spiritual mission, remembering how upon first meeting Jesus, "No talk of God then, we called you a man." He highlights the reprisals if Jesus' message draws undue, harmful attention by both the Roman and Jewish powers, warning, "We are occupied, have you forgotten how put down we are? I am frightened by the crowd, for we are getting much too loud." Whatever Judas' aspirations for any kind of political revolution, he opposes Jesus' methods from the opening of the musical. I could sum up his repeated message to Jesus as: "Why do it *that* way? My way is better." As the musical progresses, Judas has inner conflicts about whether to betray Jesus or not, lamenting his reward for his treason as "blood money," but he nonetheless proceeds with the arrangement. Perhaps, as *Superstar* portrays it from the beginning, Judas is not greedy for the thirty pieces of silver—he is covetous of things going *his* way and according to *his* limited perspective. By not embracing Jesus' radical vision, Judas lets greed, not love, lead.

The students who chose to write about "Judas Iscariot, Greedy Disciple" in *128 Stories* most often focused on this aspect of greed and the promotion of self-above-other in their applications. I was most drawn to the students who identified themselves with Judas as the guilty party in some form. This self-calling out, to me, is one of the most difficult yet rewarding uses of the autocritographical approach, and it links clearly to both the temple-cleansing and "heal yourself" motifs I wrote about earlier in this chapter. In my own autocritographical writing when analyzing texts by authors of color who suffer intersectional oppression, I quite often found myself as the "bad guy" in those stories. *I* was the advocate of the high, Eurocentric, male voice in literature that black womanist scholar Barbara Christian decries. *I* was one who, metaphorically, approved of black oppression without rabid white supremacy, the one Frederick Douglass would sarcastically give "the proud name of being a kind master" (3). In identifying with the oppressive force, I repeatedly experienced the liberation of what the Bible might call "repentance," a deep and painful acknowledgment of mistakes I made. I have thus chosen two students whose applications of the Judas narrative find them recognizing and ruing their own greed, impelled by reflection on Judas' actions.

One female student writes an application in which she sees herself in the Judas role of greedily wanting things her way. She narrates how, in the midst of their two hectic lives, she continually attempts to monopolize her boyfriend's free time to make up for the busy-ness of their school and work schedules. She confesses that, in general, "I often guilt trip him about activities that he has already planned and try to sway him into cancelling in order to hang out." In an example she provides, she tries to convince him to abandon his previous commitment to supporting one of his long-time friend's inaugural football game. She insists that he come to an event she herself is hosting, even though she would be unable to socialize with him. Her boyfriend's firmness about the original commitment "led to my disappointment and a quick argument." In the name of her own grasping at her boyfriend's attention, she sows the seeds of discord. By means of the self-reflective autocritographical mode, however, this student sees the nature of her greed by looking through the perspective of her boyfriend, and how "it was important to support his friend from childhood."

I am reminded in this student's story of another important Judas reference in John's gospel, also found in *Jesus Christ Superstar*'s song "Everything's Alright." When Mary anoints Jesus' feet with an expensive perfume, Judas complains about the waste of money and the potential sale to raise money for charity—an overtly reasonable justification. John calls Judas out for his real motives in John 12: "He wasn't really concerned for the poor but was actually a thief. He kept the money box and would steal from it" (Moore *Book of John* 85). Likewise, given the fact that this student could not really "hang out" with her boyfriend at the event she was hosting, her motives for wanting him there are not as "reasonable" as they might appear on the surface. Jesus' insightful response shows his adeptness at perspective-shifting: "You always have the poor among you, but you don't always have me" (Moore *Book of John* 85). Similarly, the young woman's boyfriend knows that there will never be another debut football game for his friend, whereas her job often involves setting up of events he could attend. Priority goes with ephemerality. So, even though this student's self-identified resonance with Judas appears to lack the import and deep betrayal aspects of the biblical account, her association with Judas' dissembling selfishness and limited viewpoint link her to another facet of the "Greedy Disciple" that awakens her.

Another female student's application of "Judas Iscariot, Greedy Disciple" links her story to Judas' act of self-seeking betrayal. Her narrative not only resonates with Judas as treacherous, it also has a kiss as the central act. She begins with critiquing the biblical story itself, reflecting "I have been pondering about why Judas would betray Jesus or how he could justify his actions to himself, much less to God." This young woman then recollects a time in her mid-teens when she succumbed to the strong temptation to kiss a male acquaintance whose affections were already set on her friend's sister. Remembering her own action of betrayal, she begins to see herself in the biblical story: "Nobody likes to think how they have betrayed Jesus or other people. . . I especially do not like to think about the really stupid [thing] that I did when I was young that I still cannot justify to myself, much less to God." Despite her "not liking" doing so, this student takes the courageous step to call out her own betrayal, reflect on it, and grow from the self-reflexive process.

In trying to seek meaning in the biblical story, this young woman delves into her own story. She ponders a mix of reasons for wanting her disloyal kiss. Aligning with the text's section's "greed" subtitle, was it just selfish desire for the young man, relatable to Judas' desiring things to go his way? Was it jealousy for her friend's sister, paralleling Judas' resentment at Jesus' popularity? Was it revenge for her friend's sister being involved with this student's old boyfriend, as Judas was perhaps seeking payback for Jesus not operating politically the way Judas wanted? The student's application doesn't resolve the single ultimate cause of her betrayal, and perhaps wisely so, if all these factors were in play. She ends her writing with two biblically-espoused actions: she expresses gratitude for her current partner, whom she appreciates as removed from the turmoil of the contentious social rules surrounding friends and romantic relationships. Finally, she confesses remorseful concern for those she wounded previously:

"I can only hope for the best in the lives of the people that I hurt." I see this student, by working through the confessional aspect of her application, emerge more like Jesus' other notable disloyal follower—Peter—whom Jesus asked three times, "Do you love me?" for each of the apostle's denials of Christ. Love can lead the one who is willing to re-examine the heart, no matter the betrayal.

Judas' story ends, of course, with his own feelings of remorse, but his means of seeking atonement is through returning the thirty silver pieces and committing suicide. The flatness of Judas' character in the Bible leaves considerable room for his vilification, and this fact only becomes more amplified by the fact that the "superstar" Son of God was betrayed by one of his closest friends. For his treasonous act, great philosophers and theologians have labeled Judas the ultimate sinner. Perhaps the best-known of these is Dante, who places Judas in the frozen lowest circle of Hell, with Satan forever chewing on him. Of course, this gnawing symbolizes the work of guilt that Judas obviously felt at this death. However, the numbing conditions even more represent the distance from this book's central theme, as Kim Paffenroth explains: "The worst betrayer, the one who knowingly destroyed his relationship with the Son of God, thereby rejecting the greatest offer of *love*, is surely the most icy, the most cut off from *love*" (28; emphasis added). Acts of greed and betrayal remove us from the three kinds of love spoken of in the two greatest commandments: love of God, neighbor, and self. Both the flatter biblical and more rounded musical portrayals of Judas convey a human struggling with this precept and the downfall of the failure to let love—in all its venues—lead.

Pilate: Politics (In)action

The last thread of the Passion Week story I wish to explore in the students' writing—inspired by my re-examination of *Jesus Christ Superstar*—is the role of Pontius Pilate. Like Judas, Pilate's biblical portrayal is rather flat, and he also suffers the same easy blame that the "greedy disciple" does. This factor, along with my simplistic view as an eight-grader of a Roman provincial governor's political role in

Judaea, left me open for a shock when I first saw the rock opera. While much of *Superstar*'s musical affect came from the harder-driving elements of Judas' songs like "Heaven on Their Minds" and "Damned for All Time," the song that actually moved me the most was "Pilate's Dream." In it, Pilate foresees that his dealings with a Galilean will lead to "thousands of millions crying for this man. And then I heard them mentioning my name and leaving me the blame." This brief critique of the oversimplification of Pilate echoes the same issue that Judas brings up in the line "Just don't say I'm damned for all time"—namely, these adversarial people are more than one-dimension characters; they, too, experienced human emotion and inner conflict to which many readers/viewers can relate. Moreover, by having even a small amount of empathy, the potential autocritographer can resonate with the negative traits and consequences of textual characters and take these as cautionary lessons.

I wish to address one clear deviation of *Superstar* from Pilate's biblical account. Matthew 27:19 states that the dream actually came to Pilate's wife—apocryphally named Procula—who then told her husband, "Don't have anything to do with that good man. I have felt terrible all day because of a dream I had about him" (Moore *Book of Matthew* 179). Tim Rice made the artistic decision to merge the two: "We had planned for Procula to have the dream, but then Barry Dennen[, the actor who would eventually portray Pilate,] came along, and we were so pleased with him that we decided to bring him on early in the recording" (Nassour and Broderick 41). One could argue that the removal of Procula amounts to an act of sexism on Rice's part, in the long tradition of erasing or silencing women's voices. I would counter that the biblical narrative itself gives no meaningful importance to Procula's words, as we know nothing of Pilate's inner thoughts concerning them. The monologic "Pilate's Dream" thus creates an entry point for the audience to see themselves in Pilate's place, just as the reader response approach in the Bible at Literature does.

Including the dream into the play's narrative with such haunting music and lyrics makes an important statement about how love can try to lead from unexpected places. A female student connects to Pilate's wife because of the mysterious power of a dream she once experienced. Her great-grandfather's symptoms of Alzheimer's disease had grown to the point of requiring him to reside in assisted living. She recalls, "I had a nightmare in which he was lying on the ground and couldn't get up. There were several people walking around him, yet no one would stop to help. He finally stopped asking for help and just lay on the ground." Two amazing things happened the next time she went to the care facility. First, she discovered that her great-grandfather had been persistently receiving an overdose of sleeping medication, keeping him more sedated than he needed—or wanted—to be and thus asleep on her many visits. She also witnessed, after telling the nurse that he had accidentally spit out a pill he was supposed to take, the staff ignore her request for a new one. Witnessing his helplessness in the face of the facility's dereliction connected her instantly to her mysterious and prophetic dream. Within weeks, this young woman's grandfather had expedited her great-grandfather's departure from that location to "a new home [that] treats him wonderfully" in Philadelphia. Moreover, because of this student's dream and family intervention, her great-grandfather was wide awake and interactive the day when she said goodbye to him before he moved north.

    Modern Western thinking has tended to de-emphasize the role of dreams and placed them into the realm of impractical curiosities. Because of both their non-logical tendencies and their ultimately enigmatic origins, dreams simply do not work well with the societal drive for explainable rationalism. Thomas Moore, long a practitioner of dream exploration in his therapy work, asserts, "Dreams come from a place that is very deep and mysterious. Given our backgrounds that extend so far back in time, and *all that stirs us*, as well as our material lives, we are very deep and profound people. All of this comes out in our dreams" (Peay; emphasis added). That which stirs us can come from both the explainable and the unexplainable, the Great Mystery that the divine represents. Dreams present us with the milieu in which the rational mind relaxes just enough for an opening to that creative, perspective-shifting energy to irrupt into consciousness, unfiltered by reason. For Procula and this female student, this exemplifies itself with compassionate concern for the innocent, both truly examples of love leading, only in this student's case those in power—the student and her family—chose to act, whereas with Procula, her husband chose political inaction that ultimately led to Christ's crucifixion.

Another female student divulges an even deeper experience of resonance with Pilate as guilty through passivity in the biblical story. She particularly focuses on Pilate's symbolic washing of his hands as he refuses to personally act to prevent Jesus' condemnation by the Jewish leaders. "It was a symbol that he considered himself to be free from blame and guilt," this student emphasizes, "if the innocent man were to be executed." She then applies this symbolism to an incident with her college girlfriend. This friend's brother sold drugs on the same campus, but this student herself never tried to pry into her friend's personal life too intently, much less call out the brother for his activities. One evening, a young man overdosed in her dorm, and she watched in horror as the student's seemingly lifeless body was taken out to the ambulance. She then overheard the drug-selling brother ask, "Do you think he will rat me out?" This student sees in retrospect how her inaction made her complicit in the young man's overdose. She opens up, "As I go back, I feel like Pontius Pilate. I can even relate to him. I had washed my hands of the matter, slid the truth under the rug. And just like Pilate said to the Jews, 'Kill him yourself,' I, too, felt as though I had let my friend's brother kill [my dormmate]." Although in the end the young man survived, this young woman expresses that just the imagined reality of his death takes on new meaning: "Standing by and watching others do bad things made me just as guilty as if I had done them." Seen through the lens of Pilate's fecklessness, her pasts inaction becomes a fault she now determines not to repeat.

A male student also finds himself aligning with Pilate's inaction in the Passion story. This student, the head porter at a new car dealership, relates the story of being tired at the end of a day's work and unmindfully passing off a customer complaint to one of his assistants who is lacking in both authority and customer care skills.

"The last thing I wanted to do," he recalls with regret, "was deal with a guest." The assistant's clumsy interaction angers the guest even more, and by the time this student intervenes, the customer is aggravated almost beyond reconciliation. The young man first asks, "What could we do to make this situation better?", to which the customer's response of "Nothing, I am fed up with this shitty place!" recalls the anger of the crowd at Pilate's plea to acquit Jesus. He luckily avoids the trap of Pilate who, in turning Jesus over to the mob, cannot undo the crucifixion process. He is able to satisfy the customer with some recompense far more effective than Pilate's release of Barabbas. Afterwards, this student receives a "dressing down" for not doing his job, but his retrospective application of Pilate's "just handing down" the responsibility for Jesus' fate perhaps indicates a rethinking of how he could have let love lead proactively instead of reactively.

Another scene involving Pilate in *Jesus Christ Superstar* that riveted me was Jesus' whipping. Having heard the Passion story exclusively narrated from the Bible up to that point, I found it easy to avoid imagining what that moment was like; the entirety of its mention in the Gospels is the short sentence that Pilate "had Jesus flogged" (Matt. 27.26, Mark 15.15, John 19.1). In fact, Christ's suffering in general felt sanitized to me until I saw *Superstar*. The static representation of immobile, slow-suffering of Jesus on the cross that I had seen in so many crucifixes could not match the intensity of that re-enacted whipping, especially driven by Lloyd-Webber's musically discordant crescendo. When I later viewed Norman Jewison's film version of the musical, I watched Barry Dennen's Pilate match the music's intensification as he counts each lash up to thirty-nine. *Superstar* was consequently my visceral introduction to the sufferings of Jesus that I had learned *intellectually* were in the name of humanity's salvation but had never experienced *emotionally*. This depiction catalyzed the "desanitizing" of Jesus' torture in the Bible and evoked a deep, empathetic imagination about this figure that, despite the overemphasis on His divinity, even Pilate sees as a human sufferer after his flogging, exhorting in John 19:5 "Look! The man!" (Moore *Gospel of John* 125).

Another male student utilizes the ordeal of Jesus' trial before Pilate and subsequent torture and crucifixion to draw out the theme of the link of suffering to service he sees in the story of Peter/Abdul-Rahman Kassig. While most of Gary's class write their applications relating to themselves or their family and friends, occasionally students find a strong connection with those beyond their close social circle. The student reveals his bond with Kassig in the fact that they both served as Army Rangers. At the time of this student's response, the news had just reported that Islamic State militants had beheaded the captive Kassig. He discovered that Kassig had received a medical discharge from the Rangers but had returned to the same region where he had served militarily but this time as a humanitarian worker. The student comments, "He chose willingly to return to a war-torn part of the world with the sole intent of relieving human suffering," and gingerly draws a connection between Christ's courage to metaphorically perform the same task. Although he respectfully asserts, "I do not want to be so bold as to state that Peter Kassig was Christ-like," he cogently relates Kassig to Jesus via the motto he learned as an Army Ranger: courage is being afraid but going on anyhow. This student concludes his application with his own grateful memories of awakening to Christ's suffering via the cinematic Passion play of his generation—Mel Gibson's *The Passion of the Christ*. The student affirms of Kassig, and obliquely of Christ, "Understanding all too well the dangers he was facing with this undertaking, [he] chose to go, regardless . . . Peter Kassig, thank you for reminding us what it means to live a fulfilled and meaningful life."

I believe that this student's application becomes even more profound once further details of Kassig's life emerge. In delving into the aid worker's story, I find strong reasons to go deeper into the comparisons of Kassig with Jesus and the Passion Week events. Jesus ponders the suffering to come in his moments of agony in the Garden of Gethsemane. Kassig, writing a letter to his parents while in captivity with the Islamic State militants, echoes this fear, "I am obviously pretty scared to die…If I do die, I figure that at least you and I can seek refuge and comfort in knowing that I went out as a result of trying to alleviate suffering and helping those in need" (qtd.

in Westcott). Asked about his switch from the military to humanitarian work, Kassig remarked in 2012, "I can either be in a position to deliver tens of thousands of antibiotics for women and children, or I can be another young man with a gun" (qtd. in Meuse). Here I grasp this Peter proactively embracing the words Jesus spoke to Simon Peter after the latter had cut off the high priest's servant's ear in the moments of Jesus' arrest. "Put your sword back," Jesus commands Peter in Matthew 26:52, "Whoever lives by a sword will die by a sword" (Moore *Book of Matthew* 171), or, as in the words of "The Arrest" in *Superstar*, asks, "Why are you obsessed with fighting?"

Kassig was captured and imprisoned with a devout Syrian Muslim who influenced Kassig's conversion to Islam and his changing his name to "Abdul-Rahman," which can translate to "servant of the most merciful." By all accounts a sincere conversion and not an expedient to be released or shown mercy, this change of heart emulates the condemned thief's conversion next to Jesus on the cross in Luke 23:42. Abdul-Rahman's chosen name not only exemplifies the criminal's request for mercy to his Lord, it also evidences his parallel to the Suffering Servant, who shows mercy though treated unmercifully. Moreover, in the student's words, both found power in their "willingness to succumb to the cruelty of humanity for humanity's sake." Finally, the letter that Kassig wrote to his parent vividly displays the work of love in the dynamics of Kassig's life. In first saying thank you to his parents, Kassig writes, "Your love and patience are things I am so deeply grateful for…Don't worry, Dad, if I do go down, I won't go thinking anything but what I know to be true. That you and mom love me more than the moon & the stars" (qtd. in Westcott). He directly attributes his mission of mercy with the love he received from his parents. I see a potent connection with 1 John 4:19: "We love because He first loved us" (*New International Version*). Thus, love leads not only because of embodied examples, but because love is the very nature of the Divine that we are mysteriously created to reflect.

This final student paper contrasts with the others I have discussed in this chapter in that it finds an admirable quality to amplify rather than finding a negative one to avoid, as with profaned temples, selfish actions, and irresponsible inactions. Still, each student's entry into her or his chosen biblical episode comes from personal resonance with people *as people* in the Bible. Although my strong religious upbringing in the Episcopal and Presbyterian churches had given me much knowledge of the Gospel narratives, neither any Scripture reading nor any sermon from the pulpit had infused those stories with a relatable emotionality or a radicalness that spoke to my young mind. My experience of *Jesus Christ Superstar* in the eighth grade, even before I had the critical skills to contemplate it, was my own significant moment of resonance with individuals who were simply characters in a story I had heard repeated, possibly too often to even be invested any more. The humanizing and politicizing aspects of *Jesus Christ Superstar* empowered a view shift in my consciousness that brought Jesus to life for me as more than the mythologized, "meek and mild" Son of God. He became a more fully-realized human, engaged in the realms of human politics and emotions. Perhaps just as importantly, the rounding of the other characters in the story—especially antagonists like Judas and Pilate—permitted the same question of "What of myself is in them?" that many students I have highlighted in this chapter ask.

Using dramatic and musical aesthetics as their tools, Tim Rice and Andrew Lloyd Webber are just two people in a line of many who collaborate with the Gospels to awaken new perspectives. Dan Harmon, Colleen L. Reece, and Julie Reece-Demarco also work to create alternate approaches to the Scriptures in *128 Greatest Stories from the Bible* via a narrative context. Just as these writers craft fresh and nuanced meanings from the Scriptural accounts, so each student autocritographer's use of memory, empathetic imagination, and self-reflection collaborates with their texts in "The Bible as Literature" to create personal meaning. After such collaborative introspection, the student's changed inner world can then manifest in the outer one. In this way, when compassionate contemplation results in personal and then political transformation, this is a sure sign that love is leading from the radical—root—level.

Acknowledgements
I would like to thank the following students (from the fall 2014 semester of "The Bible as Literature") whose responses I included in this chapter—Jose Flores, Carmi Jiménez, Hali Kudler, Jon C. Lee, Jessica Pane, Lourdes Saenz, and Cayla Sanelli.

Works Cited

Beckwith, Michael Bernard. *Spiritual Liberation: Fulfilling Your Soul's Potential*. Atria Books/Beyond Words, 2008.

The Bible. New International Version, Biblica, 2011.

Douglass, Frederick. *A Narrative of Frederick Douglass, An American Slave*. 4th ed., Dow & Jackson's Anti-Slavery Press, 1845.

Fallon, Kevin. "How John Legend Became the Black Jesus We Need in *Jesus Christ Superstar: Live in Concert*." *Daily Beast*, 27 Mar. 2018, www.thedailybeast.com/how-john-legend-became-the-black-jesus-we-need-in-jesus-christ-superstar-live, Accessed 17 Sep. 2018.

Malone, Peter. *Screen Jesus: Portrayals of Christ in Television and Film*. Scarecrow Press, 2012.

Meuse, Alison. "For U.S. Soldier Turned Aid Worker, The Goal Was to Help Syrians." *NPR*, 15 Oct. 2014, www.npr.org/sections/parallels/2014/10/15/356122509/for-a-u-s-hostage-facing-death-syria-meant-a-new-life. Accessed 16 Sep. 2018.

Moore, Thomas. *Gospel—The Book of Matthew: A New Translation with Commentary—Jesus Spirituality for Everyone*. SkyLight Paths, 2016.

---. *Gospel—The Book of John: A New Translation with Commentary—Jesus Spirituality for Everyone*. SkyLight Paths, 2018.

Nassour, Ellis, and Richard Broderick. *Rock Opera: The Creation of Jesus Christ Superstar from Record Album to Broadway Show and Motion Picture*. Hawthorn, 1973.

Paffenroth, Kim. *Judas: Images of the Lost Disciple*. Westminster John Knox Press, 2001.

Price, Robert M. *Jesus Christ Superstar: The Making of a Modern Gospel*. E-book, eBookIt.com, 2011.

Peay, Pythia. "At the Intersection of Psychology and Spirituality: Part Three of my interview with former monk and psychotherapist Thomas Moore." *Psychology Today*, 17 Jan. 2014, www.psychologytoday.com/us/blog/america-the-couch/201401/the-intersection-psychology-and-spirituality, Accessed 16 Sep. 2018.

Webber, Andrew Lloyd, and Tim Rice. *Jesus Christ Superstar*. NBC, 1 Apr. 2018.

Westcott, Lucy. "'Pretty Scary to Die:' ISIS Hostage Kassig's Letter to Parents." *Newsweek*, 6 Oct. 2014, www.newsweek.com/pretty-scared-die-isis-hostage-kassigs-letter-parents-275613, Accessed 16 Sep. 2018.

Chapter 6

Jesus at the Intersection: Where Feminist Meets Womanist

Gary L. Lemons

In her vision of womanism, Alice Walker compares it to feminism through a color-based simile—"womanist is to feminist as purple to lavender" (xii). As figurative shades of difference between the ideas of female for female equality, human rights, and social justice—the two ideologies are interlinked especially in the connection between "[a] black feminist [and a] feminist of color." From the Introduction of *Let Love Lead* to the ongoing representation of autocritography as a strategic genre I employ to teach "The Bible as Literature," not only have I revealed how concepts of feminism and womanism have undergirded its pedagogical foundation, but I have also demonstrated their integral significance in my spiritual evolution. This chapter further builds upon the idea that Jesus' message of love for humanity—male *and* female—is rooted in the liberating agency of faith and hope.

I continue with my particular interest in how students I have taught in "The Bible as Literature" comprehend this message in their responses to texts I utilize in the course to foreground Jesus' acts of love as models for revolutionary activism in service to human salvation. Also, framing this chapter as a Class Discussion, I again feature the interpretive analyses and self-reflections of students from the fall 2015 course, as well as those who most recently completed its spring 2018 session. In fact, the opening section of this chapter functions as a preface to how I purposely came to liberate my thinking about feminism and womanism related to my pedagogical practice in the 2018 version of the course. In it, I openly and directly promoted Jesus' works of love in a feminist-womanist context.

Class Discussion Part III: Sisters in the Struggle, Family Matters

Of the narratives I assigned students to read in *128 of the Greatest Stories from the Bible*, the story "Mary and Martha, Sisters of Different Priorities" (198-200, ref. Luke 10; John 11-12) continues to draw my attention. In one student's personal, narrative response to it in the fall 2015 version of "The Bible as Literature," I would realize how intrinsic class discussions focused on women's relationships with Jesus could be literarily *and* literally enlivening. Specifically, the student's "reader response" to the story is integrally linked to how Jesus responds to the sisters in the narrative.

The story of Mary and Martha begins when the sisters invite Jesus to their home—along with his disciples and other folk. As the narrative develops, he has to deal with some real issues of "different priorities" between the sisters. Apparently, many people in their community have experienced the kind-heartedness that they possessed; they have a "reputation of hospitality." Often folk are invited to their home in need of food and a place to stay. From the beginning of the story, the sisters clearly have a longstanding friendship with Jesus, as they "invited [him] to stay with them anytime He came to Bethany" (199). Of the two sisters, Mary loves his teaching. When he visits the home, she "delighted in sitting at [his] feet and hearing." In this case—her sister, Martha, is the one with the primary task of preparing the meals and cleaning the house, "even when she felt overwhelmed by the magnitude of the task she faced." However, Martha never stops doing her work—even though she has begun to feel "resentment" toward Mary as "[m]ore than the usual number of guest had appeared." Mary was no help once again: "[s]itting at the Master's feet, listening to His words." At this point, enough is enough for Martha—"A pang went through [her], and a lump formed in her throat. If only she could also sit at the master's feet and hear what He said."

Here the narrator intervenes with some questions: "Why didn't Mary realize the burden she placed on her sisters? Why didn't she offer to take her place supervising the endless chores, the roasting and baking, the bread making and serving?" In self-reflection, Martha thinks to herself that her feelings are not warranted. Martha knows how much her sister loves to hear Jesus teach. She knows that Mary does help in some of the necessary tasks of "cooking and cleaning" their home. Martha reflects: "[Mary] just couldn't bear to be out of Jesus' sight when He came, even to help with the serving." But she thinks maybe she should follow her sister's lead and "just [walk] away from my tasks and [join] her" (199). At the same time, Martha knows if she stops serving, the people will suffer—"[n]one would be given food or drink until their bellies loudly protested." Needless to say, Martha is conflicted in these family matters.

 To resolve her concerns, Martha approaches Jesus and shares them: "Lord, dost Thou not care that my sister had left me to serve alone? Bid her therefore that she help me" (199). I believe this is, indeed, a bold move by Martha. I am sure Jesus knows before she speaks that she has an attitude of "resentment" toward Mary, who in the moment is struck by her sister's feelings of neglect. Caught up in Jesus' teaching to the invited guests, herself, and the sisters' brother Lazarus, Mary has no idea that Martha feels this way. Relating this scene, the narrator comments: "Like a child, [Mary] stood with bowed head and quivering lips. What must Jesus think of her? She scarcely dared raise her head enough to look at either Him or Martha." Interestingly, after a while, Jesus comments in "a voice that held more sadness than condemnation." Actually, what he says to Martha sounds a bit puzzling: "Martha, Martha…Thou art careful and troubled about many things" (200). The reader might ask, what does Jesus know about the "many things" that "troubled" her? What one does understand—especially after reading the "The Poor Widow's Mites"—is that Jesus is an observer. Just as it saddens him to watch the rich people give large sums of money to be publicly honored, perhaps, it makes Jesus unhappy to witness Martha's attitude of "resentment."

 While her thoughts about serving the needs of the invited guests are to be recognized and respected, perhaps, she should have taken time—as she also desires—to listen to Jesus' teachings. Nevertheless, Martha takes Jesus' words to her as a compliment rather than a "condemnation." Even so, the narrator asks, "[W]hy did He address Martha instead of her slothful sister?" (200). What an interesting choice of words the narrator uses to describe Mary. The term "slothful" has a number of negative connotations, especially related to *laziness*. This suggests that instead of Mary being compellingly drawn to the teachings of Jesus, she is simply "sitting at [his] feet" because she has no desire to work—or help her sister. Jesus knows this is not so. For in response to his complimentary words to Martha, she begins to shed tears in "shame at having complained." Openly admitting one's feelings can be painful, yet as the reader witnesses in this moment, the sisters come together in comradery as "[t]enderhearted Mary sprang to her sister's side. She wrapped her arms around Martha"—saying to her, "I will help you...Then we both shall sit at Jesus' feet."

How the sisters come to terms—uniting in their desire to be on equal terms with "hearing" Jesus' teaching—is communicated in a position of communal humility. Time and time again, those who sincerely believe in the "Master" teacher often position themselves at his feet, rather standing with him. Symbolically, this resonates as Jesus illustrating Divine love for humankind through the mastery of his storytelling. Also, the setting of people sitting together at the feet of Jesus (as he sits) suggests an atmosphere of informality, rather than one in which the Teacher stands in an authoritative position of lecturer (or "high" priest). What Mary *and* Martha comprehend at the end of the story is that, while laboring to serve people is a good thing, service to others should not be about *self*-promotion. As such, it will always lead to *resentment* if what one does is not publicly recognized. The narrator of the story understands this idea, ending it with the fact that Jesus' time as a visitor to the sisters would come to an end:

> In saying Mary had chosen that good part that would not be taken from her [having listened to the Master's teachings], *Jesus wanted Martha to focus on what was even more important. He would not always abide in the home at Bethany. Martha must learn to store up His teachings, as Mary did, against the time of His departure. Everyday duties would*

always abound. The opportunity for the sisters to hear Him would not. (200; emphasis added)

I have learned in teaching the life of Jesus and the acts of love he presented that time spent in personal reflection about what it means to serve others is not about public recognition. While my desire is that my teaching as a pro-feminist and womanist black man will be acknowledged by my students as life-transforming, I must not allow academic egotism to override calling to practice what I teach in "The Bible as Literature" about Jesus as the "Master" Teacher of love, faith, and hope. As exemplified especially in one student's response that follows, issues of gender and labor are also interlinked to culture and generation. In her personal reflection of the story, she (Maria Silva) addresses what gender meant to her grandparents coming from a country outside the U.S. to visit her family:

> If I wanted to impress [them, after each meal during the week stay with them in my home, I would have to] pick up all the plates and wash the dishes...Wondering why this was the case, [I was told by] my father that I should work in love to please her grandparents. I recall my grandfather called out, asking why I had asked for help. [One day], he then came over and lectured me about [my request]. [B]ecause I [am] a female, I had to clean the kitchen. He continued on about how my brother was tired from eating the meal and needed to rest. I was in disbelief of his reasoning; however, out of respect I lowered my head and began to clean. My brother eagerly ran off knowing his duties had been relieved...Soon I realized that this expectation was warranted beyond the kitchen.

On another occasion before the grandparents left to go back to their home country, the grandmother also began telling her about duties ascribed to females in the home. This occurred when the granddaughter had asked her brother to help her with a cleaning task. She states that her grandmother,

> had been drinking tea at the table when she overheard me and quickly...[began] to lecture [to me] that I was a female, and therefore it was my responsibility to fold the laundry. She then smiled sweetly and resumed her tea drinking as she walked

back to the table. Infuriated I began to resent my brother. How did he get to [leisurely enjoy our grandparents' visit], while I attended to the household chores? The next day when my father came home from work, I pleaded the unfairness I had felt the previous few days. He listened to my frustrations then pulled me into a hug and explained that he did not agree parents; however, [given their age], I had to obey their commands. [My father] asked me to remember that they would soon leave.

Ultimately, this student comparing herself to Martha in the story and learned this from her "resentment" toward her sibling. She continues,

Like Martha, I did not see the good in the presence of a loved one such as when Jesus visited her family's home. Rather I focused on tasks and in turn they consumed my compassion and formed into jealousy. When it came time for my grandparents to depart, this newfound understanding allowed me to see the pain in their eyes as [my grandfather] hugged us and [my grandmother] broke into tears. At the time we were unsure when we would see them again, and the importance of quality time [with them] reigned in my thoughts. My brother and I are much older now. We have been blessed to see our grandparents on multiple occasions over the years; however, I see them with new eyes. They still have expectations of me to play the role of what they believe should that of a "woman," and to please them I abide to most of these anticipations. Yet I no longer resent my brother when he [does not help me with the household chores].

A New Course of Action: What Did This Require?

In closing the Class Discussions as a re-envisioning in the fall 2015 semester course of "The Bible as Literature" with the story of "Mary and Martha, Sisters of Different Priorities," I include it here to mark my eye-opening transition in reconceptualizing the course. While holding no antipathy toward anyone for having *not* chosen to incorporate my pro-womanist teaching standpoint into the course, I had not overtly affirmed my *female* students' critiques of patriarchy. Why not? From the time I began teaching this course in 2014—in not professing a radical pedagogical standpoint that examined biblical narratives from a pro-feminist/womanist perspective—in actuality, I perpetuated patriarchy in the name of the "Father-God" I had grown up knowing in an ultra-conservative, black religious setting. Was this my purpose in teaching the course? As I stated in the opening chapter of *Let Love Lead,* in gratitude to have the opportunity to teach a course focused on biblical literature, I did not want to cause trouble. Students would drop the course, I thought; thus, I would not be able to teach it.

While growing up having taught the Bible in Sunday school and Bible study in black church settings, in truth, I had deeply internalized the *anti-*feminist idea that any critique of patriarchy—as portrayed in the Bible—would be viewed not only as heretical but as blasphemously in defiance of the "Word of God." Ultimately, however, as the Spirit of love would have it, in my calling to teach "The Bible as Literature," I would come to the realization that excluding feminism from the course was about self-betrayal. Everything that I had come to know about the liberatory power of feminism conceptualized in the feminist writings of bell hooks, Alice Walker, Audre Lorde, Patricia Hill-Collins, and Layli Phillips Maparyan—among other black/feminists and womanists of color—had been hidden in my ego-driven, professional desire to have students affirm my work in our biblical course work together.

Little did I know at that, after teaching the fall 2015 version of the course, my fear of blasphemously teaching the Bible from a pro-feminist/womanist perspective would come to an end when Susie Hoeller (as noted co-author of *Let Love Lead*) would introduce me to the work of Sarah Bessey in her book *Jesus Feminist: God's Radical Notion That Women Are People Too, An Invitation to Revisit the Bible's View of Women* (2013). Moreover, in line with this happening, one afternoon in 2015 at the university where I teach, while checking my mailbox in the English department office, I found a package sent to me from Neil Averitt. I found it contained a book titled *The Single*

Gospel: Matthew, Mark, Luke and John Consolidated into a Single Narrative (2015). Just as I had never heard of Sarah Bessey's name or her book, I had never heard of the Neil Averitt or his book. For some time prior to this moment, I had begun to think that the direction and focus of my course should change. The message: teach "The Bible as Literature" about the life of Jesus from a pro-feminist/womanist standpoint. Amazingly, the primary course materials I needed to do so had been sent to me. Without doubt, as I began to reconceptualize the course, I would embark upon a new life-transforming journey recovering the revolutionary nature of my being a pro-feminist/womanist, black male professor in con*texts* of the supernatural. Revising the course syllabus, I envisioned it accordingly, as stated:

Course Objectives:
1. This semester we will explore what Leland Ryken calls the "ingredients [that] make up this new approach to the Bible" (11). During the semester, we will read about the life of Jesus as narrated in *The Single Gospel*. Not only will this text take us into the life of Jesus, it will allow us to engage stories about the lives of various individuals with whom Jesus interacted—particularly related to the politics of gender.
2. We will examine it through Sarah Bessey's "invitation [to us] to revisit the Bible's view of women." Both *The Single Gospel* and *Jesus Feminist* will not only help us to understand how gender is represented biblically, but will enable us to see ourselves more deeply as human beings.
3. Most importantly, the study of Jesus' interactions with people will help us to comprehend the complexities of human experiences in a biblical (con)text.

Course Outcomes:
1. By the end of the course, your critical analyses and interpretations of *The Gospel* and *Jesus Feminist* will have brought you closer to the complex realities of your everyday life experiences.
2. Having read the narrative of Jesus' life in "The Bible as Literature," your study of it may be viewed as a mirror for

your *own* self-empowerment—having provided you will literary analytical, interpretive, and stronger writing skills.
3. Studying the biblical life history of Jesus not only provided you with a deeper intellectual knowledge, it also moved you to think about the emotional *and* spiritual dimensions of literary studies.
4. Having analyzed and interpreted Jesus' personal experiences and those of the individuals he encountered (in his thirty-three-year life journey), you created a pivotal pathway to comprehending your own personal life struggles—in and beyond this classroom.
5. My hope is that readings in *The Single Gospel* and *Jesus Feminist* offered you a new vision of "the Bible as Literature," offering you a broader, global of human experience(s).

In this revised version of the course, while I still did not employ the term "autocritography" to describe the papers students wrote in response to the readings assigned, I nevertheless placed emphasis on the importance of critical self-reflection. Thus, I refer to the students' writings as "reflection" papers. In all the courses I teach, students write papers (in a "folio" format) throughout the semester as the foundation for class discussions.

This is how I framed the requirements for the "reflection paper" (70% of the course work) composed for the folio (as stated in the syllabus):

- The folio students produce and present papers from in class (throughout the semester) will contain the REFLECTION PAPERS focused on *The Single Gospel* (with support cited from *Jesus Feminist*).

Format for the Reflection Paper:
1. Each Reflection Paper should include an in-depth discussion of thematic aspects of the readings in *The Single Gospel* related to Jesus' experiences connected to people in his life (for examples: relatives, friends, children, co-workers, teachers, religious and government leaders, among others). Center your reflection(s) around issues of gender, class (as in economic status), (dis)abilities, nation-state affiliation(s),

among other relational dynamics you discover in the readings assigned each week.
2. Think about writing your Reflection Paper with some of these themes *and* issues in mind—trust, unity, love, acceptance, loyalty, patience, forgiveness, commitment, transformation, liberation, community, jealousy, domination, oppression, power, discrimination, abuse, hatred, and the list goes on and on...You certainly may contemplate other themes and issues not listed here.

Important notes:
1. In your Reflection Paper include a response to the reading assigned from *Jesus Feminist* using at least *one* quotation from this text (relating it to the representation of female identity as it appears in the reading assigned each week from *The Single Gospel*).
2. Most importantly, see the "Discussion Questions" Sarah Bessey asks at the end of *Jesus Feminist* related to each chapter. Respond to one or more of the questions for each chapter in your Reflection Paper.
3. All Reflection Papers must be typed, single-spaced.
4. Overall, your Reflection Paper must be at least 300 words in length.

Jesus is the Real Deal in *The Single Gospel*
"I Am the Way and the Truth and the Life" (John 14:6, NIV)

> In the end Christianity is about Jesus Christ. Everything that Christians want to claim about God is captured in that life that Christians believe is the "Word made flesh." Jesus is the Eternal Wisdom embodied; Jesus is the utterance of God that shows us God; Jesus is the definitive revelation of God to humanity.
>
> Ian Markham, Foreword to
> *The Single Gospel*

Having introduced students to the new course direction in teaching biblical narratives based on the life of Jesus, I would become more able to show them the path that Jesus took as the revolutionary model of pro-woman(ist) activism. In reading and interpreting Jesus' life-calling and labor for human liberation, students would find Averitt's *The Single Gospel* and Bessey's *Jesus Feminist* (as the primary course texts), particularly enabling *and* spiritually insightful. I would witness the transformative agency of the love Jesus personified as I interacted with students' analytical, interpretive, and personal reflections about these texts in the spring 2018 offering of "The Bible as Literature." Not only would I experience this power within the students' autocritographical writings as they shared its life-saving effects in their everyday lives, I would also interpret it as a profound affirmation of my pro-womanist calling in the college classroom. Teaching *The Single Gospel* and *Jesus Feminist* set me on yet another spirit-filled path of hope by connecting my spirituality with my academic positionality.

Before settling on *The Single Gospel* as one of the core texts for my womanist concept of the course, I read Ian Markham's "Foreword" to it. He states that what makes this book interesting is Averitt's work toward the "harmonization" of the writings that compose the New Testament Gospels as recounted by Matthew, Mark, Luke, John. Growing up reading them in church, I never examined ways these authors' writings differed in how they documented Jesus' life and his works. No one—ministers or pastors—in the churches I attended ever pointed out differences in their accounts. Markham says, "In our heads we have a 'single Gospel,' but nowhere does that 'single Gospel' exist" (xiii). In actuality, as he points out, Averitt took on the work (for nearly a decade) to create consistency in the four writers' documentation of the life of Jesus. In effect, Averitt:

> has created the single Gospel…And it works. The narrative is a delight to read. It combines the best of scholarship with an accessible. Wisely, he uses the most familiar phrases from the King James Version. Footnotes helpfully illuminate some of the mysteries of the text. He really is quite brilliant.

> Do linger over the introduction. The impulse behind this project is beautiful. (xiii-xiv)

I found Markham's words so compelling that when I read the book's "Introduction," I clearly comprehended why Averitt *personally* spent so many years working to harmonize the Gospel. As he reveals to the reader in conceptualizing his labor toward consolidating it, he recounts his upbringing in a family of scientifically-oriented folk who rarely attended church or read the Bible. He states, "My parents were scientists—geologists who were more inclined to study what they could see and measure, the stones and rock formations that make up the physical universe . . . And so I grew up virtually without a religious education" (xv). However, his life as a young adult would completely change after having a major motorcycle accident during his travel in France and being in a hospital connected to a Catholic church. During his time in recovery, he listened to communal messages from believers of the Bible, but he was not personally touched by them. Yet, even has he would go on to be educated as a lawyer—in reflecting upon his academic training—he states, "The rational secular laws I had studied in law school didn't seem to be providing a similar [community] structure for people's lives or making them particularly happy. There were a lot of alienated strivers in our world. But what was the alternative?" (xvii).

While our religious and educational backgrounds are markedly different, I can relate to Averitt's critique of how his intellectual evolution in a secular institution of higher learning had not offered him a sense of community that he had experience while hospitalized and coming into contact with Christian-identified folk. As I have written in Chapter 1 of *Let Love Lead*, my education toward becoming an English professor in majority white colleges and universities did not provide me a sense of community where I felt accepted as a black person. My spiritual *re*-awakening would come when I began studying the writings and lives of pro-feminist and womanist black/women *and* men. For Averitt, as he goes on to write in the "Introduction" to *The Single Gospel*, spiritual awakening—as an "alternative" to his secular education—would take place in a trip he took to Greece. He recalls,

> One alternative began to appear when I first encountered a true community of faith, and saw what lives lived in Christian understanding might look like. This experience could happen to a person anywhere, but in my case it happened on a visit to a place in Greece call Mount Athos…[i]t did not seem likely to be the place of my spiritual awakening. After all, I had gone there as a cultural tourist…I was a visitor. (xvii)

While visiting Greece "to see the architecture and the unique institutions surviving from the classical world," Averitt meets a group of monks. One of them offers "[him] a line from the Psalms, 'Be still and know that I am God'" (xvii). Feeling drawn to attend one of the monks' early morning (3:30 AM) ritual services, he notices the lamps that burn in the darkness are filled with olive oil in "bowls of colored glass, often red…And they symbolized, at least to me, a different way of looking at God—not distant, transcendent, remote, but rather as something personal and close by. *They conveyed a sense that the infinite was accessible by looking within yourself*" (xviii; emphasis added). That Averitt would symbolically envision the presence of God in this moment through red glass, candle-lit bowls is imaginatively insightful—especially in his comment that these configurations enabled him to self-reflect, to see "the infinite…by looking within [himself] yourself." This is precisely what I teach as the transcendent, inner Spirit of love that autocritography (author)izes. What has been the result of Averitt's spiritual awakening related to his authorization of *The Single Gospel*? He says, "I had come to realize that I wanted to know more about Jesus and his life. And as I came to learn more, I found that my own truth had changed" (xix).

Like Averitt—from the time I began teaching "The Bible as Literature" in 2014 to 2018 when I invited co-authors Scott Neumeister and Susie Hoeller to join me in writing about my conceptual *re*-vision of the course—I, too, have "wanted to know more about Jesus and his life." Another reason why the *128 of the Greatest Stories from the Bible* would not continue as a primary text in the course is the fact that after 2016 it was no longer in print. As disappointed as I was, upon receiving *The Single Gospel* and reading its "Foreword" and "Introduction," I knew this was the leading for me to revise the course focus. One thing I know for sure: my faith in Jesus rooted in works of healing and life-saving transformation deepened when I read Averitt words about how:

> [t]he words [delivered by Jesus in his] Sermon on the Mount have not encouraged me to set aside my judgments, but rather not to judge in the first place...for another thing, faith has opened the door to a different way of looking at all the business and practical dealing of daily life. It made it suddenly clear that it is possible to live in the world by different values, and to perceive both troubles and opportunities in ways very different from our society's customary practices. (xix)

For me, studying and teaching the Bible through the vision of womanism enabled me "to perceive" more deeply the mission *and* teachings of Jesus.

In sharing his personal story of coming to see the revolutionary community bridge-building agency of Jesus calling as "Immanuel (which means 'God with us')," as recorded in Matthew 1:23 (New International Version), I receive Averitt's book work in creating *The Single Gospel* as a material symbol of my aim in teaching "The Bible as Literature." Averitt illuminates his desire to reach a varied readership:

> This version of the gospels strives to make the original material more readable...This book puts the incidents of Christ's life into one sequence...At the end of the day, my goal has been to create a Platonic form of the Bible story—not something with the shine of novelty, but something comfortable and familiar, the biblical narrative as it exists in our mind, and as we think we remember it.
>
> I hope that the story in this form will speak to several different groups of readers...It does so in a form that is accessible to everyone. The teachings of Jesus do not focus on particulars of ritual and doctrine. They address instead the wonderment of mankind's relationship to the infinite, the self-knowledge that comes from a study of the human heart, and

the true community that binds together all the parts of God's creation. (xxi—xxii)

Narrating the life of Jesus in a consolidated format offers the reader a story "that is accessible to everyone." *The Single Gospel* helped me to promote self-reflection as a critical pedagogical tool to solidify an interactive community foundation upon which to structure class discussions in which all my students could feel included. At best, its simple narrative consistency creates a portrayal of Jesus as the prophetic messenger of hope in touch with the "human heart."

"Jesus Made a Feminist Out of Me" (Too)

> I want to be outside with the misfits, with the rebels, the dreamers, second-chance givers, the radical grace lavishers, the ones with arms with open, the courageously vulnerable, and among even—or maybe especially—the ones rejected by the Table as not worth enough or right enough...Jesus made a feminist out of me.
> It's true.
>
> Sarah Bessey, *Jesus Feminist*

When Susie Hoeller first mentioned *Jesus Feminist* to me, I was provoked by its title. As someone who is always intrigued by book titles, this one alone compelled me to reflect on a number of things—but foremost, what black/person of color reared in traditional, conservative Christian terminology would refer to Jesus as a "feminist"? Outside of Christianity the term "feminist" itself is loaded with negativity. Moreover, in black communities—whether in or outside the church—this term is racially fixated on white women, particularly those who are lesbian-identified. Considering this, what black would positively identify himself with this label? Nevertheless, in the evolution of my identity as a black man who would come to identify himself as *pro*-"feminist," I have embraced my alliance with feminism—personally and professionally. Additionally, in having decided to teach *Jesus Feminist,* I have begun a new spiritual journey in which I profess an allegiance to the idea of Jesus as a feminist.

Personally, professionally, politically, *and* spiritually—I find this idea radically revolutionary. Yet again, I find myself thinking "outside the box." This is why I chose to open this section of this chapter with Sarah Bessey's words related to her idea that "Jesus made a feminist out of [her]." Like her, I am on the outside of much of what this "Man"-centered life is all about, linked to patriarchal, systemic and institutionalized forms of domination and oppression. Having own my identity as a "black male outsider," I boldly made the decision to connect *Jesus Feminist* with the study of the life of Jesus with *The Single Gospel*.

The quote I chose as the epigraph above is cited from Bessey's "Introduction" to her book. Like Averitt, she openly speaks personally about her relationship Jesus related to the book's concept. I am drawn to her willingness to share her position as a Christian-identified white woman who desires "to be outside with the misfits, with the rebels, the dreamers, second-chance givers, the radical grace lavishers, the ones with arms with open, the courageously vulnerable, and . . . especially—the ones rejected by the Table as not worth enough or right enough." Considering what the *outsider* positionality Bessey calls for—in her willingness to own the transformative empowerment of Jesus in her life—I believe that he "made a feminist out of me," too. In line with the Bible-centered study of Jesus' life, as I state in the syllabus, Bessey "offers us a deeply personal and insightful examination of Jesus transforming her into a feminist." As a devoted biblical scholar, she opens our eyes to see a vision of feminism that counters stereotypical ideas of it. She states,

> I know feminism carries a lot of baggage…There are the stereotypes…man-haters, and rabid abortion-pushers, extreme lesbians, terrifying some of us on cable news programs, deriding motherhood and homemaking. Feminism has been blamed for the breakdown of the nuclear family…[and] the downfall of "real manhood"…Most of what has passed for a description of feminism is fearmongering misinformation . . . Modern Christian feminism is alive and well, from social justice movements to seminaries and churches to suburban [as well as urban] living rooms, worldwide…At the core,

feminism simply consists of the radical notion that women are people, too. (11-13)

In teaching *Jesus Feminist* in fall 2018, I accepted Bessey's "invitation to revisit the Bible's view of women...exploring God's radical notion that women are people, too." I knew this would begin a new pedagogical, hopeful course of action. Believing in all I brought to the college classroom—as a black male professor whose personal, political, pedagogical *and* spiritual life had been transformed by the writings of bell hooks, Alice Walker, Audre Lorde, and many other black\feminists and womanists of color—I could teach Jesus as the revolutionary embodiment of hope *and* love.

In the previous chapter, I included students' written responses from the fall 2015 version of the course based on *128 of the Greatest Stories from the Bible* and *How to Read the Bible as Literature*. Complementing each other, these works supported my having chosen them as the primary course texts. By studying them, students in that concept of "The Bible as Literature" certainly gained a sense of the Messianic calling of Jesus. Those students' "reader responses" deeply convey how Jesus' compassion for women struggling against sexism and classism, as authorized by patriarchal religious laws, was life-transforming. In this chapter, reviewing the spring 2018 revised version of the course, I feature the "discussion starter" papers produced by students reading *The Single Gospel* and *Jesus Feminist*. What follows is my representation of the "new" course direction (as indicated in the syllabus):

> This course will focus on the life of Jesus from a biblical standpoint—with particular regard to how he deals with women in his treatment of them. Studying *The Single Gospel* in collaboration with readings from *Jesus Feminist*, we will comprehend ways in which Jesus radically defied the ruling hegemonic ideas of patriarchy. As such, this course will foreground Jesus' life as a model of active "community service." From this standpoint, we will literally (and literarily) transport what we learn about Jesus in this class(room) to the "living"(room) of people's everyday lives. In other words, it is simply not enough to study "The Bible as Literature." My idea

for this class is to make its principles of servant-hood livable in this contemporary moment of global discord and separation.

On a Radical Course Revision: Jesus Was the Reason

In the Sermon on the Mount, Jesus taught us to do the following:
> But seek ye first the kingdom of God, and his righteousness; and all these things shall be added unto you. (Matthew 6:33 King James Version)
>
> Susie Yovic Hoeller, *Lean on Jesus: Christian Women in the Workplace*

This "smoothing out" of the four gospel accounts is actually one of the main virtues of a consolidated story…While there may be four authoritative gospel accounts, there is only one underlying gospel. There was only one life of Jesus…The four gospels illuminate this one underlying reality from their four different vantage points, but bringing those four accounts together will give our most rounded and nuanced portrait of Jesus and his life.

Neil Averitt, *The Single Gospel*

After years of reading the Gospels and the full canon of Scripture, here is, very simply, what I learned about Jesus and the ladies: he loves us.

He loves us. On our own terms. He treats us as equal to the men around him; he listens; he does not belittle; he honors us; he challenges us; he teaches us; he includes us—calls us all beloved. Gloriously, this flies in the face of the cultural expectations of his time—and even our own time.

Sarah Bessey, *Jesus Feminist*

I stated in the Introduction to *Let Love Lead* that when Susie first began visiting my class on "The Bible as Literature" in 2014 as a guest-speaker, she brought copies of her book *Lean on Jesus:*

Christian Women in the Workplace. She gave a free copy to every student in the class. As I also shared, I was not aware she planned to do this. I listened to her inspiring talk about the purpose for writing *Lean on Jesus*, and after class I kept thinking about it related to my own pro-feminist scholarship and teaching. Having completely read the book before my class met the following week, I decided to add it as a secondary reading in complement to the required texts—*128 of the Greatest Stories from the Bible* and *Reading the Bible as Literature*. I prompted my students to think about the contemporary reality of "Christian [w]omen in the [w]orkplace"—from the professional standpoint of Susie's critical standpoint she offers in her book—because I desired to discover what they learned from her perspective. As she shows in Chapter 8 of *Let Love Lead*, student responses to particular chapters in *Lean on Jesus* convey how Susie's relatable "spiritual wisdom and practical advice" not only works to empower "all women"—but to compel all men to "lean on Jesus" as a radical agent of self-liberation and esteemed supporter of women's equality.

Each time Susie came to "The Bible as Literature" as a guest-speaker over subsequent semester, she would give out copies her book. Moreover, as I stated in the previous chapter, Susie would eventually introduce me to *Jesus Feminist*. Studying it, after having become committed to my students' reading *Lean on Jesus*, I knew my thinking about required readings for the course had begun to take a new direction. I gained a clear sense that the life of Jesus, his earthly mission, spiritual teachings, and accomplishments would become the new focus of the course to freedom after simultaneously studying the work of Neil Averitt in *The Single Gospel* and that of Susie and Bessey. Yet, as I have shared, before adopting *The Single Gospel* and *Jesus Feminist* in my spring 2018 offering of the course—I had chosen *128 of the Greatest Stories from the Bible* as a primary course text. However, even in all the readings I assigned for students to read in it (including Old and New Testament texts), many of the students wrote about narrative representations of Jesus' life. Their writings regularly illustrated the thematic personification of love in his actions, especially related to the lives of women.

Presenting Jesus and his embodiment of the healing power of love was not my primary intention when I first taught *128 of the Greatest Stories* in the course in 2014. I would only move on after reading *Lean on Jesus, The Single Gospel* and *Jesus Feminist*, as I gained the courage to employ Averitt and Bessey's books as primary texts for the course in spring 2018. In becoming aware of the progressive writings of Hoeller, Bessey, and Averitt—I wanted students to read these works to deconstruct biblical forms of patriarchy, gender, class, mental, and physical conditions—linked to religious domination and oppression. Not only would my pedagogical point of view shift to a more overt feminist/womanist approach to biblical literature—I would also include a community service component to the course. In having students share the writings ("Discussion Starter" papers) they produced during the spring 2018 semester, I fearlessly owned the idea that this *re*-vision of the course would challenge all of us—teacher and students. I additionally desired for students to share their work in a community outside of academia. This was my purpose for pursuing a community partnership: to think inclusively about Jesus as a revolutionary pro-woman(ist) Savior *for* all human beings.

Thus, in this chapter—focused on my representation of the spring 2018 offering of "The Bible as Literature"—I once again undergird my commitment to demonstrating the emancipatory power of love Jesus manifests as the radical messenger of hope. Re-envisioning the concept of "The Bible as Literature" was, in truth, not a difficult task at all. Even when I began teaching this course in 2014, I possessed a clear internal sense of its sub-plot. Having taught black/feminist and womanist (female *and* male) writers of color, over time, I learned how to subvert institutionalized systems of domination and oppression. As I shared in Part I, what had kept me from boldly professing a pro-feminist/womanist standpoint in teaching the course was a fear that students (especially males in the class) would not be open to my approach. I simply backed away from what I knew my students needed to challenge biblically—especially related to issues of sexist oppression. However, in 2018, I determined to reclaim the revolutionary path I had begun years before teaching literature against sexism.

In hindsight, Susie Hoeller—having introduced me to *Jesus Feminist: An Invitation to Revisit the Bible's View of Women*—led me on an insightful journey of self-reflection. I received this "invitation" as a clear affirmation of my calling to teach the life of Jesus in a pro-feminist and womanist context.

Works Cited

Averitt, Neil. *The Single Gospel: Matthew, Mark, Luke and John Consolidated into a Single Narrative.* Resource Publications, 2015.

Bessey, Sarah. *Jesus Feminist: An Invitation to Revisit the Bible's View of Women.* Howard Books, 2013.

Walker, Alice. *In Search of Our Mothers' Gardens: Womanist Prose.* Harcourt Brace and Co., 1983.

Part III

Lean on Jesus as a Passageway to *Jesus Feminist*

> Trust in the LORD with all your heart, and lean not on your own understanding…
> Proverbs 3:5 (New King James Version)

Chapter 7

Let Love Lead in Business

Susie Hoeller

I will begin by exploring the meaning of *love*. In English, the word *love* is widely used as a noun, verb, adjective and adverb. Here are some examples:

NOUN: "Love Is Like an Itching in My Heart" (Holland/Dozier). This is the title of a Top 10 hit song by The Supremes, released in 1966 by the Motown record label.

VERB: Yoko Ono once said: "The regret of my life is that I have not said "I love you" often enough.

ADJECTIVE: William Shakespeare wrote a famous play about Romeo and Juliet's love affair.

ADVERB: The nurse on duty at the emergency room tenderly and lovingly bandaged the injured child's leg.

Many Types of Love

There are many types of love: romantic love (sexual, intimate); familial love; love between friends; the love of comrades in arms; patriotic love of home and country; and the love of nature and God's other creatures. People often say how much they love their jobs, sports teams or hobbies. Of course, women are known to love shopping.

Here, I am interested in a different kind of love, often called agape love. This is a pure form of love. It is the love that Christ has shown to the world by his teachings, his life, death and resurrection. For people, this is where the love object may or may not be "lovable" or even personally known to the "lover." The lover acts in a selfless manner to benefit or care for another, outside of family and friends.

Think of:

- the brave New York City firefighters who ran up the stairs of the burning Twin Towers on 9/11, when everyone else was running down;
- the small businesswoman who generously shares profits with her employees;
- the young man who takes his elderly neighbor to her medical appointments for nothing in return;
- Nelson Mandela, unjustly imprisoned for twenty-seven years by the apartheid regime in South Africa, who then led the country with love by not shedding the blood of his oppressors;
- volunteers who feed the hungry, clothe the naked and visit prisoners; and
- the all-volunteer "Cajun Navy," which rescued hundreds of people during Hurricane Harvey.

Gary's Leadership

Our educational system revolves around testing, competition for grades and scholarships all based on individual student achievement. Is it possible to find agape love in this system?

Yes, I found this agape love in a college classroom. Three years ago, I was a guest speaker for Gary, a professor of English at the University of South Florida in Tampa. For his "The Bible as Literature" class, Gary asked me to speak about *Lean on Jesus,* a small book I had written to encourage women to lead, not for individual career success, but to make our workplaces more just and humane.

I gave my talk and answered questions from the students. I was surprised when the students openly shared their own experiences in the workplace. They described the struggles they had faced and overcome as well as the temptations they had given into. Gary's students were not afraid to discuss their fears or failings with each other. They expressed their agape love for one another in that classroom and in the papers they wrote reflecting on my book (which I discuss in Chapter 8). They were learning the course material not as solitary, atomized individuals but as a cohesive group, seeking the best for one another.

Where did this spirit of love come from? It came from Gary. He treats his students with the utmost respect and dignity, all the while challenging them to do their best work. In his classes, the students truly get to know each other, they sincerely congratulate each other on successful assignments, and they help each other learn critical thinking skills.

The students' cooperative relationships with each other and Gary go well beyond what Corporate America calls "teamwork." In today's political climate where exclusionary nationalism and xenophobia are rising around the world, Gary creates a welcoming and encouraging environment for a diverse student body to learn not just from books or lectures but from one another. Because his classes are held at night, on an urban public university campus, the students represent different races, ethnicities, religions and ages. Many are the first members of their families to attend college. Some are older, mid-career adults working full time during the day and attending college at night. These are not students from similar backgrounds and life experiences like one typically sees in a college fraternity or sorority. I spoke to other classes at Gary's invitation, and the unique student engagement was always the same.

What a difference from my law school in the late 1970s. Back then, law students were known to tear pages out of library books to prevent other students from reading the assigned cases. Stiff competition for grades and class rank, a place on the law review and finding a position with a prestigious law firm after graduation were law students' goals, not collaboration.

The Lack of Love in Business

In the business world, where I have spent my career to date, there is little talk of "love" unless someone is gossiping about the latest case of sexual harassment. "Agape love" is clearly not at the forefront of our market economy. Like academia, our business world is based on competition. Companies seek market dominance and profits above

all else. As the Nobel Prize-winning economist Milton Friedman writes,
> There is one and only one social responsibility of business—to use it resources and engage in activities designed to increase its profits so long as it stays within the rules of the game, which is to say, engages in open and free competition without deception or fraud.

The lack of love in our capitalist system explains the growing appeal of socialism. Communism, socialism's close relative, has been discredited because it became a totalitarian and murderous regime in the former Soviet Union, China and smaller countries which embraced it. But socialism, especially what is known as "democratic socialism," variations of which are found in Western Europe, Canada and on Israeli kibbutzim, is increasingly seen by many people as a much better economic system than capitalism. This attraction is especially strong for American millennials, coming of age in the period of highest economic inequality in our history. Red flags are waving in the streets of Seattle, and democratic socialists are being elected to Congress.

The appeal of socialism is because people are taken care of by the government and not left behind, like what happens to too many people with naked capitalism. Whether they are *well* taken care is a matter up for debate, but nevertheless socialism is a system seen as promoting equality, human rights and compassion. In fact, some modern-day socialists point to the communal living and sharing practices adopted by the early apostles of Jesus Christ as described in the Book of Acts, chapters 2-5.

Let me return to my discussion of capitalism. It is clearly under serious attack today. With few exceptions, its leaders and supporters are doing a poor job of defending it against an oncoming socialist wave. Yet it is indisputable that capitalism and free markets have created the greatest amount of wealth and the most goods and services in human history. No other economic system even comes close. A corollary is that capitalism is lacking in love.

Many of the current financiers and captains of industry in Corporate America do not understand this fundamental truth. These individuals are blinded by the deadly sins of pride and greed. To cover their tracks, these people establish "corporate social responsibility" programs which are often just public relations spin. They set up charitable foundations, often with monies made dishonestly. Philanthropy is good, but it does not make up for cheating people and cutting corners in the first instance. Vast inequality, a declining middle class and millions of Americans with no realistic chance of escaping poverty are economic conditions which history shows lead to social unrest and chaos. These conditions lead to the rise of authoritarian regimes (both from the left and the right).

Can Capitalism and Free Markets Be Saved?

Milton Friedman did not support the concepts of corporate social responsibility and government regulation of business because of his belief that free markets produce the best outcome when it comes to the exchange of goods and services. He was a market fundamentalist, but he rightly valued human freedom and realized that government bureaucrats can end up oppressing the very people they are supposed to be helping.

In my view, the solution to the problem of economic inequality, which is becoming more extreme, is not true socialism, where the government controls the means of production and individuals become less free. Socialist economies stagnate over time since people become too dependent on the government. There is little incentive to invent, to create and to become an entrepreneur. The greatest inventors and innovators are not found in socialist countries. The records of the patent offices around the world prove this statement to be true.

A significant number of more visionary business leaders have come to understand that for capitalism to survive, it cannot be driven by profits and investor returns only. These people operate their firms following principles of robust business ethics, servant leadership and/or conscious capitalism. These modern-day business philosophies, when implemented properly, can make capitalism more humane. Let's quickly examine them.

Robust Business Ethics

Robust business ethics means designing a holistic ethics policy and enforcing it universally, even when it means the loss of profits. Robust business ethics policies and actions go beyond mere legal compliance, because adhering to the law is a minimum standard of conduct. The following scenarios illustrate the concept of business ethics.

- It is not illegal in the United States to send manufacturing jobs to overseas "sweatshops." However, an ethical company will not use sweatshop labor to increase its profits.
- At the time of this writing, it is not illegal in most states for restaurants to serve drinks with plastic straws. An ethical company, knowing that disposable plastic straws entering our oceans are killing sea turtles and other marine life, will stop providing them (unless a customer has a medical need for this type of straw).
- The company's leadership realizes that discrimination based on race, national origin, ethnicity, gender, age and disability, as well as sexual orientation and gender identity, is morally wrong, even if the latter two categories are not protected by the law in the state where the company is headquartered. The company implements and enforces an anti-discrimination policy that goes beyond the law.
- The CEO of the company has been found to have violated the company's ethics policy. The company will discharge him and not reward him with a golden parachute severance package.

Unfortunately, we see that some companies miss the holistic aspect of business ethics. They may act ethically in one aspect of their business operations but not in another. For example, a company pays fair wages but manufactures products which harm human health.

An Example of an Ethical Company—Texas Instruments

When I worked in the legal department of Texas Instruments Incorporated (TI) in Dallas, all employees were handed the booklet "Ethics in the Business of Texas Instruments." I still have the 1990 booklet and always show it to my business law students.

Here is an excerpt from the first page:

> TI's reputation for integrity—for honesty, fairness, candor and respect in all business dealings—dates back to the founders of the company. That reputation is a priceless asset...We will not let the pursuit of sales, billings or profits distort our ethical principles. We will also place integrity before shipping, before billings, before profits, before anything. If it comes down to a choice between making a desired profit and doing it right, we don't have a choice. We'll do it right.

But more important than the booklet is that I always saw the company act in an ethical manner. I had a unique vantage point when I was asked to serve as the secretary of the company ethics committee for a term. Because of attorney/client confidentiality, I cannot describe specific facts, but I can say that I saw bad actors fired or disciplined even if they were making money for the company. If their actions violated the company's ethics policies, there were real consequences. TI's commitment has proven to be unwavering over decades.

However, as we have seen in the news, so many other organizations ignore and cover up ethical and even legal violations committed by their top executives or revenue producers, unless and until a whistleblower goes public or a journalist writes an exposé. Many people think that obeying the law means they are ethical. The law is the floor when it comes to conduct, not the ceiling. Just because an action is legal does not make it ethical. Others mistakenly think that acting ethically will damage business success. History shows the opposite is true. Ethical companies are more successful, not less successful.

What Is Servant Leadership?

The modern concept, promoted by former AT&T executive and management expert Robert Greenleaf, is that business leaders must put the needs of others first and focus on developing their employees' skills and opportunities. Companies which currently proclaim their adoption of servant leadership include Nordstrom and Starbucks. Robert Greenleaf was a Christian, and he based his concept of servant leadership on Jesus Christ.

Conscious Capitalism

This business philosophy was first articulated by John MacKay, the founder of Whole Foods Markets, and it is also promoted by Kip Tindell, the former CEO of The Container Store. It includes servant leadership, which is a management practice. But conscious capitalism goes beyond mere management to consider the intrinsic societal value of the business itself for all the stakeholders impacted by the business. Profit and investment return for shareholders are not the sole purpose for the business. Stakeholders include management, employees, the community and the environment.

Two now-deceased business leaders—Aaron Feuerstein, the "Mensch of Malden Mills" and Dame Anita Roddick, the founder of the Body Shop—are inspiring models of conscious capitalism in action. Feuerstein continued to pay all his employees after his textile mill burned down. Roddick led the movement to ban the cruel and unnecessary animal testing in the cosmetic industry. She also pioneered ethical sourcing of ingredients to build up global communities instead of just exploiting their workers and natural resources.

Looking Backwards for a Moment

It is not just modern business leaders like the founders of Texas Instruments, Robert Greenleaf, John Mackay, Kip Tindell, Aaron Feuerstein and Anita Roddick who have given us examples of how businesses should be operated to benefit society and not just make money for the shareholders and executives. After all, socialism and communism emerged and expanded as alternative philosophies in the mid-nineteenth century and early twentieth century when capitalism was not only naked—it was truly predatory. Let's take a quick look at two historical advocates for capitalism to reform itself.

Rerum Novarum

In 1891, Pope Leo XIII issued his ground-breaking Encyclical, *Rerum Novarum*, on the rights and duties of capital and labor. Here is an excerpt:

> The following duties bind the wealthy owner and the employer: not to look upon their work people as their bondsmen, but to respect in every man his dignity as a person ennobled by Christian character. They are reminded that, according to natural reason and Christian philosophy, working for gain is creditable, not shameful, to a man, since it enables him to earn an honorable livelihood; but to misuse men as though they were things in the pursuit of gain, or to value them solely for their physical powers—that is truly shameful and inhuman…To defraud any one of wages that are his due is a great crime which cries to the avenging anger of Heaven.

Social Creed for the Workers

Protestant churches led by Methodists were not oblivious to the terrible social conditions of the industrial revolution. In 1908, they published the "Social Creed for Workers," calling for the abolition of child labor, a ten-hour workday, no Sunday labor, and workers compensation for industrial accidents.

Back to the Present

Robert Greenleaf did not hide the fact that his principles of servant leadership had biblical foundations. He then advocated that servant leadership can and should be adopted in secular organizations. However, since the publication of his book *Servant Leadership* in 1977, Christianity has become unpopular in many elite and progressive circles. This has happened because many churches have remained too patriarchal and homophobic. The ever-widening and horrific pedophile priest scandal in the Roman Catholic Church has eroded its moral authority. But one should never tar Jesus Christ with the sins and theological errors of his human followers.

Christians should stop being afraid of bringing agape love into the marketplace. The irony is that many Christians will not hesitate to wear a visible cross or crucifix, tack up a Bible verse in their office or cubicle, put a fish symbol on their vehicle or even bring their Bible to work. But then they act like everyone else in the workplace—they don't let love lead.

How Do We Let Love Lead in Business?

As individuals, no matter our position in the business world, the first step is to study the relevant teachings of Jesus Christ. We cannot put into action what we do not know. Jesus taught us how we should live in all aspects of our lives, including our participation in commercial activity. Let's look at some of these teachings from the Bible, and it will be obvious how following them will always let love lead.

Seven Ways to Let Love Lead

The seven "Deadly Sins" of greed, gluttony, envy, lust, anger, sloth and pride have infected our society. However, we can look to

Jesus's teachings and see seven ways for us to let love lead in our business dealings and personal lives.

Jesus instructed his followers to pay fair wages when he spoke about the "cries of the harvesters." See James 5:1-6.

In the famous "Good Samaritan" parable, the Samaritan traveler did not discriminate against, but stopped to help, the injured Jew alongside the road. See Luke 10:25-37.

The story of the master, who, traveling to a far country, left his three servants in charge while he was away, shows us how to practice stewardship. See Matthew 25:14-30.

Jesus tells his followers to be honest and pay their taxes. See Mark 12:17.

He teaches us about the proper relationship between money and serving God. See Mark 8:36 and Matthew 6:24.

If we follow the Master, we will build our businesses and careers on a strong foundation. See Matthew 4:24-28.

We will act with generosity and will not judge others harshly. See Mark 4:21-24.

Conclusion

We started this chapter with a discussion of Gary's leadership model for academia which is based on agape love. This model is also desperately needed to transform capitalism. Business today, even small business, has become so complex that firms must be able to establish teamwork and collaboration among their employees, suppliers and customers. Businesses that cannot do this fail. But because our market economy is based on competition, many businesspeople have great difficulty working in a collaborative manner. This is true especially for people who are educated in a system which emphasizes individual student grades and performance. How does a student who has spent years studying alone and competing against other students then morph into a team player at work? The answer is with great difficulty.

Now even if a business is successful in building a collaborative culture, problems will arise if the team leader is unethical. Then the team members are encouraged to "go along to get along." No one will speak up to stop wrongdoing. Or if someone is brave enough to become an internal "whistleblower," that person is typically kicked off the team, humiliated, and may lose his or her job. The solution is for businesspeople to lead with love. Doing so will inspire people to always choose honest dealing over corner-cutting. Businesses need to make a profit, and profits are not intrinsically evil. Profits are only evil if they are made by exploiting and harming people, creatures and our environment in illegal and unethical ways.

As a business attorney, I can suggest many reforms to corporate and commercial law which would make capitalism work better for all stakeholders, not just investors and top executives. One example would be to require executives in public companies to act in a fiduciary manner towards all stakeholders not just investors, as corporate law requires now. Another legal reform would be to require public companies to cap executive compensation and institute generous profit-sharing plans for all employees. These actions would help, but they are at the margins.

The only reform which will save capitalism is to let love lead.

Works Cited

Friedman, Milton. "The Social Responsibility of Business is to Increase Its Profits." *The New York Times Magazine*, 13 Sep. 1970, pp. 32-33; 123-125.

Greenleaf, Robert. *Servant Leadership: A Journey into the Nature of Legitimate Power and Greatness.* Paulist Press, 1977.

Methodist Social Creed for Workers 1908. www.umc.org/what-we-believe/methodist-history-1908-social-creed-for-workers.

Rerum Novarum Encyclical of Pope Leo XIII on Capital and Labor. 1891. w2.vatican.va/content/leo-xiii/en/encyclicals/documents/hf_l-xiii_enc_15051891_rerum-novarum.html

Texas Instruments Incorporated Original Ethics Booklet—1961. Revised 1968, 1977, 1987 and 1990.

Chapter 8

Students Learn How to *Lean on Jesus*

Susie Hoeller

I graduated from law school in 1976, when very few women were law students and practicing attorneys. In fact, when I started at Vanderbilt Law School, there was no women's restroom in the law school building. Needless to say, our small group of female students changed that situation by occupying one of the men's restrooms until it was converted for our use. During my career, I was typically the only woman in the room when working with high-tech companies.

As a female attorney working in a male-dominated profession, I was very disappointed when Sheryl Sandberg, the Chief Operating Officer of Facebook, published *Lean In* in 2013. This best-selling business book urged women to act aggressively to achieve leadership positions, success and personal wealth in Corporate America. In my view, Sandberg missed the point. Having more women strive to reach the top rungs of the corporate ladder does nothing to restrain the greed and conflict which dominate too many places in our current business world.

This is why, as a direct response to *Lean In*, I wrote *Lean on Jesus: Christian Women in the Workplace* in 2014. My goal is to encourage women to bring agape love into the business world to change it in a humanitarian and socially responsible direction. (The book is for men, too.)

Changing Ourselves, First and Foremost

Christians (and other people of faith and goodwill) cannot make workplaces and our society better unless we all focus on changing ourselves for the better. My book deals with common temptations at work and provides both scripture verses and passages from other

Christian writers, including songwriters, to help readers overcome these temptations.

My Reflections on Students' Papers on *Lean on Jesus*

After speaking about my book to Gary's students at USF for three different classes from 2014-2016, I was pleased to read the students' papers providing their personal reactions to specific chapters in the book. Because of the encouraging and sharing classroom environment Gary has created for his students, the students responded to my book in very heartfelt ways.

Most writers do not have the chance to receive personal reactions from their readers. What a privilege it has been to speak to these students and then read their writings reacting to my book. It is not just a privilege, it is a blessing. *Lean on Jesus* has seventeen chapters and an Afterword which discuss various temptations found in the workplace, as well as ways to follow Jesus in a positive and affirming way.

Four chapters were commented on the most. For each of these chapters, I will provide an excerpt (indented) followed by the most interesting student comments, sometimes abbreviated for clarity. I will start with two of the chapters concerned with common workplace temptations.

Chapter 3: "I Heard It through the Grapevine"

This chapter deals with gossip, which is certainly a juicy temptation for everyone.
Excerpt:
> Baby Boomers immediately recognize this Motown hit recorded by both Marvin Gaye and Gladys Knight and the Pips during the 1960s. Every office has an internal grapevine and it constantly hums with breaking news about other employees and the boss. The grapevine can be positive . . .

But news *aka* gossip that is untrue or malicious travels on the grapevine too—sometimes much faster than the good news...

Are we ever the source of slanderous gossip in the office? Or are we merely the avid listeners or repeaters of same?...

Whenever you are tempted to engage in gossip or criticize others behind their backs; take a deep breath and fill your mind with Scripture verses like these:

> But I tell you that everyone will have to give account on the day of judgment for every empty word they have spoken. For by your words you will be acquitted, and by your words you will be condemned. (*New International Version*, Matt. 12.36-37)

Student Responses to Chapter 3

Taylor: "Hoeller refers to the gossip that occurs at work to be a 'grapevine'...This grapevine is the one that creates drama. I honestly don't know even why it exists because if something isn't true, I don't know why it would even be mentioned. However, this happens often. We all have been victim to a negative grapevine. I feel, though, that these are easy to overcome, because if something is said about me and I know it is untrue, I just ignore the things that were said. The people that truly care about me either already know it's not true or will ask me personally to find out if it is true."

Taylor continues: "This particular chapter impacted me as soon as I started reading it. My [restaurant] workplace contains a lot of females...My male coworkers are always very easy to get along with, as well as MOST of my female workers. This is with the exception of one coworker. While her name will not be mentioned, I have encountered problems with this particular coworker...From the beginning she did not like me...However, it eventually got to the point where she was calling me names to other people and saying she wanted to fight me. As you can imagine, I was appalled because I did not know what I had done to her. I had never been rude to her and always treated her with respect, which is why I was very confused when I had heard all this was said by someone that had barely spoken to me. I decided to ignore the comments that she had supposedly made, because I didn't know if the people that were telling me this were telling the truth, or they just wanted a reaction out of me. I left it alone…I understand that not everyone will like me. I get it. However, if you have a problem with me, I can't fix it if I don't know what the problem is!...Confront me with it…I would not be mad if someone came up to me and told me that something I did bothered them. The Bible states: 'A soft answer turns away wrath, but a harsh word stirs up anger' (*ESV Study Bible*, Prov. 15.1)."

Arielle: "The only thing that isn't addressed [in this chapter] is when the gossip is about you. I have a story about a gossip situation that happened just this past weekend at work. I work at a bar, which is already a delicate enough situation when it comes to maintaining your moral and ethical integrity. I'm constantly surrounded by alcoholics, drunks, slutty females, womanizing men, young people acting 'grown up,' and ancient people clinging to a past youth. What makes my job tolerable and even fun are the people I work with. That's why when I heard gossip about me from those people I cherish, it was a particularly nasty blow. I am the only female at the bar who is single and not dating, and I guess that's just difficult to believe for some of my coworkers…on Friday, one of the female bartenders who has seniority over almost everyone else…told me to my face that I was exchanging sexual favors for food and drinks, specifically from one of the bouncers I spend a lot of time with. The male server I was working with that day heard that and told me he also thought I only 'hang out with the big guys to get favors.' This was so upsetting that I nearly cried and started a heated argument (these things tend to happen hand in hand when I'm furious).

Arielle continues: "Instead of lashing out at them, I told her calmly, while staring at her dead on, that what she had said was a lie, that the idea was repulsive, and that I had yet to do anything sexual with any employees which was something which wouldn't change…"

Chapter 4: "Overcoming Envy"

This chapter discusses this common temptation and contrasts it with jealousy—two different emotions which are often confused as one.

Excerpt:

> Have you ever been envious of a person in your office who gets promoted ahead of you? Have you gone home upset because you believe you deserved the job instead? I can answer "yes" to both questions. Something I am ashamed to admit.
>
> Envy is one of the "seven deadly sins" identified by the Catholic Church and some Protestant churches. It is incredibly destructive.
>
> When will we face the truth? There will always be people with more money than us, people who are better-looking, and people with more worldly goods and accomplishments. Being envious of other people is the very antithesis of Christ-like behavior. When envy raises its ugly head in our lives, it shows our lack of faith in God's promises.
>
> Whenever we have envious thoughts, we should re-read the Old Testament story of Rachel and Leah (Genesis 29-31) and the New Testament story of the prodigal son (Luke 15:11-32). These stories reveal how envy ruined family relationships.
>
> Here are two Scripture verses to help us overcome the temptation to envy our co-workers or anyone else for that matter.
>
>> A heart at peace gives life to the body, but envy robs the bones (*New International Version*, Prov. 4.30).
>>
>> But if you harbor bitter envy and selfish ambition in your hearts, do not boast about it or deny the truth. Such "wisdom" does not come down from

heaven but is earthly, unspiritual, demonic. For where you have envy and selfish ambition, there you find disorder and every evil practice. (*New International Version*, Jas. 3.14-16)

Envy and jealousy are similar sinful attitudes. The two words often used inter-changeably, but there is a difference between them. Envy is where we are upset about the good fortune of another or want something the other person has. Jealousy occurs when we are afraid that someone will take what we already have away from us, like our spouse's affection or our position at work.

Envy and jealousy are both forms of coveting prohibited by the Tenth Commandment: "You shall not covet your neighbor's house. You shall not covet your neighbor's wife, or his male or female servant, his ox or his donkey, or anything that belongs to your neighbor" (*New International Version*, Exod. 20.17).

Student Responses to Chapter 4

Krystal: "Envy is a feeling that I, unfortunately, have felt many times throughout my working career. I pride myself on being a team player and working as hard as I can to do the best job I can do. My grandmother always told me to learn everything I could and what I was told to do well, because at some point it would pay off. She also went on to add that it's a skill that I would learn for life. Since I began working at the age of sixteen, I've taken my grandmother's advice and have applied myself in every job that I've done. I guess that is why I felt envious of any person who got a promotion when they only put in half the effort I did. People who would barely work or barely apply themselves except with the minimum effort always upset me. How did people like this get ahead? How did the bosses and supervisors not see who the harder worker was? These feelings of anger and envy mixed together are as Hoeller describes in this chapter. 'It [Envy] is incredibly destructive.' If I allowed it to completely take over me, I would fall down this never-ending void of unhappiness. After expressing my issues over what was going on at work, my grandmother helped to bring me down. She told me that my time would come and that I just needed to continue to work hard and have the faith that things will work out. As always, she was right. Within the following year I got promoted into the supervisor position at my office. It really showed me that feelings of envy and jealousy are not healthy. It's important to stay positive and know that God has a plan for all of us."

Jon: "The theme of this chapter is the danger of giving in to envy and jealousy. Additionally, this chapter discusses how caving into such petty and futile emotions actually demonstrates a failure to remain faithful to God, and his promises to us....The author correctly points out that in addition to being one of the seven deadly sins as identified by the Catholic Church, it is also a violation of the tenth commandment...The desire for earthly possessions can be a very toxic influence in life, especially if that desire goes unchecked. Such has been the case for much of my adult and professional life. I can now readily admit that I invested twenty-four years in amassing assets. I spent a miserable twenty-four years believing that my net worth was the only thing that mattered, and that the only way to affect positive change was to do so monetarily. I purchased property, invested in stocks, and participated silently in business ventures with the intent of creating wealth."

Jon continues: "The Recession of 2007, however, could not have cared less about the plan I had in place or the fact that where I stood financially represented seventeen years of non-stop work. As a result, everything I had done was virtually wiped out in a period of one hundred days. One hundred days was all it took to negate a lifetime of work. Assets were sold for pennies on the dollar. Retirement funds were liquidated to clear upside-down assets. An exit strategy of comfort was redefined as a plan of desperation, and I became bitter. I hated anyone and everyone who made it to the other side of the storm. I despised those that declared bankruptcy instead of paying their debts. I broke from colleagues, and associates for fear of what I might do or say, but mostly because I hated them for surviving intact. I moved from a 4000-square-foot golf course home on Amelia Island to a 1000-square-foot townhouse in Tampa, and straight into the bottle. I drove anyone and everyone that ever cared for me away, and I did so as quickly as possible. I spent six straight years violating the tenth commandment on a daily basis, but what I came to understand was that I had been breaking it for seventeen years in reality. I had always coveted what others had;...It is funny to recall now, but when it all came crashing down around me, I had only three things left to cling to: my wife (only by the grace of God, I assure you), Fr. George Corrigan (who I scarcely knew prior), and God. I found a strength in my wife that was unbeknownst to me when times were good, and I fell in love again..."

Briana: "As a child and teen, envy is quite common, since you are surrounded by individuals that want to show off their newest toy or their latest name brand fashion item. However, envy is something that has personally followed me into my young adult years...Especially being in a sorority, you find yourself wishing you had certain attributes or things that the girls around you had. Recently, I have incurred envy in multiple forms: wishing I had someone's beautiful curls, being envious of a friend that got a new car and hoping that one day my body would look as good as the girl that every man has desired. While some may think these are thoughts we all face at this age, Susie Hoeller reminds us that 'when envy raises its ugly head in our lives, it shows our lack of faith in God's promises' (13). While one girl may be experiencing the best years of her life at that moment and may get everything handed to her, that does not mean that my life won't be as prosperous and that I am unlucky in life. Faith in God's promises should be the driving force that pushes me through every hardship I encounter. Hoeller's statement that 'there will always be people with more money than us, people who are better looking, and people with more worldly goods and accomplishments' actually made me realize how envious of a person I really am (13). All of these statements are things that have brought my personal downfall and made me second guess myself throughout college. However, it also helped me conceptualize a major evil within my life. There is always going to be someone who is better than you at something, someone who has one more of everything you hold dear to your heart. If you let this measly comparison get to you, you will fail to see how much you really have. You will fail to see how God has blessed you with what he has given you. This passage helped me realize that my beauty is enough, my accomplishments are enough, and that someone else's attributes shouldn't diminish the light that mine bring.

Briana continues: "This chapter also addressed jealously which is something that experience more so at home rather in public. Growing up it has always been a competition between my sister and I for my mother's attention...I realized this jealousy of the relationship that my mother and younger sister have together is a sin...."

Chapter 2: "Lead by Serving"

Here I discuss not only Bible verses describing the nature of "Servant Leadership," but I also insert some "geo-political commentary."

Excerpt:

Sitting down, Jesus called the Twelve and said,
"Anyone who wants to be first must
be the very last, and the servant of all."
(*New International Version*, Mark 9.35)

Throughout history, political and religious leaders have come and gone off the world stage. Many have been evil, most have been mediocre, and some have been pretty good. But no leader has ever impacted the world for good like Jesus. No leader has even come close!

Just like Europe, we are becoming more and more of a post-Christian society. Many Americans, especially young people, are skeptical of Christianity and some are openly hostile. They see it as oppressive instead of a beacon in a world of moral darkness.

Skeptics and enemies of the church are clueless about what life is really like in countries without a Judeo-Christian history. They simply take for granted the hospitals, nursing homes, schools, colleges, social service organizations and charities which were founded by Christians and Jews since the founding of our Republic. They take for granted our rule of law and its biblical roots. Let them go experience life under the rule of a tyrant. I have been for short trips to countries where Christianity was cut off under Soviet communism or never really took root in the first instance. It is survival of the fittest in these places.

If the skeptics and enemies of the church were sent to actually live in countries without any Judeo-Christian influence (and no American troops to protect them); they would run back to our shores as fast as they could.

Jesus selected twelve men to become his disciples. He also taught women about the Kingdom of God and treated them with dignity. This was despite the prevailing culture where women were seen as mere property.

The disciples, women of faith and crowds of the curious followed Jesus around Israel and Samaria for the three years of his public ministry. He was not just their leader. What many non-believers miss is that Jesus was their servant. He led by serving.

> For even as the Son of Man came not to be served but to serve, and to give his life as a ransom for many. (*New International Version*, Mark 10.45)

Wherever he went Jesus healed the sick, the blind and the lame. He brought the synagogue leader's daughter and Lazarus back to life. He washed the disciples' feet. He calmed the Sea of Galilee so they could travel safely. He provided loaves and fishes for the multitudes. He broke bread with his followers. He freely gave his life for them and for us.

Jesus told many parables about the relationship between masters and servants. There is the parable of the bags of gold found at Matthew 25:14-30. The master gave one servant five bags of gold, another two bags and a third servant one bag. The master went on his journey. When he returned, the servant with five bags now had ten because he had invested wisely. The servant with two bags also had invested and presented the master with two more bags. The servant with one bag of gold was afraid to lose it and had buried it with no increase.

The master commended the first two servants for their faithfulness and put them in charge of many things. The master admonished the third servant and ordered that he be cast out.

> So take the bag of gold from him and give it to the one who has ten bags. For whoever had will be given more, and they will have an abundance. Whoever does not have, even that will be taken from them. And throw that worthless servant outside, into the darkness where there will be weeping and gnashing of teeth. (*New International Version*, Matt. 25.28-30)

Ostensibly, the lesson of this parable seems cruel. After all, the third servant did not steal the bag of gold or lose it. He just failed to invest it like the other two servants. But we have to go deeper into the parable to understand the true meaning. The story is not about bags of gold—it is about wisely using the skills and resources God has given us.

It is not enough for a Christian to try to live a life free from sin. Jesus wants us to use our skills and invest our resources to build the Kingdom of God, not waste them like the servant who buried the gold in the ground.

Christ called us to be leaders—leading all men and women to Him with a servant's heart and actions. Being a servant is taking care of other people's needs not just our own.

> Each of you should use whatever gift you have received to serve others, as faithful stewards of God's grace in its various forms. (*New International Version*, 1 Pet. 4.10)

Whenever we get caught up in chasing our own personal success and ignoring the needs of others, we need to step back.

> No one can serve two masters. Either you will hate the one and love the other, or you will be devoted to the one and despise the other. You cannot serve both God and money. (*New International Version*, Matt. 6.24)

Student Responses to Chapter 2

Jeffrey: "The theme of 'Leading by Serving' is that, to be a true leader, you have to serve God. That does not mean to avoid anything outside the church…What I took from [this] chapter is that if I don't use the talents or resources I am given, they will waste away. I think everyone, including myself, has been born with skills unique to them, and our task is to use those skills in the most effective way. Early in life, I was always a natural in math and loved Japanese culture. The two seem unrelated now, but hang on. This year I changed my major from Biomedical Sciences to Computer Engineering; one, because I was slowly starting to understand that I had more of an interest in engineering than medicine; and two, I was quickly starting to understand that I didn't want to spend another six-plus years in school ... I've decided I'm going to invest my resources and time into going after my childhood dreams. Using my talent for math and love for Japan, I hope to get a degree in Computer Engineering and work for some tech company based out of Tokyo."

Amy: "Personally, I felt like Chapter 2, 'Lead by Serving,' was very inspiring because I myself was a leader at some point. During the last two years of my high school career, I was the president of my school's anime club, which was really nerdy of me then, but I don't regret it either. Either way, this chapter reminded me of the club that I led, and I reflected on how I did as the president...one day out of the blue [while here at USF] I received a message from one of the club members who was a freshman while I was president. She told me that...she was inspired to be a leader like me. I remember getting choked up that day..."

Jeremiah: "I found Chapter 2 intriguing, because within the chapter, Susie Hoeller talks about the parable of the bags of gold. She mentions this, but she compares the bags of gold to our spiritual gifts and resources...This hit me hard. As I was reading I just felt a sense of encouragement from God. I feel like at times Christians are apathetic towards their gifts; they compare what they have to what others have and discredit themselves in the process. Myself for instance, I feel like at times my voice isn't good enough to lead worship. What I'm doing here is taking credit away from the God who gave me my gifts. I am saying what He has given me isn't good enough. I am like the pot telling the potter he made me wrong (Isaiah 45:9)."

Kirra: "The theme of Chapter 2...is the importance of serving and giving back to the community. This chapter stood out to me because I find that I have gotten so consumed in my own personal endeavors, that I have forgotten the importance of finding time to give back to my community...As I reach the end of my time at college, however, I find myself burned out and wanting to be selfish...[But] as I come to this realization, I know that by serving others I may find my true passion and happiness. I think this may have been the push I truly needed to explore my options to create a more selfless future for myself."

My Encounter with a Student's Criticism of Chapter 2

The first time I spoke in Gary's class about my book (in 2014), during the break, a female student asked to speak to me after class. I told her certainly, I would be happy to do so. On first appearance, I assumed she was Muslim because she was wearing a hijab (head scarf). During our conversation, she confirmed this because she angrily accused me of being anti-Muslim because I had written: "If skeptics and enemies of the church were sent to actually live in countries without any Judeo-Christian influence (and no American troops to protect them), they would run back to our shores as fast as they could."

Certainly, it is reasonable for her to make that assumption based on the broad claims in my sentence. However, it was not my intention to attack Islam and Muslims in any manner. In fact, the only system I had criticized in the chapter was Soviet communism. This is because the Soviets had made atheism the official state "religion," destroyed thousands of churches, murdered thousands of Christian clergy and persecuted Jews.

Nevertheless, I must confess that I personally believe a society TRULY based on Judeo-Christian values would be superior to other societies from a human rights perspective, especially when it comes to the status of women. Sadly, in my view, naked capitalism, racism, and a host of other nasty "isms" have infected historic Judeo-Christian values today in America. But there is hope to reclaim these precious values if we will only let love lead!

Chapter 17: "Our Mission and the Cross"

This chapter is concerned with discerning God's will for our lives. Excerpt:
God placed each and every one of us on this earth with a unique mission.

> For You formed my inward parts; You covered me in my mother's womb. I will praise You, for I am fearfully and wonderfully made; Marvelous are Your works, And that my soul knows very well. My frame was not hidden from You,
>
> When I was made in secret, And skillfully wrought in the lowest parts of the earth. Your eyes saw my substance, being yet unformed. And in Your book they all were written, the days fashioned for me, When as yet there were none of them. (*King James Version*, Ps. 139.13-16)

Understanding and fulfilling our mission is what we aspire to do. In the meantime, we can be overwhelmed at work and lose sight of our mission. It is easy to become physically and spiritually exhausted in the daily grind of earning a paycheck, running a business, teaching students or treating patients.

Jesus freely sacrificed his life for us. We believe this but at times we can be tempted to give up on our discipleship. We read in Matthew 4:1-11 how Jesus was tempted three times by Satan. Jesus resisted and did not abandon His mission. If we keep our eyes constantly on Jesus, we can resist all of Satan's temptations, no matter how alluring they appear to be.

Just like Jesus continued with His mission to save us from our sins, we must view our workplace as a mission field. All around us, there are lost souls to be saved. Will we lead others to Christ or turn them away?

After his resurrection, Jesus did not remain on earth to build His church. He gave that job to us. Building His church is not just about physical structures, bible studies, becoming a missionary or working in a non-profit humanitarian organization. We can build up the body of Christ in every situation we are involved in. We can scatter the seeds of faith everywhere we go.

> But you will receive power when the Holy Spirit comes on you; and you will be my witnesses in Jerusalem, and in all Judea and Samaria, and to the ends of the earth. (*New International Version*, Acts 1.8)

We simply don't exercise our Christ-like power as much as we should. Our faith can be shaky at times especially when we have our own troubles or see innocents who are victims of crime, accidents, illnesses, and poverty. We question why God allows so much massive human suffering in wars, genocides and natural disasters . . .

All I can say is that our faith, like our bodies needs to be continually nourished. We need daily food and water to be healthy—not occasional food and water. To build a strong faith that overcomes doubts, we have to pray and "water" our minds with the Scriptures every day, whether at home, at work or at church. Don't go a day longer without this essential nourishment!

Jesus, even after enduring horrific scourging, had to carry the Cross he was crucified on. We have to carry our crosses as well.

> Whosoever wants to be my disciple must deny themselves and take up their cross daily and follow me. For whoever wants to save their life will lose it, but

whoever loses their life for me will save it. (*New International Version*, Luke 9.23)

Mother Maria Skobtsova, a Russian born nun, is not a household name for most American Christians because she comes from the Orthodox tradition. Americans are much more familiar with Christians from the Protestant and Catholic branches of Christianity. Mother Maria was arrested by the Nazis for rescuing Jews in Paris. She died a martyr at the Ravensbruck concentration camp during WWII.

In addition to putting her faith into action, even unto death, Mother Maria was an inspiring Christian writer. Here is a beautiful passage she wrote about taking up the cross.

> Let the cross lie on human shoulders, along the path of human God-likeness. The human heart should also be pierced by the two-edged swords, the soul cutting weapons, of other people's crosses. Our neighbor's cross should be a sword that pierces our soul. Our soul should co-participate in its neighbor's destiny, co-feel, co-suffer. (71)

Student Responses to Chapter 17

Krystal: "This particular chapter stood out to me because it speaks about our mission and essentially our destiny. I'm still trying to work out what my destiny is, but I know what I love doing, and I'm hoping that God has a plan to put me on a path…at work my current mission is to assist people who are sick and are in need of assistance in getting their lives back together. As Hoeller states in this chapter, 'Understanding and fulfilling our mission is what we aspire to do' (60). I think that right now God wants me to be where I am, because

I'm meant to help people with their health. Sometimes a simple smile goes a long way in helping to make the patients feel better when they come through our doors. I try to remember that this is my mission even when I am faced with tough moments with some of the patients themselves or other coworkers."

The response of the students to my book was overwhelmingly positive, for which I am grateful. Some students in addition to their personal reflections and application of passages from the book to their lives, offered suggestions for additional topics. However, I wish to note that, in addition to the student who objected to my statements about Judeo-Christian culture in Chapter 2, a second student objected to my use of the word "tribe" later in the book.

Chapter 14: "Remember the Good Samaritan"

Excerpt:
> American businesses, non-profit organizations and government agencies have been encouraging diversity and inclusion in the workplace. Working with people from foreign and diverse backgrounds can be difficult for many Americans, especially if they have not grown up in cosmopolitan urban areas.
>
> Whenever you are tempted to be fearful of or disparaging of someone who is from a different country or ethnic background; re-read the story of the Good Samaritan found at Luke 10:25-37.
>
> Even people who have never picked up the Bible know this story. Our fifty states even have "Good Samaritan" laws. These laws protect individuals who voluntarily and reasonably help injured people.
>
> The Samaritan came upon a Jew, who had been attacked, robbed and left half dead alongside the Jerusalem to Jericho road. Two earlier Jewish travelers, a priest and a Levite had passed by and not stopped to help the injured man. But the Samaritan

took pity on him, bandaged his wounds and brought him to an inn, and paid the innkeeper for his care.

The Samaritan went out of his way to help the Jew even though the Jews looked down on the Samaritans because they did not strictly adhere to Mosaic Law, among other reasons.

The message of this story is not just that we should stop and help injured people. The story teaches more than that. We must not be prejudiced against people because they are not the same as us.

We have to honestly ask ourselves if we harbor prejudices against other human beings just because they are not members of our own "tribe." If we do, then we are breaking the commandment to love our neighbor as ourselves.

Angela's Response to Chapter 14

Angela: "Chapter 14 deals with issues of prejudice and discrimination. The author begins the chapter with a statement of fact that living in the world, people will come across others that differ from them and expected norms. The author says to be tolerant of people of varying backgrounds one should be kind to these people from different 'tribes' by remembering a Bible story. Hoeller simplified the issue of race, which I infer the chapter is about from her use of the word *tribe* which is often used to condescend to people of African descent, to a farcical extent. Racism is not about prejudices because people have not encountered people of different races; it is almost impossible not to encounter people of other races in a globalized world. Racial prejudice and discrimination in the U.S. are based in America's colonial past and is continued on today by a complex system of internalized, ingrained beliefs in individuals and institutionalized racism that makes these beliefs acceptable. In a world where, tonight, Darren Wilson was not even indicted for killing a young black boy, remembering a Bible story is not enough to fight against racism, and to suggest it is disgusting."

My Response to Angela

First, I did not use the word *tribe* to refer to or condescend to Africans or people of recent African descent—rather I used it to refer to a social group. I could have used *nation, ethnic group, social class*, or similar words. The fact is that many people commonly use the word *tribe* without any thought of connecting this word to Africa. After all we have Native American tribes in the U.S. David Brooks, a prominent New York Times columnist, often complains about the "tribalism" which is tearing apart American politics.

Tribe is a word derived from the science of anthropology. The truth is there are tribes all over the world and tribalism, where people are kind only to members of their own social group, is a huge problem. The term *racism* is commonly used in the U.S. because of our ugly history of slavery, Jim Crow and discrimination and violence against African Americans. But tribalism is actually a much broader concept than race. A recent example of "tribalist" conflict occurred during the 1990s' civil wars which broke up the former Yugoslavia into six smaller countries.

The student wrote that it was "disgusting" to suggest that a Bible story could be used to fight racism. I believe because of her anger about my use of the word *tribe*, she missed my point. I had included the Good Samaritan story because it is not just about helping an injured person. Rather it is about *helping someone else who is different from yourself.*

The full meaning of the parable of the Good Samaritan is that a Samaritan stopped to help an injured Jew at a time when Jews despised Samaritans as a lower "tribe." This full meaning is a warning against racist and discriminatory thinking and behavior. This is why Jesus told the parable. I am sorry that the student was offended by my use of the word *tribe*.

One last point: the student, living in diverse Tampa Bay, stated that it is almost impossible to not to encounter people of different races in a globalized world. Frankly, she is wrong about this. I would be happy to take her to parts of Canada where she will never see a black person or to Taiwanese cities where she will never see a

Caucasian. The truth is that many places in the world are not ethnically or racially diverse, even in a so-called "globalized" world. In these places, there can be a greater fear of the "stranger" than in diverse metropolitan areas.

Conclusion

The point of bringing up Angela's criticism of this chapter as I conclude is not to defend myself. The point is to show that people from diverse backgrounds can interpret the same words very differently. I intended my very short chapter about the Good Samaritan to bring a message of love but not to claim that prayer alone could defeat racism, although I do believe that prayer is much more effective than what most people think. I leave readers with this reflection by Father Bryan Massingale about Dr. Martin Luther King, Jr.:

> King never advocated "pray-it-away" solutions to personal or social problems. He was deeply realistic about the intransigence of evil and how it yields only in the face of determined action and persistent challenge. He knew that prayer alone is insufficient for social change and is too often used as an excuse by Christians to avoid facing difficult social issues.
>
> Yet he insisted that prayer is an essential dimension of social engagement and never a secondary force in the quest of justice. King scholar Lewis Baldwin maintains that King believed that the struggle against the triple evils of racism, poverty, and war required "the combination of prayer, intelligence, and sustained activism." King's own prayer life is a witness against opposing spiritual maturity and action on behalf of justice.

Lean on Jesus is a concise book, designed for busy people looking for spiritual guidance as they make their way in business and in life. It contains wisdom from the Scriptures and all three branches of Christianity—Catholicism, Orthodoxy and Protestantism. It has been a privilege to share it with Gary and his students. I learned a great deal from their papers. If I decide to publish a second edition, I will certainly consider their comments, suggestions and criticisms.

Works Cited

The Bible. New International Version, Biblica, 2011.

Brooks, David. "The Retreat to Tribalism." *The New York Times*, 2 Jan. 2018, p. A15.

ESV Study Bible. English Standard Version, Crossway Bibles, 2008.

Hoeller, Susie. *Lean on Jesus: Christian Women in the Workplace.* West Bow Press, 2014.

The Holy Bible. King James Version, Hendrickson Bibles, 2011.

Massingale, Fr. Bryan. "How Martin Luther King, Jr.'s Prayer Life Moved Him to Act for Justice." *U.S. Catholic*, 12 Jan. 2018, www.uscatholic.org/articles/201801/how-martin-luther-king-jrs-prayer-life-moved-him-act-justice-31263. Accessed 4 Feb 2019.

Skobotsova, Mother Maria. *Essential Writings.* Edited by Helene Klepinin, Orbis Books, 2013.

Chapter 9

Jesus Christ: The Champion of All People—Regardless

Susie Hoeller

As the new year of 2019 begins; it is time for all Christians to recognize Jesus Christ as a champion of the equal human dignity and worth of all people regardless of gender (or any other attribute or characteristic). Certainly, the Canadian author Sarah Bessey makes a convincing case for gender equality in her 2013 book *Jesus Feminist*.

Up until now, most Christian denominations have been patriarchal institutions. Of course, the Roman Catholic Church is the most prominent example with its male-only priesthood. But it is not just Catholic clerics who have subordinated women in the church. Protestant and Orthodox churches have used bible "proof-texting" (based on a couple of passages in Paul's letters) to limit the participation of women and girls in their churches.

But in our #MeToo era, many Christian women and girls are finally refusing to submit to the unequal treatment in their churches. For example, a Greek Orthodox college student in Tarpon Springs, Florida, recently challenged the annual Epiphany celebration where only young men are permitted to dive into the bayou to retrieve the gold cross and receive the spiritual blessing associated with its retrieval.

Is this just a spirit of worldly rebellion influenced by our politics and the media? After all, the same week that the Greek college student publicly challenged her church and ended up on the front page of the *Tampa Bay Times*, the largest class of female representatives in history was seated in the U.S. House of Representatives.

In my view, the answer is no. A recognition of Jesus as a feminist springs from the need for a spiritual cleansing of the churches. Of course, there have been female theologians advocating for gender equality in the church for some time. But their scholarly work may not have resonated outside of the academy. This is why books like

Sarah Bessey's *Jesus Feminist* are so powerful because they are written for women and men in the pews and the public at large, not just for scholars in the universities and seminaries.

The best thing about Bessey is that she does not attack anyone or engage in theological debates. She does not fall into the trap of bible proof-texting. Rather, Bessey is a talented storyteller. She tells stories about her family, her friends and the churches she has attended. In this way, she is following in the footsteps of Jesus, who taught his audiences by telling stories.

Jesus, fully God and fully man, understood the nature of human memory. We all remember stories, whether children's fairy tales, novels, songs or movie plots, much more than lists of facts or commandments. We can understand the Good Samaritan, the woman caught in adultery, the widow and her mite and the fear of Peter during the storm on the Sea of Galilee. Jesus used stories to teach us what it means to live in the "Kingdom of God."

I cannot remember now how I first found *Jesus Feminist*. I know it was not in a church library. I think I happened upon it in the Christian books section of my local Barnes and Noble. The cover stood out on the shelf because of its bright yellow color and its simple yet profound title in all caps "JESUS FEMINIST." More importantly, the title seemed so radical at first, since I had never seen Jesus described as a feminist. I was familiar with the usual names for Jesus such as the "Son of God," "Son of Man," "Prince of Peace," "Good Shepherd," and "Lamb of God." But neither the Bible nor a Catholic litany ever speaks of Jesus as a feminist. My curiosity was piqued, and I immediately purchased the book. I took it home and read it in one sitting—just like how I read thrilling novels. It is similarly engaging.

I then recommended this book to Gary. He read it and placed it on the reading list for his "The Bible as Literature" class. Using the autocritographical learning style which Gary champions, the students wrote reflective papers about what Bessey's writing means to them. These papers are not like the typical "book report," where a student describes the plot, the characters and the setting. Rather the students write about how Bessey's message can be applied to their lives, past, present and future.

I read all the student papers commenting on my book *Lean on Jesus* and Sarah Bessey's book *Jesus Feminist*. The two books were written for different audiences and for different purposes. *Lean on Jesus* was written to help women in workplaces act like Christians and not leave their faith at home or in church. *Jesus Feminist* was written to show readers how Jesus made a feminist out of Bessey and to encourage women to fully exercise their spiritual gifts in freedom, unshackled by ecclesiastical and societal tradition. Bessey described feminism as follows:

> At the core, feminism simply consists of the radical notion that women are people too. Feminism only means we champion the dignity, rights, responsibilities and glories of women as equal in importance—not greater than, but certainly not less than- to those of men, and we refuse discrimination against women. (Bessey 13-14)

My book deals with Christian ethical conduct in business—an essential subject but not one stirring up the same level of controversy, passion and even anger as a discussion of gender roles in the church and society.

Here are some moving excerpts from Gary's students' papers:

Keith: "I enjoyed chapter four of Sarah Bessey's book and agree wholeheartedly with her comments on the centrality of studying scripture and scrutinizing attempts by people to manipulate it and/or take scripture out of its historical context....The author points out the negative effects of inequality between the sexes:

> When women are restricted from the service of God in any capacity, the Church is mistakenly allowing an imperfect male-dominated ancient culture to drive our understanding and practice of Christ's redeeming work, instead of Jesus and the whole of Scriptures. (69)

If you are a believer in Jesus Christ, that means you have been born into his family. You are his sister or brother, and the Bible has now become your family history book. So, why would you allow someone else to explain your family history to you?...It is a gift and a responsibility to read and understand the Scriptures for ourselves."

Kennedi: "Why should [Paul] tell women to be silent and not the men? It was only when I read the background context, which Bessey provides, did I understand. Bessey says:

> ...when Paul wrote his letter to the Corinthian Church, they were in disunity and disorder. They were quarreling. He wrote to them as a pastor and a friend...Paul clearly wanted everyone to be involved in the ministry of the church...so he took the time to go through each of the disordered groups with specific corrections...Paul's intention was to restore order to the community of God. And that order didn't include the silencing of all women any more than it included a blanket forever-and-ever prohibition on prophesying or speaking in tongues. (Bessey 65-66)
>
> My favorite part is when Bessey tells us what the word 'quietly' means translated into Greek, the language originally used by Paul to write these letters. It does not mean silence as we English speakers would assume. The Greek word used is actually *hesuchia*, which according to Bessey means 'stillness'—more along the lines of peacefulness or minding one's own business. It is not about talking versus not talking; it's about learning in a still way..." (Bessey 67)

Kennedi continues: "My issue with the patriarchal view of women in church, started at a young age. I wondered why I wasn't given the same attention in the church by the elders as my male friends were. I wondered why I was 'put on a pedestal' and told to smile constantly when my male friends weren't. Why was I always being told I'd be a lovely wife someday, but my brother was never told he'd make a great husband? Why couldn't I deliver the message on kids days, a day when the children led service, but I could sing? Why were all the singers on that day always girls and the 'preacher' always a boy? I noticed these things, and as I got older, I began to question them when I was simply told by older women in the church or my relatives, 'The Bible says women shouldn't preach.' Okay. I'll admit, I accepted that for a time. But when I began to be told that a woman could preach if she had a 'spiritual (that means male) covering' over her, that's when the wheels really started turning. 'So, you're saying I can preach once I get married?', I'd asked my aunt, a *very* religious non-denominational woman, when I was twelve years old. She simply replied yes—but I wasn't done. 'Why isn't it the same for men?' I'd asked. 'Why can an unmarried man preach, but an unmarried woman can't?' I then mentioned the youth pastor at our church, who was male and currently unmarried. Her response was, since men were the spiritual leaders, they could preach with or without a covering. Their marital status had no weight. 'So, a male preacher's wife means nothing, but a woman pastor's husband means everything?' She softened it up a bit after that, saying how it was a man's job to treat women with respect and 'love her as Christ loves the church,' to quote Ephesians 5:25.

Kennedi concludes: "The conversation ended eventually, but I still never got over it. The whole 'submit to your husband' never sat right with me (and it still doesn't) . . . Now because of the idea that women should be submissive to men, we see all types of rape on women becoming more and more commonplace. We see all types of sexual misconduct against women becoming a day to day thing. Society sees women as objects because they are only here to 'affirm her husband's leadership.'[1] This idea suggests we have no motives on our own. All we want to do is serve our husbands. Our husband wants more kids? Fine. He wants us to stay home? Fine. He does not want me working? Fine. The men decide, they're the leaders, *right?* Since women have no motives of their own, since they only want to serve their husbands, we must not care that we get paid the same as our male co-workers who do *less* than us. We don't care about getting cat-called on the street, feeling unsafe by ourselves…Why is it that the thing men fear the most about going to prison, is the very thing

---

[1] The student referenced this term from an article titled "Six things submission is not" by John Piper, author and founder of desiringgod.org

women fear the most when walking down the sidewalk?...I had someone tell me once, 'Liberals ruined feminism for me.' Let's change that. How about, misogyny ruined *society* for me."

Keith: "As for *Jesus Feminist*...there are a few things that have already put me off to the author. The first thing is the cover, 'Exploring God's Radical Notion That Women Are People, Too.' This strikes me as a not so subtle insinuation by the author that the male population does not currently treat women as human beings. I flatly reject this claim. While there are individuals among the male population that have chosen to treat women horribly and as objects, I firmly believe that the vast majority of the male population does treat women appropriately. Another sticking point for me is the author's claim that there is the 'perennial topic of whether women should be allowed to teach or preach or even read Scripture aloud.' (3) Ironically, she makes this statement right after she admits her disdain for strawmen and women. I personally have attended a dozen churches (including two in communist China) over the last fifteen years, and I have never seen women kept from teaching, preaching or reading scripture. In fact, it has been my experience that women are the most audible, faithful Christians and easily outnumber the men in the church congregations."

Tiffany: "That idea, Jesus as a feminist, is not taboo to me. Why wouldn't Jesus be a feminist? He was born to a virgin mother; being born to a virgin mother, personally, would give me an unwavering and overconfident belief in the power and strength of all women. I don't know why all men are not feminists. Why not believe your mothers can do all the things you can? After all they gave birth to you. They nurtured you, fed you from their bosom to keep you alive. They were your life support before you knew what life was. Why not root for all things like them? I second Sarah Bessey's notation,

> Let's head outside. I want us to sit around a fire pit ringed with stones and watch the moon move over the Pacific. I want us to drink good red wine, dig our toes into the cool sand, and wrap in cozy sweaters. . .And I want us to talk about this—really about womanhood, church, the labels, and where we go from here., Because the vicious arguments, the limits, the you're-in

-but-they' re-out, the debates, and the silencing aren't working, are they? [No! They aren't working at all.]. . .I'll be honest: some of the words I have to say might rub you wrong. You might disagree [It don't matter, Bessey; speak on, sister!] with the particulars, but that's okay—stay with me [Alright now, Bessey]. Let's sit here in hard truth and easy beauty, in the tensions of the Now and the Not Yet of the Kingdom of God, and let us discover how we can disagree beautifully. (Bessey 1-2).

Tiffany continues: "Bessey is begging women to speak up and out. Forget this idea of the 'male-ego' and speak candidly about the past, the present and future of women in this world, and if we disagree let us disagree beautifully. As women we cannot continue to allow the World or men to emasculate us, yes, I said emasculate. I believe that women are born with masculinity and then taught to be feminine, but we never lose the masculine the part of ourselves. Masculinity, to some people, just means man or having muscle (muscular); but masculinity goes deeper than a physical appearance. It is about an inner strength, an inner natural aggression. Women are taught to be feminine because too much aggression leads to corruption and fighting; someone had to be softened down to keep order. So, society chose to soften the gender that lacks the physical appearance of masculinity, even though they possessed the highest amount of inner strength and aggression. Why does the lioness hunt for the food? Why does the mother bear protect her cub, even at the cost of death? Why do they tell us to never mess with a woman scorned?"

Tiffany concludes: "Women have mastered masculinity so well we can turn it on and off, but mostly we keep it off. Turning it on would interrupt the status quo of life, and what have we learned about disturbing the status quo? That is corruption and corruption is punishable by death, and in our case, rape. One of the most common tactics used to emasculate women—rape. 'The debates and the silencing aren't working, are they?' (Bessey 2). Maybe I took Bessey's words more aggressive than what was intended, but why not picture Jesus as a feminist? Why not see women as both masculine and feminine beings?"

Avram: "Oh, man, do I have a lot to discuss here. I hate when sexist men use scripture to allow themselves to be dominant over their wives or anyone else with whom they serve Christ. Sarah Bessey said it perfectly when she said, 'He wanted each individual to use his or her gifts, strengthening the church' (Bessey 119) . . . Women in the church are just as important as men. I am Coptic Orthodox, which is an Apostolic Church from when Saint Mark the Evangelist came to Egypt to spread Christianity. In the 2,000 years my church has been around, we have experienced so much martyrdom, a Christian scholar named Tertullian is reported to have said, 'If the Martyrs throughout the world were to be put on one side of the scale and the Coptic martyrs alone on the other side, the latter would outweigh the former.'[2] Now were all the people who were martyred men? Absolutely not! Men and women both were killed for the sake of Christ, so how can one say that men are dominant over women? The question that arises is then. 'What baggage shows up on your emotional doorstep when you read scriptures about submission in marriage and to men? Does the context of Paul's writings to the early Christians help you grapple with those issues?' (Bessey 327). A lot of times men will use the phrase, 'Saint Paul tells women to submit to their husbands,' but they are ignorant to the rest of the chapter…in the book of Ephesians, 'Wives submit to your husbands, as to the Lord…Husbands love your wives, just as Christ also loved the church and gave Himself for her, that he might sanctify and cleanse her with the washing of water by the word, that He might present her to Himself a glorious church, not having any spot or wrinkle or any such thing but that she be holy and without blemish. So, husbands ought to love their own wives as their own bodies; he who loves his wife loves himself. For no one ever hated his own flesh, but nourishes and cherishes it, just as the Lord does the church' (*New King James Version*, Ephesians 5.22-20)."

---

[2] Tragically, the persecution of Coptic Christians in Egypt continues to this day. www.theguardian.com/world/2018/jan/10/christians-egypt-unprecedented-persecution-report

Avram continues: "Men need to understand the phrase *after* 'Submit to your husbands' if they truly want a successful marriage. When Saint Paul says, 'as to the Lord,' he is referring to a submission of trust, not a submission of servitude. So, men, can we truly say to our wives, 'Trust me, I will do everything for the edification of our marriage,' or are we going to continue to use scripture in a way to pervert our sanctity with women? Let's not be uncultured swine, and let's truly be able to tell the women we are going to be married to 'Trust me, I will do everything for the edification of our marriage' as Christ has done everything for the edification and salvation of man."

Avram concludes: "Christ was the Master Builder of the world. And I am not just talking about the creation of the world. I am also talking about the building of relationships with others. . .Christ was able to build a friendship between those who followed him. Saint Matthew was a tax collector, while Saint Peter was a fisherman. Before Christ, I am sure those two men would never have sat in the same room, let alone love each other. Christ built a world where we are here to serve the underserved, care for those who have no one and live a life that truly imitates Him. Sarah Bessey is a woman who wants men to understand that we are equal. She is right, and the Bible supports this. We must not use the Bible as an allowance for sexism. especially Saint Paul. Saint Paul continuously talks to men about how they ought to respect women and even give their life for them, if required."

As you can see, students reacted strongly to Bessey's book. Here are my thoughts to conclude this chapter:

The word *feminist* means different things to different people. After all we have pro-abortion and anti-abortion feminists. Anti-feminists characterize feminists as "man-haters." Womanists rightfully believe that the feminist movement from the time of the suffragettes through the 1970s activism and even today has been too focused on issues involving white and upper/middle class women. In fact, as the centenary of the nineteenth Amendment to the U.S. Constitution will be celebrated in 2020, writers are now examining how the suffrage movement left black women behind—advocating for the vote for white women only.[3]

An insightful take on what feminism means comes from the greatest singer of our time. Who can forget when in 1967 Aretha Franklin first sang these lyrics in "Do Right Woman, Do Right Man" (Moman/Penn 1967)?

> A woman's only human
> You should understand
> She's not just a plaything
> She's flesh and blood just like her man

Or what baby boomer can forget when in 1971 the Australian pop sensation Helen Reddy reached the top of the charts worldwide with her feminist anthem "I Am Woman"? Or when, in 1973, Billie Jean King defeated Bobby Riggs in the "Battle of the Sexes" tennis match which drew millions of television viewers?

It was not just feminist writers and politicians in the 1970s like Gloria Steinem, Betty Friedan, Simone de Beauvoir, Bella Abzug and Shirley Chisolm who ignited a new wave of feminists, but it was also cultural moments in music, sports and entertainment. For me as a college and law student and then a young lawyer entering a male dominated profession, all of these influences were significant. I was also a female pioneer in ice hockey and sailboat racing, not just the law.

Until I read *Jesus Feminist*, I never really connected feminism with Jesus Christ. This is because starting from childhood I worshipped in traditional churches, both Protestant and Catholic. Men were the ministers and deacons or priests and bishops. The role for women was limited and secondary—teaching children Sunday school, choir membership or participating in a women's bible study. Since I had never aspired to becoming a minister or priest, I did not focus my attention on the lack of opportunities for women to become servant leaders in Christ's footsteps.

---

[3] See, e.g., Brent Staples, "When the Suffrage Movement Sold Out," *The New York Times*, February 3, 2019 at page SR1.

Many modern-day feminists are critical of Christianity because of traditional teachings placing women on an unequal footing with men. Clearly these teachings need to change, as Sarah Bessey advocates. But merely because of the foibles of Christ's followers, no one should miss out on the gospel message which Jesus taught—to love God and love one's neighbor as oneself, or put another way—treat others and you would like to be treated. Christians are called to "let love lead," and that is what we must do in our words and deeds: "There is neither Jew nor Gentile, nether slave nor free, nor is there male and female, for you are all one in Christ Jesus" (*New International Version*, Gal. 3.28).

Works Cited

Bessey, Sarah. *Jesus Feminist: An Invitation to Revisit the Bible's View of Women*. Howard Books, 2013.

The Bible. New King James Version, Thomas Nelson, 1982.

The Bible. New International Version, Biblica, 2011.

Franklin, Aretha. "Do Right Woman, Do Right Man." *I Never Loved a Man the Way I Love You*, Atlantic, 1967.

Part IV

A Visionary Invitation: All Are Welcome

He loves us. On our own terms. He treats us as equals to the men around him; he does not belittle; he honors us; he challenges us; he teaches us; he includes us—calls us all beloved. Gloriously, this flies in the face of the cultural expectations of his time—and even our own time…Jesus loves us.

Sarah Bessey, *Jesus Feminist: An Invitation to Revisit the Bible's View of Women*

Chapter 10

Access Granted: Feminine Mystical and Mundane Pathways

Scott Neumeister

Blessed are the pure in heart, for they will see God.
                Matthew 5:8 (New International Version)

    I have learned in writing autocritographically to reflect not only on past memories but also on present-moment situations as material to inform my critical writing. From the very first course I took with (Dr.) Gary (L. Lemons) at the University of South Florida, he would give the same response to any experience, current or previous, that we students brought up in class as meaningful: "Write about it." This technique of looking at the relatedness of written texts with the ongoing texts of our personal stories creates the opportunity for realizing the connectedness of human experience. Recognizing the recurring themes of life and literature brings a solidarity between our lives and the lives of the Other, whatever the differences might be. In Chapter 5 of *Let Love Lead*, I use the occasion of the revival of *Jesus Christ Superstar* to both explore the musical's impact on my life and frame my examination of the students' writing in Gary's "The Bible as Literature" course related to *128 Greatest Stories from the Bible*. In this chapter, I dialogue with another semester's class who wrote in response to their readings in *The Single Gospel* by Neil Averitt and *Jesus Feminist: An Invitation to Revisit the Bible's View of Women* by Sarah Bessey. I am basing my framework for this dialogue on a piece of my personal story related to the most important (young) woman in my life—my fifteen-year-old daughter, Catherine.

    I was recently asked about how Catherine received her name. My memories took me back to the time several months before her birth. Her mother and I had bandied about seemingly endless name ideas, some based on how they sounded, others as tributes to family members or close friends. I know how important a name can be in establishing a person's lifelong social interactions, in both positive and negative ways. For example, my middle name—Leslie—was generally "hidden" from my peers, yet it still incited much gender bullying as being too "feminine" when I was young. Moreover, the meaning and historical usages of a name can carry significance and hidden connotations. At this time nearing my daughter's birth, I had a growing interest not only in Russian history but also in saints of both the Orthodox and Catholic churches. The name Catherine kept recurring in my explorations—Catherine I (the first female Russian empress) and her granddaughter-in-law Catherine the Great, as well as the saints Catherine of Alexandria, Catherine of Siena, and Catherine of Genoa. These women all were pioneers, whether in political or religious arenas. So, in the name Catherine, I saw women both of earthly influence and with a depth of spirit willing to seek the divine.

One of the main etymological possibilities for the name Catherine is the Greek *katharos*, meaning pure. For me, this root carried a strong connection to the verse from Jesus' Sermon on the Mount: "Blessed are the pure (*katharoi*) in heart, for they will see God" (*New International Version*, Matt. 5.8). This purity transcends the limited meaning of some kind of spotless moral behavior to become, as Kenyan author Pamela Mandela Idenya indicates, a purity of intention and vision in seeking the divine. Catherine of Siena (1347-1380) and Catherine of Genoa (1447-1510) were examples of these "pure of heart" mystics who indeed had powerful, direct experiences of Jesus and who left behind written accounts of their encounters. In my original exploration of the name, I had purchased *The Dialogues of St. Catherine of Siena*, a first-person narration of the saint's ecstatic visions and interactions with Christ. I had skimmed the book, but with much to accomplish before my child's birth, I had not read with a deep, critical eye. Now, writing this chapter and prompted by the recent inquiry into Catherine's name origin, I decided to return to this book, as well as delve into the writings of Catherine of Genoa, *The Life and Doctrine of Saint Catherine of Genoa*.

Both Catherines lived in a time when men severely limited the influence of women in the Church and access to the divine was mediated by the male priesthood. These saints remarkably circumvented the patriarchal and hierarchical barriers the Church had constructed between themselves and the divine. Their lives exemplified how, as Sarah Bessey states in *Jesus Feminist*, "Jesus ushered in a crazy upside-down kingdom...where the least is the most honored...This is the Kingdom of love" (80). This fact is particularly true for Catherine of Siena, who became the first female Doctor of the Church, along with Teresa of Avila. The move of the feminine into venerated religious positions of power that acknowledged personal access to divine communion is an indication of the "crazy upside-down kingdom" breaking through. Grace M. Jantzen explains, "The connection of questions of power to questions of mysticism is obvious as soon as one stops to consider that a person who was acknowledged to have direct access to God would be in a position to challenge any form of authority, whether doctrinal or political, which she saw as incompatible with the divine will" (186). The experience of these female *katharoi* epitomizes "the least" being the most honored—honored with seeing God—as well as a shift, as bell hooks titles her book on feminist theory, from margin to center. I would argue that, just as Bessey's *Jesus Feminist* bears the subtitle *An Invitation to Revisit the Bible's View of Women*, the depths of biblical writing reveal an "access granted" status to women and all historically marginalized groups.

What are the principal qualifications for this access? A purity of heart and a willingness to let love lead. Despite what might seem the impossibility of both Catherines' mystical encounters, I found as I began to deeply explore their writings that their received spiritual messages were consistent with Bessey's emphasis: love itself is the key to the "kingdom of love," unlocking the door to the divine. I repeatedly uncovered this motif throughout their own words concerning their visions. "It is, indeed, through the effect of love that the soul becomes another [Christ]...The soul unites herself with God by the affection of love," Catherine of Siena asserts (20). In recalling her divine ecstasies, she conveys these words she repeatedly heard from God, "Look at those creatures who, among the beauties which I have given to the soul, creating her in My image and similitude, are clothed with the nuptial garment (that is, the garment of love), adorned with many virtues, by which they are united with Me through love" (19-20). Catherine of Genoa likewise received instruction directly from Christ, whom she refers to as "My Love," that reinforces its primacy: "Take always for your support this word, Love, with which you will go on your way, direct, pure, light, watchful, quick, enlightened, without erring, yet without a guide or help from any creature; for love needs no support, being sufficient to do all things without fear; neither does love ever become weary, for even martyrdom is sweet to it" (18). In discovering this theme resonant with my concurrent writing of this chapter in *Let Love Lead*, I had allowed the serendipitous question about my own daughter's name to lead me fully into the experience of the Catherines—the *katharoi* that could see God. Thus, I am, as per (Dr.) Lemons' maxim, "writing a paper about it."

The theme of love uniting us to the divine and to each other, a love that is beyond fear (and even beyond reason), does not solely resonate personally with me in European women of the Middle Ages, oppressed as they were. My graduate studies of African American literature since the time of my daughter Catherine's birth have brought me into literary contact with Sojourner Truth, the remarkable former slave and abolitionist from the nineteenth century. Truth's experience with the divine reminds me of the Catherines' mystical encounters and reinforces this same, love-linked motif. In an interview with Harriet Beecher Stowe, Truth narrates her direct encounter with Jesus while revisiting her old slave home, as much an exercise in memory for her as reader response work is for Gary's students:

> An' I begun to feel such a love in my soul as I never felt before—love to all creatures. An' then, all of a sudden, it stopped, an' I said, "Dar's de white folks, that have abused you an' beat you an' abused your people,—think o' them!" But then there came another rush of love through my soul, an' I cried

out loud,—"Lord, Lord, I can love EVEN DE WHITE FOLKS!"

Here, Truth's surmounting of her understandable hatred for her oppressors epitomizes a love, as Catherine of Genoa conveys, "sufficient to do all things without fear." Truth expresses the same transformative nature of the deep encounters with Jesus that Bessey is emphasizing in her text.

All of the above-mentioned folks embody what Bessey would label (as in *Jesus Feminist*'s Chapter Six title) "Patron Saints, Spiritual Midwives, and 'Biblical' Womanhood." Recorded both in the Bible and outside of it, the stories of women who embody the faith, hope, and love I wrote about in Chapter 4 of *Let Love Lead* suffer from historical underrepresentation. Bessey, when imagining a personal bookshelf filled with texts of individual significance and inspirational texts, sees the disconnect between women's scarce literary presence and the power and example of their spiritual stories: "It's not a conspiracy theory. The status quo is simply what sells . . . [Women] don't get the shelf space they deserve. I wanted those stories" (89). The reader response work from the female students in "The Bible as Literature" course operated in two ways that address this "shelf space" issue. One of the prompts that Bessey gives as a discussion question for Chapter Six is the following: "What women stand out as 'saints' and midwives in your spiritual journey?" In several of the students' responses that I will highlight from Gary's "The Bible as Literature" class from spring of 2018, they give a place of preeminence to the female versions of "another Christ" (as Catherine of Siena would call those "clothed in love") in their own lives. However, even more than honoring these embodiments of love, the students themselves often narrate their own moments of experiencing "love to all creatures," as Sojourner Truth calls her epiphanic comprehension. In keeping with my own autocritographical moment, I will be using both Saints Catherine and Sojourner Truth as my major female touchstones for the wisdom and "crazy upside-down" power of letting love lead.

I Can Do All Things: Breaking Conventions

The first female student I will engage in my dialogue, pondering the question of her own patron saint, initially does not shy away from finding strength and inspiration in two masculine figures in the Old Testament: Job and David. However, given Bessey's focus on females, the student then identifies a pair of biblical women with whom she has previously resonated—Ruth and Naomi. Feeling a correlation with her life story, the student connects with the struggles of her two "spiritual mamas," as Bessey refers to them, in losing everything yet still finding solace in each other and faith in God to persevere. In this aspect she sees that Ruth and Naomi parallel her initial selection of Job in affirming her own "staying faithful in my season when a situation didn't come my way." She also feels encouragement in her struggles with morality as she moves on to contemplate the "sinful woman" who anoints Jesus' feet in the Gospels and receives forgiveness. The student quickly transitions from these women in more traditional roles, however, to write in detail about a new inspirational figure whom she had not heard about until reading Bessey: Anna from Luke's gospel. Anna, as the only prophetess mentioned by name in the New Testament, holds a position higher than even the priest Simeon in Luke's account. Across the age and stature difference between herself and this elderly female seer, the student identifies with the character's persistence, just as she appreciates in Ruth, Naomi, and Job: "I see myself in Anna because, even though the Bible says that she was very old, she stayed true to her calling even when things did not go as planned." I note additionally that the student admires the same quality in Anna that she discerns in the "sinful woman" and David: people "after God's own heart" whose desire for intimacy with the divine—despite even personal missteps—never wavers.

In contemplating these women's societal roles, this student begins by agreeing with Bessey's assertion that "I am a biblical woman because I follow in the footsteps of all the biblical women who came before me" (97). The student imagines her ongoing "walk" as encompassing an entire range of possibilities, not just a narrowly-defined image of womanhood. Indeed, by finding "spiritual mamas" in Ruth and Naomi, she is grasping what feminist biblical scholar Phyllis Trible observes in the book of Ruth as "the struggles of Naomi and Ruth for survival in a patriarchal environment." The student sees that, despite Anna's lacking the same "shelf space" as male prophets with entire books of the Bible (like Ezekiel or Isaiah), God's calling to seek and speak divine inspiration extends to women just as much as men. Any system, patriarchy included, that seeks to limit human potentialities capacitated by divine plans, then, stands at odds with true biblical personhood. The student declares, "I am wanting to pursue God's purpose, and that doesn't make me less of a woman. I don't live by a stereotype." Bessey's approach, which places Jesus as the ultimate biblical trailblazer, reinforces the student's expansive and hopeful vision: "As we follow in the footsteps of our Savior, we are led away from the world's [limited] way of looking at life and conflict, community and creation, marriage and children, aging and youth, suffering and friendship" (100). Just as Jesus extolled the *katharoi*—the pure of heart who will see God—this student, resisting human restrictions, pursues in steadfast devotion "the bliss of fellowship with and knowledge of God," as Alyce M. McKenzie recognizes (42). In this student's following of both "spiritual mamas" and "papas," biblical women and men both of high position and of none desiring to see God, she seeks to embody the work of letting love lead.

Another female student, who simultaneously works as a preschool teacher, speaks about taking inspiration from her "patron saint" of a mother who has given her revelations in both her intimate relationships and her classroom roles. When this student was in middle school, her mother, having for years submitted to the prescribed role of solely being the keeper of "marriage, children, a nuclear family unit," received the inspiration to work with students and become a teaching assistant. The student's father, angry at his wife for accepting this calling and thus supposedly neglecting her wife and mother duties, responded with "a couple years of tantrums and yelling, of thrown dishes and threats." Eventually, her mother had to quit the job that she loved and had fulfilled her avocation outside of their home due to his raging. Following the constricted model of what she had witnessed at home, the student subsequently got engaged to her high school boyfriend, a close approximation of her controlling father, at the age of nineteen. Her mother then pulled her aside and, with a solicitous urgency underpinned by years of suffering abuse and restrictive oppression, asked, "Do you see my life? Do you want this for yourself? Please don't do what I've done." Awakening to the direct implications of her mother's life as a cautionary tale, the student called off her engagement and has since that time carefully avoided men, or *anyone*, who would seek to limit her desire to be "strong, intelligent, and assertive."

The student's hagiography of her mother did not end with simply warding off the disempowerment of a controlling partner. Her "spiritual mama's" midwifery also enabled the student to pursue the exact lifework that her mother had been denied—in children's education. By responding to her own summons to become a teacher, this student is carrying forward her mother's stymied mission and is sensing the depth of her mother's legacy as expressed through her. Each year she enjoys a classroom with new girls whom she—along with some empowering parental allies—encourages with "affirmations attesting to their bravery and power." Along these lines, in order to broaden her young female students' conception of what is possible for them in their future, she has replaced the princess dress-up station in her classroom with a doctor, veterinary, firefighter, and police officer one. This stance has not been without some parental opposition, however, and so this teacher/student has been called upon to muster the spiritual fortitude to remain the "strong, intelligent, and assertive" woman that her mother evoked in her that allows her to engender the same qualities in her female students.

Through both pedagogical and role model influences on her students, this teacher/student is also extending the empowering message that her mother conveyed to her: don't let limited thinking or societal roles set you up for restraints on your divinely-gifted capacities. Her message, as well as her mission, aligns with what Sojourner Truth declares: "Let individuals make the most of what God has given them, have their neighbors do the same, and then do all they can to serve each other" (qtd. in Stanton 927). To these ends, this teacher/student continuously selects and reads stories of influential female role models to her class. She sees herself assembling all these role models and their lessons onto both her own and each of her student's "memory's imaginary bookshelf," as Bessey terms it (96). Ultimately, however, the woman whose story started the bookshelf is her maternal patron saint. As she sees it, her mother's book, although having "dog-eared pages and bent spine . . with redacted paragraphs," is "the foundation," a book of love that lead to the difference in this student's life—and now vicariously, the student's students' lives.

With You Always: Love Seen and Unseen

Another student finds reconnecting with her estranged mother as the moment she realized the maternal spiritual impact she had, even after years of blaming her mother for being absent. This student beautifully weaves the reading from *The Single Gospel* about the Prodigal Son into describing her own version of a Prodigal Mother. When she was eleven years old, the student, her four siblings, and her single mother split up due to her mother's inability to care for all of them properly. In the intervening time, the student—and separately, her siblings—had built many resentments and imagined what a horrible person her mother must have been to abandon her own flesh and blood. To numb the assumed meaning of the silence and separation from her mother, the student confesses, "For years I told myself my mother was dead, and I would never see her again. I convinced myself I was motherless." But in a miracle of grace, eventually all five siblings would reunite with their mother, this student being the final one to do so. Her mother finally was able to meet with her right after the student turned twenty-one. The two held each other in an embrace that seemed eternal yet was not long enough to make up for the lost ten years. Her mother then related the story of how the other siblings had all wasted no time upon reuniting in unleashing their pinned-up hate and resentment accumulated over the years. The student reflects on that moment, "How could I hate her? I was no longer worried about the situations of the past. I was . . .

excited for our future as mother and daughter." She movingly rewords the biblical father's acclamation upon seeing his prodigal son, "For this, my mother, was dead, and is alive again. She was lost...and is found."

In her reader response, the student is specifically dialoging with Bessey's chapter "Moving Mountains One Stone at a Time," which explores the theme of miraculous divine grace working in tandem with faithful, repeated action. The student's moved mountain was the seemingly insurmountable odds against reuniting with her mother. However, I also observe in the student's words a new realization for the way love manifested in her life because of her mother—both in presence and absence. The student describes her realization that both the first eleven years she experienced with her mother *and* the growth opportunities she had after her mother released her into foster care planted a two-part legacy in her: one of love and connection, and one of independence and strength. She rejoices both in the fact that "To this day I pray I can be half the parent she was," as much as her assertion, "I took control over my own life a long time ago." Thus, her mother first served as a saint who "nurtured, nourished, sourced, [and] watched over" (Bessey 90) her directly until the age of eleven. Then, her mother's painful-but-solicitous absence served as a "spiritual midwifery" that "helped give birth to some new part" (Bessey 90) of the student, one that relied on faith in struggle to emerge.

I find in this reader response a story with strong parallels to the one of my mentors, Dr. Wayne Dyer, whom I mentioned in the introduction to Chapter 4. Toward the end of his life, Dyer often reflected on how many moments, both painful and pleasant, empowered his journey to becoming a spiritual teacher. One such critical phase was during his childhood. Dyer's mother, Irene, with three boys and abandoned by their father, made the same heart-wrenching decision as the student's mother: to place two of the children into an orphanage and one into a relative's home so that they could receive better care. As Dyer grew into a self-help author who taught self-reliance linked with a spiritual dependence on the divine, he reframed his early childhood experience as stemming from a pre-birth conversation with God. He narrates this imagined dialogue in a conversation with Hay House president Reid Tracy: "[God said,] 'What do you want to do in this lifetime?' And I said, 'Well, I'd like to teach self-reliance.'...Then He said, 'Go into the orphanage, and while you're in the orphanage, you're going to be there for ten years, and in those ten years, you're going to learn to rely upon yourself'" (8). In his memoir *I Can See Clearly Now*, Dyer constellates moments in his life that led him toward the divine: "As I look back, I can see that my entire career was beginning when I was that young boy in an orphanage...how each step led to a higher step on the ladder toward God-realization" (336). Paralleling the student's ten years of familial separation, Dyer's decade of training in "picking up the stones, one after another, after another" merged with a trust in a God who collaborates in moving mountains. Moreover, just as the student "can see clearly now" the depth of her "spiritual mama's" love, Dyer pays tribute to Irene: "She lived and breathed that loving Spirit...[she] extended love where she had received only mistreatment...Yes, Mother, you inspire me!" (*Inspiration* 189-190). I find undoubtedly that, in both the student's and Dyer's self-reflection, sometimes love leads from visibly shining lights, sometimes from invisible ones as we faithfully pick up stones in the darkness.

Where Two or Three Gather: Love in Commun-ion/ity

"Can I take a moment and be real?" one student asks pointedly in her response to *Jesus Feminist*'s call for saints and midwives. "For the past four years, I witnessed my parents' marriage falling apart." Her strength through this time in the wilderness? "The women that have been there for me along my journey and that have blessed me with their teachings." Despite her being raised for nineteen years in a Christian household, the dissonance between her ideals of a perfectly harmonious home and the reality of its brokenness grew almost too much to bear as her parents' marital bond dissolved. Each week she saw their pious masks put on for Sunday church then removed once the family got home to argue. Referring to the bleeding woman in Matthew 9:20 who touches Jesus' cloak, this student reveals, "I realized I had to grab hold of God's garment and not let go but rather hold on tight because something was coming…God started placing people in my path that would talk to me about their personal lives and testimonies that I realized were going to be similar to mine eventually." Just to be in dialogue with women who could hold the space for this student to go through her wilderness walk was as healing of an outcome as the bleeding woman's touch on Christ's hem.

When her parents finally did separate, however, this student felt a love beyond the fear and confusion the situation might have engendered, because spiritual midwives had prepared her for a birth into a new phase of her life: having divorced parents. In her words, these saints "shepherded her" along the way and empathetically "shared their stories of their parents divorcing." Equally of importance, they offered their closeness. "To this day," the student asserts with hope and appreciation for their loving presence, "they continue to be there for me, and I am able to look up to them as role models" with wise advice when needed. This connection of love to community echoes Alice Walker's reflection on her baptism, a symbolic plunge into "murky water": "How deeply did I love these who stood around solemnly waiting to see my 'saved' head reappear above the murky water. This experience of communal love and hope for my well-being was my reality of life on this planet" (23). Catherine of Siena echoes this manifestation of divine love expressing itself in communal action, "The love a soul sees that God has for her, she in turn extends to all creatures. She immediately feels compelled to love her neighbor as herself for she sees how fully she herself is loved by God" (*Passion for the Truth* 38). The student then concludes in the spirit of this communal love, "We have to have Love…if we would only love our brother or sister as Jesus loves us, what great things we would do and be a witness to," an affirmation of the same theme of the saints named Catherine and Sojourner Truth, as well as of this book.

Another student begins her writing critiquing love within the female community of the church and its relationship to biblical love of self. In her reading from *The Single Gospel*, she resonates with the humility Jesus espouses in the Luke 14 parable about not immediately assuming the place of privilege at a wedding feast. However, she struggles with her own attitude that at times can *look* like this humility but is in fact poor self-love. This leads into the student's reflections on Bessey's exhortation in the foreword, titled "Let Us Be Women Who Love," and its portrait of a woman "loved for her true self." She admires particularly Jesus' example of revealing his depths, his weeping at the death of Lazarus and therefore being "raw in his emotions…[He] didn't care what anyone thought, he didn't pretend to be strong for his people." The student finds most disempowering what she sees as a lack of love within the church community for those such as herself who are working out the struggles of revealing her true self. She longs for the loving vulnerability of "frank discussions about things women have been conditioned to feel shameful about, such as sexuality and body image." As she has experienced nominal church "sisterhood," she professes that "Women are mean to other women," often "talking shit about girls we don't even know" and "bothered when a woman looks better than us." Indicating a deep need to feel acceptance, this internalized belief in the tyranny of appearance cloaks itself in the preemptive judgment of others. The chronic fear of personal imperfection turns outward into criticism, perpetuating a cycle of protection and then projection.

The student's fear of other women's judgments is only surpassed by one other thing: "I am…someone that actively stands up for men, but I am afraid of them. I am afraid of their rough hands and steel minds." She admits that the first man to hurt her was her father. This primary wound of the Other has led to a string of hurts that resulted in harmful experiences of "hatred and rage" from which she finds difficulty in recovering a loving heart. Recalling an argument with her boyfriend just before writing her reader response, she admits that she now has begun repeating to herself, "Be a woman who loves; be a woman who loves," as a reminder of how to counter her well-worn habit of angry thoughts and words. Her poignant disclosure clearly demonstrates her need for a love that transcends her current frame of mind: "I don't know a lot about love. I don't know what to do with it. I don't know how to show it or accept it." In both her worry about the harsh scrutiny of other women and her anxiety about men's intellectual and physical aggression, the student waits paralyzed in self-defeating fear.

Even amid her despair, however, Jesus calls out to this student just as he did to the disciples terrified in the storm on Lake Gennesaret: "Don't be afraid...Take courage!" His next words speak even more directly about the presence of divine love. Translated at times as "I am here!"—the *New Living Bible* suggests the original Greek's ambiguity: "The 'I AM' is here!" (Mark 6.50). Paraphrasing and expanding on 1 John 4:18, Bessey asserts, "As we follow Christ in the counsel of the Holy Spirit, resting in the love of our Abba, we no longer fear—for there is no fear in love. We do not fear slippery slopes, we do not fear each other, we do not fear change, and we do not fear our own selves or what people can do to us" (164). Bessey includes both "fear of each other" and "fear [of] our own selves" because, as Christ spoke in the second great commandment, love of neighbor and self are intimately linked. Improper self-love—whether too little or too great—blocks our ability to experience connectedness with the Other because it falsely emphasizes a "worthiness hierarchy." This student now hears Jesus' compelling words to take courage, to love self and Other with proper humility. She also is beginning to see the examples of that kind of love in action by reading *The Single Gospel*, which "always reminds me that Jesus is a good man, someone that I should also want to be." This student's closing sentence leaves open the possibility for escape from her fear-driven rejection/protection cycle: "One day I will wake up, and I will be a woman who loves." Perhaps following love's leading that she has gotten from Jesus' words and deeds from her "Bible as Literature" course, she will experience an epiphanic moment like Sojourner Truth and exclaim in realization, "Lord, Lord, I can love EVEN MY FATHER, EVEN THE HATERS, EVEN MYSELF."

Need of a Physician: Therapeutic Love

Another student also writes of her frustrations in finding love in the world, rooted in her unhealed past wounds. She, unlike the two students whose writing I dialogued with above, had major difficulties with her mother, whom she would definitely *not* label her as a "spiritual mama." This student's story, though, and whom she designates in her reader response as her patron saint indicate that the flames of love and hope are still alive in her, as much as how "The Bible as Literature" class enables a care of those flames. She begins her writing discussing an encounter she had during the day on which she wrote her response. Having just come from a counseling session in which she had revealed some of her closest-kept secret wounds, she was accosted by an overenthusiastic Christian proselytizer who sat down next to her on campus and began to ask the usual questions: "Do you know Jesus loves you? Do you know without a shadow of a doubt that you will go to heaven?", and so on. Despite trying to answer politely, she resisted the push to see God in the exact way the evangelizer did, "Even though she was basically telling me that I was doomed to hell and a sinner." The student laments the lack of compassion, the one-size-fits-all approach, and the undertone of "you're not good enough" that she felt from this missionary who was supposedly an emissary for the love of Jesus. Frustrated and angry, the student returned to her studying, diving into *Jesus Feminist* and preparing to respond.

In what might be a divine synchronicity, the student then read Bessey's story in the "Moving Mountains One Stone at a Time" chapter dealing with the exact same topic as what the student had spoken to her counselor about that same day: a young woman's sexual abuse at the hands of a parental figure. In the student's case, it was more than one of her mother's male partners: "I waited for my mom to pay attention, to not focus so much on keeping a man," she agonizes, "[but] a man was always more important to her." Abandoning what the student designates as the "sacred role" of protecting her child, her mother permitted the abuse. "So I hate my mother," the student confesses, "I will never be able to forgive my mother." In the very hours right after she had dug up and bravely spoken her "secret that scares the shit out of me…that tore my family apart that I was too afraid to share," she had encountered a person professing the Great Physician's love but not attending to her pain.

She reflects, "After the confessions I just made in my counseling session, how dare she *tell me* that I needed Jesus' love?" (emphasis added). In her reaction to her presumed unworthiness to access Jesus' kingdom, she drilled right down to the core of what she needs: not rules, not righteousness, not "some book and some journey that was acceptable to go to heaven"; she needs to *see* and *feel* love.

Despite her disheartening encounter earlier in the day, a therapeutic light shone in this student's heart because she read Bessey's moving narrative of Janelle, who came to a home called Mercy Ministries of Canada that shelters young women from just such situations. Janelle was first raped at the age of three and then trafficked by her father, ultimately finding safe harbor at Mercy. The story culminates with Janelle addressing a gathering of Mercy's "graduates," as well as Bessey herself and other volunteers and supporters. Attempting to speak her abusive life story, "Janelle suddenly stopped talking. Her voice crackled with pain; she couldn't say the next part of her story out loud. Her tongue wouldn't let her go, held with the pain of remembering" (151). After a period of grief-stricken and compassionate silence in the room, a woman's voice broke out, "It's all right, honey. We love you. We all love you. We've got you, sweetie" (151). Soon this single voice became a chorus, and Janelle, feeling empowered by this show of love, "ground shame to a powder under her feet; she finished her story, brave, in her own voice, clearly proud of herself" (151). Surely, when the student expresses that "This week, [Bessey] recognized something that is deeply rooted in me," she is reacting to her need for expressions of real love that will help her to heal and finish *her* story.

As meaningful as the moment that Bessey shared was in which love was seen and felt, it was only the capstone to all the "saintly" actions of love that made Mercy Ministries possible for Janelle and other graduates. Bessey and so many others combined had donated "hundreds of thousands of dollars over the years for their home, for their certified counselors, and for food…[had] dropped off bundles of clothes, preached the gospel with their lives" (151-152). The other virtuous people the student identifies within "Moving Mountains One Stone at a Time" as possessing this aspect of love in action are Pastor

Gaetan and his wife, Madame—the two heads of an orphanage in poverty-stricken Haiti. Their example of the daily work to keep the orphans in their care fed and healthy pulled at the student's heartstrings. Quoting Pastor Gaetan, who was asked why he chose to sleep outside on a cot in the heat with the children rather than his own bed, the student highlights, she repeats, "A shepherd will not leave his little flock" (147). She notes so stark a contrast between these remarkable caretakers and her own mother. These stone-by-stone mountain movers renounced their own comfort for the sake of children not their own; "Meanwhile," she bristles, hurting in her newly-reopened wounds, "my own flesh and blood sold me." Nevertheless, despite her suffering, the student finds hope and a calling in the actions of the Saints Gaetan as she ends her section of comments on *Jesus Feminist*. She also acknowledges Bessey's words and deeds as a spiritual midwife who, by her storytelling, brought the student to the following revelation: "We have to learn from them . . . to be people that choose love first."

I see in this student's reader response encounter with Jesus a very powerful notion of how suffering can become transformed if there is just enough opening in a person's focus on exaggerated, protective self-love to allow divine love's entrance. Catherine of Genoa, in one of her mystical reveries, speaks about this very notion, "This vision of [a person's] own misery keeps him in great poverty, and deprives him of all things which could afford him any savor of good. Thus, his self-love is not able to nourish itself…until at last man understands that if God did not hold his hand, giving him his being, and removing from him this hateful vision, he could never issue from this hell" (55). For some, this understanding of God holding their hand can be accomplished merely through reasoning or spiritual intuition. For others like the student, the divine hand must also reveal itself through human work inspired by love. As St. Teresa of Avila, another mystic, has been attributed as proclaiming, "Yours are the feet with which Christ walks to do good. Yours are the hands with which Christ blesses the world." In reading stories both ancient and modern about interventions of healing words and of loving "hands and feet," the student is able to, if only briefly, "remove this hateful vision" of life's poverty—and even more so, of herself.

The student's reader response conclusion begins colloquially, "Jesus is a cool dude. I like him a lot, and I like reading about him in *The Single Gospel*." Then, connecting right to Catherine's words, she reveals the inner transformations from her self-reflective application, "He gives me hope that I am not nothing because I don't fit into some *vision* of what a good person looks like" (emphasis added). Even more indicative of a shifted outlook, the student revisits her encounter with the proselytizer earlier that day: "I should be kind to the girl on the bench that wanted to share with me this man that she loves, and so I should recognize this as a sign of love for me." Even if that moment felt unskillful, it was an invitation to hold another's hand and to further the process of "issuing from this hell" inside of her. Her final sentence clearly lays out the heaven and hell before her: "I can spend my life being furious and hateful and bitter, or I can let go and love." She then closes with a telling, threefold repetition, "I am trying. I am trying. I am trying." This student's pure intention, her aiming at heaven, is supported in the triple-phrased exhortation of Jesus in Matthew 7: "Ask, and it will be given to you; seek, and you will find; knock, and the door will be opened to you" (*New International Version*, Matt. 7.7). If she indeed lets love lead, she is promised to be among the *katharoi* that will see God.

No Limits: When the Mystical Meets the Mundane

All the students with whom I have engaged in my three chapters of *Let Love Lead* share in the same process of reader response: turning quiet reflection on stories, both read and lived, into self-reflexive writing pieces. By highlighting in this chapter the mystical encounters of Catherine of Siena, Catherine of Genoa, and Sojourner Truth, I have desired to show that direct access to the divine is not limited by gender or other socially-constructed identity. However, I should not want to elevate the mystical aspect of their encounters as somehow better than what some might call the mundane. If the workings of the divine are all around us, if the divine is not only transcendent but immanent, then any person "pure of heart"—not morally spotless but with sincere intention—can find it, given a shift of vision.

Moreover, love is not limited to specific religious organizations such as the Catholicism of the Catherines of Siena and Genoa, nor even broadly Christian organizations such as Mercy Canada. It transcends normative religious operating contexts and can thus work its influence even in overtly secular academic loci, such as Gary's "The Bible as Literature" classroom. His teaching approach, which equalizes the importance of literary analysis and introspective memoir, creates a context which validates fully-embodied humans—with hearts, souls, and minds. The pedagogy of "The Bible as Literature" allows the class members, as the student cited above attests, to "be real." It doesn't insist on dogmatic beliefs but simply that students "set [their] mind on things above" (*New International Version*, Col. 3.2) via biblical texts, then discourse with them while "being real." In this milieu, love can lead students into a space of direct divine encounter. As I have emphasized, the effect that this experience has especially on women, whose voices have been historically diminished and whose societal roles have been limited, repeatedly manifests as empowering and healing. And as for my daughter, Catherine, I see in her the same wariness of limiting patriarchal systems—in both religious and societal institutions—but simultaneously I witness the sparks of her desire for meaning, purpose, and love that only the divine can offer. Her purity of heart, in her intentions and clarity, will continue to serve her in accessing a higher form/representation of love to lead her, just as it did all the historical and contemporary women in this chapter.

Acknowledgements

I would like to thank the following students (from the spring 2018 semester of "The Bible as Literature") whose responses I included this chapter—Slam Anderson, Manisha Brown, Kelly Prendergast, Naomi Retter, and Shyana Semprit.

Works Cited

hooks, bell. *Feminist Theory: From Margin to Center*. South End Press, 1984.

Bessey, Sarah. *Jesus Feminist: An Invitation to Revisit the Bible's View of Women*. Howard Books, 2013.

The Bible. New International Version, Biblica, 2011.

---. New Living Translation, Biblica, 2011.

Catherine of Genoa. *The Life and Doctrine of Saint Catherine of Genoa*. Christian Classics Ethereal Library, 2009.

Catherine of Siena. *The Dialogue of the Seraphic Virgin Catherine of Siena*. Translated by Algar Thorold. Kegan Paul, Trench, Trübner, and Co., Ltd, 1896.

---. *Catherine of Siena: Passion for the Truth, Compassion for Humanity, Selected Spiritual Writings*. Edited by Mary O'Driscoll. New City Press, 2008.

Dyer, Wayne W. *I Can See Clearly Now*. Hay House, Inc., 2015.

Dyer, Wayne W. *Inspiration: Your Ultimate Calling: Easyread Large Bold Edition*. Accessible Publishing Systems, 2008.

McKenzie, Alyce M. *Matthew*. Westminster John Knox Press, 2002.

Stanton, Elizabeth Cady. *History of Woman Suffrage, Vol. II*. Susan B. Anthony, 1881.

Stowe, Harriet Beecher. "Sojourner Truth: The Libyan Sibyl." *The New Yorker*, April 1863, www.theatlantic.com/magazine/archive/1863/04/sojourner-truth-the-libyan-sibyl/308775. Accessed 12 Jan. 2019.

Tracy, Reid. Interview with Wayne W. Dyer. *Hay House World Summit 2017 #28*. 2017. michellebeltran.com/wp-content/uploads/2018/09/28_Wayne_Dyer.pdf. Accessed 13 Jan. 2019.

Trible, Phyllis. "Naomi: Bible." *Jewish Women's Archive: A Comprehensive Historical Encyclopedia*. 20 Mar. 2009. jwa.org/encyclopedia/article/naomi-bible. Accessed 12 Jan 2019.

Walker, Alice. "The Only Reason You Want to Go to Heaven Is That You Have Been Driven Out of Your Mind." *On the Issues: The Progressive Woman's Quarterly*, vol. 6, no. 2, Apr. 1997, pp. 16-23.

Chapter 11

Where *Church* and *State* (University) Meet "Commissioned" for Community Service

Gary L. Lemons

As a critical aspect of "The Bible as Literature" community service collaboration in spring 2018 with the First United Church of Tampa, I shed significant light on the writings of students and their presentations as a part of its Tuesday Evening Bible Study sessions. Featured in several of these bible studies during the semester, the students' "Discussion Starters" would become a strategic element to linking our course study of with the all-inclusive mission of the church, under the leadership of its pastor, Dr. Bernice Powell Jackson. In highlighting excerpts from their papers based on readings assigned from the last chapters of *The Single Gospel* and *Jesus Feminist*, I show the compelling interactions between my students and members of First United Church who attended sessions of the Bible Study during which my students shared their writings.

The students moved through the spring 2018 semester of "The Bible as Literature," presenting their writings in sessions at the First United Church, and it became more and more fascinating for me to observe how the community service collaboration evolved—across lines of *church* and *state*, gender, race, and generational differences. In the context of the church's evening Bible studies, I began to note how my reading assignments in *The Single Gospel* and *Jesus Feminist* aligned and intersected regarding their impact on members of First United who attended the sessions in which my students offered their works. As shown in Chapter 6, students' interpretive responses to the final chapters in *The Single Gospel*—narrating the last days of Jesus' life, his crucifixion, resurrection, and commissioning of the disciples—are deeply tied to the last chapter of *Jesus Feminist* entitled "The Commissioning." In it, Bessey personally reflects upon the transforming effects Christ would have in the evolution of her life as a contemporary follower of him. Having embraced the prophetic teachings and preached words of Jesus, she asserts that she feels compelled to call all the readers of her book to take on the gender-liberating labor he performed. Those who have done so become spiritually invested in human rights and social justice—interrelated to a fundamental belief in female equality—and take on the task of activist discipleship.

Putting Words into Action
"The Commissioning" from Then Until Now

> And they went forth and proclaimed the good news of the gospel everywhere, while the Lord worked with them and confirmed their message by the miraculous signs that accompanied it . . . Now Jesus did many other miracles in the presence of the disciples, which are not recorded in this book. Were every one of them to be recorded, I suppose that the word itself could not contain all the books that would be written.
> Neil Averitt, "The Foundation of the Church" and
> "The Epilogues of John and Mark," *The Single Gospel*

> Here, come and stand in front of me.
> Stand on your own two feet, let's look each other right in the eye.
> Stand now, head up—you are loved, remember? You are love, and you are free.
> Sarah Bessey, "The Commissioning," *Jesus Feminist*

Revealing the lasting impression Bessey made on my students in "The Commissioning," in this section I include excerpts from their written responses to it. Closely listening to her words, Anthony (Martinez) cites several passages in the chapter that moved him to think about putting words into action—especially connected to Jesus' teachings about serving others. He states,

Bessey encourages, motivates, *and* commissions us to live a life as people who are called out by God to do great and mighty things in His name (*Jesus Feminist,* 191-197). [Acting in the role of a modern disciple] she says, "In the mighty and powerful name of Jesus, I commission you for the work of the gospel as a minister of Jesus Christ, to live in your world as an ambassador of the Kingdom" (192). Not only are we ambassadors but Bessey also gives some clear examples of things that we are called out to do: "I commission you in the work of healing and serving and loving and reconciliation. You are an emissary of justice, and your work from now on is to put things right, to call those things that are not as they will be" (192).

Anthony further writes:

I have been going through a season where the Lord has been working in me and through me to utilize and refine my God-given gifts and talents to converse with the lost and share and show them just how great the love of God truly is, but I have been shown that I have been hiding my gifts, distracting myself with other things, and quieting my voice because of the uncertainty of the changes that would occur if I let God use me as He sees fit.

Time and time again, during the semester, the students and I talked about actualizing our "God-given gifts and talents" toward enabling each other and those outside our classroom to believe that all followers of Jesus have been called to share them. Anthony's self-reflection reveals his humble admittance that "hiding [his] gifts" and being silent about in doubt about how they are to be employed is not following the Spirit of love's calling. The "if" Anthony struggles with here is exposed in whether he will "let God use [him] as He sees fit."

Like Anthony, many other students following the teachings of Jesus also struggled with the idea of putting their "God-given gifts and talents" into action in service to the good of others. Yet I assigned "The Commissioning" to support my challenge to students invested in the belief that the works of Jesus were, indeed, life-saving. Moreover, my aim in having students write in response to Bessey's repeated call for Jesus-led community service was to embrace its commitment to alliance building for human rights and social justice—a longstanding ideological anchor for my pro-womanist pedagogical practice. Gabrielle ("GiGi" Jackson) affirms her assertion that believers in Jesus must act out their faith in him:

> "The Commissioning" really did bring me into [an activist understanding that I must] continue to live my life [through the teachings] of Christ. While reading this chapter, I was reminded of times when family members laid hands on me and prayed over my life and health. Those memories were synonymous with the ways Sara Bessey's words were making me feel—especially when she says, "In the mighty, powerful name of Jesus, I commission you for the work of the gospel as a minister of Jesus Christ, to live in your world as an ambassador of the Kingdom" (192).

As stated above, Anthony had quoted these same words. They were obviously impactful on these two students. So much of what Bessey says to the readers of this chapter is biblically-based as signifying the factuality of Jesus calling his followers into greater discipleship after his resurrection. Her words resonate with a sermonic agency as "GiGi" (the name this student preferred to be called) points out:

> Reading these words in particular made me feel as though I was being sworn in, making a promise and commitment to the one that has called me to a life-changing purpose and promising me more than I could ever imagine…This chapter reiterates the power in helping a believer to comprehend one's purpose in life and the need to build a spiritual relationship with God in order to fully accept that purpose. It further confirms one's value as a person and the significance of love one's life. I believe the entire chapter is written as a prayer—a declaration, a thank you letter, a love letter, and a confession of hope. Bessey says, "I call you to joy, friend. I set you apart in your right-now life for the daily work of liberation and love" (195). She further tells us: "Proclaim the Kingdom of

God with your hands and your feet and your voice to every soul in your care and influence."

Proclaim the Kingdom of God: "Read in Class!"

In looking back at my hand-written notes throughout the "The Commissioning," in the margin of pages 195-196 (beginning with the words "GiGi" quotes above), I pen: "Read in class!" I absolutely agree that Bessey structures what she says in the form of a prayer as she continues (after the sentence above),

> May your soul long for prayer and for the Scriptures, may you keep secrets, may you give away your money, may you share meals and may you sit alone in silence outside under the sky and be satisfied...May you make room in your life to be inconvenienced and put out, and may you be Jesus with skin on for a few people. May you be fearless, and may you eat good food.
>
> I pray that no matter your tool or method (mothering, preaching, cooking, writing, organizing, washing, teaching, building, money making—all of your whole life encompassing it all) you will walk in knowledge of the sacredness and purpose of your calling. I pray for dreams and visions, for the active leading of the Holy Spirit...and oh, what a friend you have in Jesus...Your ministry, your work, begins now, and it began long ago.
>
> Turn around and face your life. (195-196)

In so many ways, Bessey's prayer here reminds me of Alice Walker's visionary ideas of a womanist as one who "[l]oves music. Loves dance. Loves the moon. *Loves* the Spirit. Loves love and food and roundness. Loves struggle. *Loves* the Folk. Loves herself. *Regardless*" (xi). In everyday, down-to-earth language, the prayer Bessey voices is full of love for those followers of Jesus willing to carry on the legacy of his ministry in the name of the Holy *Spirit*. I sense in the boldness of her prayer a liberating fearlessness. It proclaims ministerial agency in ways that stand against systemic patriarchal silence. Women possess "God-given gifts and talents" to share Words of the Lord to all the world. For me personally, Bessey's prayer for inspirited activism also brings back to my mind and heart Audre Lorde's prayer poem—"Litany for Survival" (which I have taped a printed copy of it on the outside of my office door at USF, as I stated in the Introduction to *Let Love Lead*). As a black male pro-feminist/womanist professor of "The Bible as Literature," it reaffirms my calling—"[r]*egardless*" to how my feminist approach to teaching the life of Jesus may be misinterpreted, in and outside the academy. Lorde says in her prayer: "For those of us who were imprinted with fear like a faint line in the center of our foreheads...this instant and this triumph

We were never meant to survive." (15-17, 23-24)

In the light of these words, Bessey asserts: "Stop waiting for someone else to say that you count, that you matter, that you have worth, that you have a voice, a place, that are called. Didn't you know . . . The One who knit you together in your mother's womb is the one singing these words over you, you are chosen" (192-193).

Sarah Bessey writes in a conversational tone throughout *Jesus Feminist*. However, it is its last chapter that coheres with clarity of the believers' calling even in the biblical tonality of *The Single Gospel*—above all, when Jesus speaks in his commission to his followers once they are ordained under the guidance of the Holy Spirit:

> '[Y]ou shall receive power when the Holy Spirit comes upon you; and you shall be my witnesses in Jerusalem and in all Judea and Samaria, and to the ends of the earth. And lo, I am with you always; even unto the end of the world.' Then he lifted up his hands and blessed them. (239)

In my comments on students' writings in the course, I continually pointed out the importance of clarity—telling them that their readers (and hearers of their words) need to comprehend as precisely as possible what is being communicated to them. It is clear to me in "The Commissioning" that Bessey is not caught up in intellectual egotism. Rather, based on how clearly my students interpret her message of "calling" for community service, she purposely employs "down-to-earth" wording. Yesenia (Schofield) writes in response to Bessey's invitation to servanthood:

This last chapter really spoke to me, and yes, Bessey definitely hit home with this one. "The Commissioning" describes everything that I've been feeling lately, especially this spring semester. First, she calls everyone to serve God through the work of the gospel as a minister of Jesus Christ. That alone was a lot to take in, but it's achievable. However, following him can seem like a hard task to complete, but it is what we were created to do. Our sole purpose is to live our lives through the teachings of Jesus and spread his message to as many people as we can through our daily activities and careers. Bessey really started to speak to me when said (as repeated by GiGi), "Stop waiting for someone else to say you count, that you matter, that you have worth, that you have a voice, a place, that you are called" (192). I've been in a "waiting" place for a while. I've felt like I needed someone to tell me all of these things . . . I've come to understand that true happiness, love, and acceptance is being able to feel worthy when you possess the knowledge of God's forgiving love . . . .

I found great relief in Bessey's words; I felt a sense of comfort when she says "...you are valuable. You have worth, not because of your gender, or your vocation, or your marital status. In Christ, you have value beyond all of that" (193). Alas, my eyes are opened to the real meaning of my life. It does matter what I do, as long as I do it in the name of Jesus. I could mop floors for the rest of my life, but if I do it for the glory of God, it will be purposeful. I nearly cried when Bessey discussed that we should live in our "God-breathed worth. Stop holding your breath, hiding your gifts, ducking your head, dulling your roar, distracting your soul, stilling your hand, quieting your voice, and satiating your hunger with the lesser things of this world" (195). I tell you these few lines mean so much to me because they describe everything I've been doing...She goes on to say, "set apart in our tight-now life for the daily work of liberation and love" (195). I have to do it. I have to go out there into this big wide world and show

God what I'm made of. No matter what it takes, I have to break free. I am worthy.

You are Worthy: Open Your Eyes and See

The idea of worthiness in "The Commissioning" is a critical point of reference thematically, as many of the students reflect upon self-value associated with the notion of a spiritual calling for activism. This chapter is figuratively eye-opening for students struggling to achieve academic authorization toward future career objectives. When professors situate academic professionalization of students as the ideological center of their success and career aspirations—particularly in a capitalist-based society—we undermine the value and necessity of self-reflection as a critical tool in the meaning of "higher" education. As stated in the previous chapter, I evolved during teaching "The Bible as Literature" (in a secular institutional environment)—having become more intentional in my interrogation of the politics of gender and critique of biblical patriarchy (as cited in my spring 2018 revision of the course syllabus). I purposely labor in the college classroom to entreat my students to utilize personal reflection as a strategic standpoint from which to engage their study of biblical narratives. With regard to issues of self-value connect to the intersectionality of gender, class, ability, and nation/religious affiliations—I position Jesus' life-stories as pivotal matter for spiritual engagement. Teaching the idea that each of them has been given particular *gifts and talents* (that they may not be fully aware of), I assert that they, indeed, have been "called" to perform acts of community service to enable others to live life more fully—especially those individuals without certain privileges associated with "skills" need to obtain a college degree, for example.

One student in the class, who goes by the name "Slam" (Tiffany Anderson), opens her discussion of "The Commissioning" citing the biblical quote Sarah Bessey incorporates as an epigraph to introduce this chapter. The passage she makes use to ground her purpose underscores her mission. Found in 1 Peter 2:9, the statement reads: "But you are the ones chosen by God, chosen for the high calling of priestly work, chosen to be a holy people, God's instruments to do his work and speak out for him, to tell others of the night-and-day difference he made for you—from nothing to something, from reject to accepted" (*The Message*). Addressing it, Slam, an activist board member of Kitchen Table Literary Arts ("a community-based creative writing center dedicated to inspiring and cultivating the unique and powerful voices of girls and women of color"), writes:

> This is going to be my new favorite Bible verse, because it says everything I am trying to do. This week I hosted a workshop in St. Pete [Florida], and one of the attendees asked me why I do what I do [as a spoken-word artist/writer]. I told her many different things as I always do when people ask me this question...The real answer is—I am a creative literary activist because it allows me to help and inspire people [to be creative], and that is all I want to do in my life. I want to show people by example that they can be and do anything creatively they desire to do, no matter what! I do what I do because I can and because it is easy, and why not? Why not use my life to encourage people, teach people, and love people? I do what I do to show people just how gracious God is. Not for money or fame or anything like that, but sadly sometimes, when you tell people all of this, they look at me with disdain and disbelief. Look at me—this homosexual, black female doing things for the sole purpose of love. I guess it is a hard concept to accept, because it cannot be explained to them in a matter of minutes. I know what it feels like not to be loved, to be hated, to be rejected, to be bullied, picked on; I know how it feels to be made to feel less. I do not wish this on anyone. From now own when someone asks me the question about why I do what I do, I going to say, "1 Peter 2:9. That is why I do what I do."

Reading "The Commissioning" confirmed all my feelings about my life, and it answered so many questions for me. One statement Bessey makes in particular grabbed me, wrapped its arms around my body, kissed my cheek, and whispered, "You are chosen" (192). I felt like she had read all [my personal reflections in the "Discussion Starter" papers I previously had

written in this class throughout the semester]. I feel like her response to me is that I should—
> Stop waiting for someone else to say that you count, that you matter, that you have worth, that you have a voice, a place, that you are called. Didn't you know [Slam]?...Stop waiting for someone else to validate your created self; that is done...Because [Slam], you are valuable...In Christ, you have value beyond all of that. You abide in love...(192-193).

The passage above is repeated in a student's response. Considering this, apparently Bessey's message to readers of her concluding chapter is that they must "[s]top waiting for someone...to validate" them. As a creative writer, Slam—like the other students citing self-affirming statements in "The Commissioning"—clearly embraces its transformative power. Students who believe in the love Jesus shared in his commission of his followers can claim its creative agency for community service. Slam ends her paper stating, "I want to spread more love."

Reclaiming Self-Value: I Am Somebody

Having courageously written about her desire to continue her activist labor for community creative awareness, Slam joins her classmates in sharing the restorative self-value of reading "The Commissioning." Student after student writing about its creative enrichment, grounded in the visionary enlightenment of Jesus' revolutionary message of servanthood, affirmed my decision to teach *Jesus Feminist* as a core text in the study of "The Bible as Literature" in 2018. Over and over again in the excerpts from students' writings on the chapter, Bessey's words about valuing oneself and not being bound up in someone else's reductive reasoning and assumptions about the quality of personhood clearly resonated in the passage: "Stop waiting for someone else to validate your created self" (193).

I look back at the close of the spring 2018 semester version of "The Bible as Literature" course when I evaluated the students' writings on "The Resurrection" in *The Single Gospel* and Bessey's last chapter, and I am simply amazed at the bold and courageous manner in which my students speak out in their interpretive analyses and personal reflections on these texts. Revisiting the papers, determining which parts of them to include in this chapter of *Let Love Lead*, I find it quite interesting to re-read my comments on them. In the margin of many of them, I wrote such phrases as—"You have been called"; "Write on"; "Don't underestimate your gifts and talents"; "You are on your way"; "Thank you for sharing"; You must keep speaking out"; "Continue to deliver the message you have been given"; "Miracles are still happening today"…and the comments kept going on and on. Taylor (Michael) remarks that Bessey's chapter,

> is soul food…If we could stop letting other people tell us we are not enough, stop telling ourselves we are not enough, and start listening to the Holy Spirit, and tell ourselves we are good enough to make change. It only takes the faith of a mustard seed to move mountains across nations and create a world where love and goodness are the driving factors [to free humanity].

Another student, Kelly (Prendergast), writes her response to "The Commissioning" as a deeply meditative prayer of *choosing*:

> I pray for the silences in the space of sentences. I pray for patience and for kindness. I pray for the ability to hold my tongue and for the ability to project my voice when necessary. I choose to live a life filled with love. I choose to lean into the pain [life can bring] and smile when it hurts. I choose, from here on, to move forward always, ever moving. I choose to find empathy when it's the hardest. I choose to love, even when it's inconvenient. I choose to always help somebody when I can. I choose to stop making excuses and instead to take action for good. I choose to hold myself responsible . . . I choose to happen. I pray for the capacity to be more forgiving. I will choose to forgive. I pray strength to embrace change, to soften my heart, to open my eyes and my ears. I choose to see, to listen. I choose to truly hear [the Spirit calling me to serve]. I pray for the power to reach for my calling…I pray for love. I will choose to love.

In line with Kelly's prayer, Manisha (Brown) writes about the personal impact of it as an affirmation of what she believes is her calling. She cites words from Bessey's prayer for her readers: "I pray that no matter your tool or method...you will walk in knowledge of the sacredness and purpose of your calling...Your ministry, your work, begins now and it began long ago. Turn around and face your life. Look it in the eye, because this, right now—this is it" (196). I will always remember, on the last evening of our spring 2018 class—utterly to everyone's surprise in class—Manisha handed out to each of us a small, soft black bag with a "Mustard Seed Necklace" in it. She then shared with us that this necklace was a symbolic representation of a creative writing ministry she had begun for young people. Inspired the prayer Bessey offers, Manisha's boldly writes in her personal response: "I am loved; I am gifted; I am chosen, and I am God's daughter whom he loves very much...Not only do I want to be a writer, but I am going to be a business woman, and a motivational speaker—not for money [but community enrichment]."

Many of the "Discussion Starter" papers students wrote in response to the final readings assigned in the last chapters of *The Single Gospel* and *Jesus Feminist* reinforce the theme of sacrificial love for community service, as Jesus personified it throughout his life and during the commissioning of his followers upon his resurrection. Through her own moments of meditation and prayer in "The Commissioning," Sarah Bessey reaffirms the legacy of Jesus' teachings centered on the revolutionary agency of servanthood. In his written response to the thematic link between *The Single Gospel* and *Jesus Feminist*—particularly related to their concluding chapters—Avram (Wassef) points out that Bessey gets to the heart of the matter regarding the essential necessity of love as a life-saving tool for social change. He says that her book is a "prime representation of how Christ wants us to treat every person, from every background, from every [national] demographic . . . She gets her point across when talking about how being yourself and loving yourself are so important to living [life fully]."

Avram quotes a passage from the chapter that solidifies the love Jesus professed—even in the face of hypocritical antagonism. As complicated and as difficult as this may be today, in "The Commissioning," loving as a self-liberating standpoint is critical to social and religious transformation, but it is still a personal choice. Bessey says, "Love yourself, and love your enemies. Love until you come to love the whole world in the fullness of God, in the full expression of the image bearer he created you to be—just that; no more, but certainly no less. Choose freedom. Choose the freedom of living loved" (194). Avram closes his discussion stating, "If people lived by this, we would not see people walking into schools and shooting the innocent. We would be able to have places where people would be able to live according to who they [as human beings], and not what people [reduce them to being as non-humans]." In line with Avram's thought here, Keith (Voney) writes,

> The words in this chapter that seem written just for my heart to hear are: "You abide in love; you can rest in your God-breathed worth" (193). It's so easy for all of us to get bogged down by the weight of the world, all the problems and all the pain, and to get down on ourselves for not doing enough [to help others], or for doing the wrong things at times. If you don't hold to your identity [as one created in the image of God], you're left to be battered and beaten by a world that continually screams that you are weak and worthless; you don't matter, and you are nothing. This leads people into a tailspin of anxiety, stress, anger, depression, and maybe even suicidal thoughts. The quote I cite above is a quick jolt to my heart, bringing it back into its natural rhythm. You/I must rest in the truth that God says you [and I] are of great worth and that you [and I] are loved and that you [and I] matter.

Life-Saving Community Love
Documenting Dialogues for Social *and* Spiritual "Kin-dom" Building

> We are a liberal Christian church. We willingly embrace such traditional liberal values as helping and advocating for the poor, protecting the environment, and recognizing as sinful

attitudes such as sexism, ageism, racism, homophobia, ableism, and religious discrimination. Our progressive and open-minded Christian witness attracts members and friends from Hillsborough, Pasco, Polk, Hernando, and Manatee Counties. Our proximity to the University of South Florida makes access to our church very convenient for USF students seeking a progressive Christian environment.

First United Church of Tampa

    As I have previously cited, one of the most compelling aspects of having chosen to revise my syllabus for "The Bible as Literature" not only centered on the selection of *The Single Gospel* and *Jesus Feminist* primary texts for the class, but also having determined to integrate a community service component into the course. This would be the first time in my college teaching career for a decade at the University of South Florida that I would choose officially to incorporate a requirement in one of my courses in which students would literally have to transport "what they learned in the classroom into the room of people's everyday lives." I quote myself here, as this is a phrase that has often appeared in articles, chapters, and books I have published related to my pedagogical theory and practice.

    After completing a workshop for faculty at USF sponsored by its Office of Community Engagement and Partnerships, I determined it was time for me to put theory into practice related to "The Bible as Literature" course. Considering the progressive standpoint in which I aimed to teach the course during the spring 2018 semester—focused on the biblical story of Jesus as a spiritual, revolutionary figure committed women's rights and an inclusive, life-saving vision of *all* humanity—I felt led to seek a "partnership" with a community of folk dedicated to his radical mission, teachings, and liberating works. Students in my course and I—in collaboration with the pastor of First United Church of Tampa, Dr. Bernice Powell Jackson—formed an inspirational, lasting bond with her and members of her congregation. I was immediately drawn to the Church's mission statement(s). In one of them, which I cite as an epigraph above, it is quite evident that

First United represents a radically inclusive body of Christ-centered believers. Having become the central focus of three sessions of First United's Tuesday evening Bible Study, during which my students presented their "Discussion Starter" papers, two communities joined together as one in the Spirit of love for Jesus' unwavering devotion to the salvation of all humankind.

In what follows, I include commentary by the pastor and members of First United Church and other individuals who attended the evening Bible Study sessions in which my students presented their papers. I begin with Dr. Powell Jackson's overall final assessment of our community service collaboration. She states,

> During my nearly decade at First United we have sought on several occasions to reach out to students to let them know there is a progressive church nearby that believes that God is still speaking, that God is Love and that church can be a safe space of extravagant welcome, seeking to follow Jesus' way of justice and peace. So, we were delighted when Dr. Lemons asked us to be their class's community partner. At every meeting we had 15-20 church members participate, always listening intently to the student presentations and seeking to provide assurance, while pushing them to think outside the boxes that religion has too often placed Jesus and God in.
>
> This was a wonderful and inspiring opportunity for our church, helping us to clarify our own understanding of the faith in the twenty-first century. If the faith of Jesus is to continue to grow, it must find new ways of listening to young people and their questions and doubts and not just at 11:00 on Sunday morning.

Before the spring 2018 semester of "The Bible as Literature" began, I recall meeting with Dr. Powell Jackson in her office at First United Church. As we sat and discussed the schedule for student presentations during semester as a part of the Church's Bible Study meetings, I looked at all the forms of culturally diverse artwork hanging on the walls of her office. One thing suddenly became clear to me as I considered the progressive mission of the Church she shared with me during our meeting. As a black female pastor of a multi-racial/cultural congregation, in a love for ministry, she exemplified womanist "universal[ism]...[c]ommitted to survival and wholeness of entire people."

I will always remember my conversation one afternoon in November 2017 with my black feminist colleague, Dr. Cheryl Rodriguez, in her office on campus at USF. I shared with her my desire to add a community service component to my course on "The Bible as Literature." Telling her about my idea of students presenting the papers they would write in the course in a progressive church setting, she immediately suggested that I consider speaking with the pastor of her church—Dr. Powell Jackson. Cheryl said her pastor would be open to hearing my idea. And so it would be. As a member of First United and one who consistently attended the sessions during which my students presented their papers, at the end of the semester, Cheryl offered her commentary on her experience of them:

> I have taught many courses in which students are required to move beyond the boundaries of the university and engage with people in the larger community. This is a transformative pedagogical strategy for students and faculty and an enlightening experience for community members. Through community engagement, students learn the value and relevance of knowledge gleaned in the classroom. They learn that people are interested in their ideas and are also very willing to support their educational endeavors. The students I teach typically enter community settings as researchers, a requirement that raises complex issues for them and their potential interviewees. So I was very interested in the idea that the students in "The Bible as Literature" course were interacting with members of the First United congregation as co-learners. That is, the students shared their intellectual and personal responses to weekly readings with members of the church. I was very moved and impressed with the students' willingness to be vulnerable and honest. In turn, congregation members had opportunities to converse with students after class sessions. There was no intellectual elitism and no issues of hierarchy. Instead, we all witnessed the coming together of

two very diverse communities of learners. This was a powerful experience for all.

Another one of the First United Church congregants, Robert G. Yizar, who attended the Bible study sessions with my students, also shared with me his deeply inspirationally creative feedback that clearly intersects the thematic foundation of Bessey's call for readers of "The Commissioning" to put their love of Jesus into action. Robert remarks:

"To teach is to learn twice." Professor Lemons, you demonstrated to FUCOT [First United Church of Tampa] that you teach for the love of teaching, giving back, providing hope, planting a seed, making a subject practical/alive, sharing your life experiences, and gaining new life experiences from your students.

"The whole art of teaching is only the art of awakening the natural curiosity of young minds for the purpose of satisfying it afterwards." Teaching is another opportunity for you to give back. You probably had many special teachers who saw something in you before you discovered it. They challenged and encouraged you. They gave you the canvas and brush to paint a masterpiece and coached you along the way. Each student has an inner drive to succeed once the right starter button is found, primed, pushed, and energized. You have given back the same to your students...mission accomplished!

"The mediocre teacher tells. The good teacher explains. The superior teacher demonstrates. The great teacher inspires." First United Church of Tampa witnessed inspired students. Keep up the good work.

Robert continues: "Professor Lemons...thanks! The topics and oral presentations of your students took me back forty-six years to my college religious studies courses with a professor and class format similar to yours. You have taken your students to the starting line of a lifelong spiritual journey. 'The Commissioning' is the doorway to experiencing the 'essence of love.'"

Moreover, Robert further states—

You challenged them to open that door and take a peek. In their presentations I heard many questions:
- What is our purpose in life? To love each other as much as we love ourselves. To take a spiritual journey. The doorway is a portal to a spiritual discovery of self-value, self-reflection, relationships, and activism.
- Who defines our purpose? We all have individual plans. Each person must discover their gifts/talents. God's spirit within us helps us to define who we are and empowers us to witness to others His love.
- Our strength is "standing on the promises of God." Do you know God's promises? God has given us more promises than commands. Why? Because he unconditionally loves us.
- What does it mean to be "called" versus "chosen"? Can you experience both? There is an expression "many are called but only a few are chosen." I was "chosen" academically (W.E.B. Du Bois' "talented tenth"), socially ("be a leader not a follower"), and spiritually ("God has smiled on me. He has set me free"). I use my life to encourage, teach and love.
- Who is God/Jesus? The spirit of God is always with us. How? God's spirit within us gives us power and the ability to "witness". He loves us. We don't see Him because we look with our natural eyes. We don't hear Him because we listen with our natural ears. We don't feel Him because we harden our hearts. We can only see, hear, and feel Him when we free our spirit.
- What is the "essence of love"? Knowing and doing the will of God is the essence of love. God is love. We know God through the revelation of His Spirit. The Spirit of God is love. God's spirit is within us. Therefore, we know/experience love through the spirit of God working within us. The essence of God and life is love.

"Love is but the discovery of us in others, and the delight in the recognition." Alexander Smith

"Love is the beauty of the soul." St. Augustine

Reinforcing the quotes cited by Robert above (regarding the self-liberating, spiritual power of love especially when exhibited "in the recognition" of service for the good of others)—I witnessed as *soul-work* my students' presentations in the Bible study sessions. Thus, in the context of St. Augustine's metaphorical vision of love being "the beauty of the soul," I close this chapter with an interview[1] between Madison Frazier (one of my students in the class) and Muriel Brathwaite (another one of the attendees during the Bible study sessions). As the two women engage each other in the dialogue that follows, it becomes clear that they have formed a loving, soulful relationship—across race and generational differences. Madison is a twenty-one-year-old white female; Muriel is an eighty-year-old black woman, full of world-travelled wisdom.

Bonding Across Differences in Community Outreach: "First United" in Love

Madison: What was your impression of the community outreach that my class was doing at your church? How did you feel about what we were doing?

Muriel: I thought that for young women and men in their early 20s, and this is what a lot of us adults said to you after, I was overwhelmed with the depth of thought that you all had. Oh, and the confidence you had with sharing that thought with not only with your peers, but with older folks as well, I thought Dr. Lemons must have done one hell of a job over the semester. I didn't know if you were that sophisticated already, but whatever he did brought out something in you, in all of you. As older people, we sat there with our jaws dropped, envying you. I think we all wondered what kind of education we had [received] that didn't allow us to have such a perception of ourselves at that age. I wasn't sure if I should attribute that to you guys' individually or to Dr. Lemons' ability to bring it out of you all. I guess

50/50. But he must have known it was going to be powerful because he dared to invite other people, older people, to share in it. And I wish he would have recorded the whole thing.

(From here to the end of the dialogue for the purpose of clarity as both our names start with "M"—I refer to myself, by my last name "Frazier".)

Frazier: Me, too!

Muriel: Did you personally know how confident you were?

Frazier: Me? No, I didn't know how confident I seemed, because I actually wasn't very confident in myself. I was worried I might not be taken seriously because we were just some young kids. I kind of felt like maybe I didn't have the authority to be speaking on these things.

Muriel: Well you must be a good faker, because you seemed very confident to me. Now tell me, what was the assignment [Dr. Lemons] gave you? What kind of guidance did you receive? What was the common theme because [all of the presentations] were so different?

Frazier: Well, Dr. Lemons gave us a rubric for each paper (which is what we presented), and as long as we met the requirements, we were able to do kind of do whatever we wanted. Each week we had a different chapter and secondary sources, and our assignment was to react to it personally. To react critically, but through the lens of ourselves, of who we were. So, we each wrote something different because we each reacted to it in a personal way. We each related to the text in a personal way, so our responses were personalized. That's why each presentation was so different from the other.

Frazier: So, what about *my* presentation specifically caused you to want to meet with me again, or to pursue a further conversation?

Muriel: I think you came near the end of the group, right?

Frazier: I think so, yeah.

Muriel: I remember thinking, gosh, this is different. Gosh, they were all so different. Maybe because I could hear you better, I was able to focus on what you were saying. Of course, when you said Africa my ears popped up. I know Africa, I know the challenges of young women menstruating in Africa. I very much related to that. I was impressed that a young white girl knew something about Africa that I didn't know. I was saying to myself: "Why did you not know that?"

but I also wanted to know *why* I didn't know [about Afripads] because that would have made life easier when I was working in Africa. But I was curious of you. You made it related to your own life, and you said you were married, and then I thought, "Maybe that's why she is interested because she is thinking about her own marriage and her own sexuality." Then I brushed that aside because you were talking about the growth and wanting to be a part of it happening. But I was just inspired that you allowed yourself to know something that so many of your peers did know or care about. A white girl from Safety Harbor, I didn't know the Safety Harbor part then, but I was impressed. So, it was a natural order to reach out to you. But how we got from there to here is a whole lot of conversation and connection. But I was interested to see how you came to feel so intensely about a situation a half a world away and very far from your own world.

Frazier: So, after our meet up, what caused you to want to pursue an actual relationship with me?

Muriel: I think you're sweet, I think you're great, but I think you're curious. I think you listen and ask questions, and honor my wisdom. And I honor your wisdom, too. I honor that when you make a date, you're punctual. It's a silly thing to honor, but it is a big plus in my book. I just like you. And I think you are the kind of young woman who I can talk about anything with. And if it is a new thing, you will ask questions and follow through. I don't know what teaches that in a young person, and I don't know what in your history has made you that way, but there is a connection. Even with a sixty-year age difference, there is an understanding. There is a lot of natural empathy between us, and you can't buy that. That may not be the perfect answer Dr. Lemons wants to hear, but that is true. I just value our natural connection. You check up on me, you ask questions, you care. I mean, I come here and sit down, and you bring me a book on colored girls. And you thought Ntozake was from Kentucky [Ntozake Shangé is actually from New Jersey], and I said, "I know of someone who is from Hopkinsville," so we started googling. That's what I like about you, you don't let anything pass. You looked on your phone first, but it didn't work. So later you looked on your computer. You remembered. That's what I like. Then you say, "Oh, it's bell hooks! Duh. Of course, that's why I was thinking of Kentucky. bell hooks, not Ntozake." Your head is going to explode one day. You're only twenty-two. You're going to have to calm down. But anyways, that's me. There is so much in my head. That's me. I remember. So, I guess you can tell Dr. Lemons that I love you because you are like me. Is that selfish?

Frazier: I don't think so.

Muriel: But I think it's more than love. I admire you. That's more than love, right?

Frazier: Muriel, you're going to make me cry. I love you, too.

Muriel: I know, me too. I am tearing up.

Frazier: That's the end of my prepared questions. Are there any questions you want to ask me? I know you said you wanted to ask me some questions about Afripad?

Muriel: Well, I already found those out, and answered them on my own. But this is free speech? I can say anything else that I want?

Frazier: Sure. But you know I wrote about you in my paper. Do you want to read it?

Muriel: No.

Frazier: Why not?

Muriel: I am scared of what you wrote.

Frazier: Well, I'll tell you then. I just wrote in a paper about *A Raisin in the Sun*, and about Lena. How you were so much like her. How you were a strong woman. Working hard every day, past the boundaries to make a path for black youths. I just wrote about how I admire you and what you have done. Nothing bad at all.

The interview ended here. Muriel then wanted to speak to Frazier off the record.

Let the Circle Remain Unbroken

When Madison told me months later after the course ended that she planned to interview Muriel related her thoughts about the student presentations at First United Church of Tampa, I was completely surprised. Across lines of race and generational differences—through "The Bible as Literature" in community service with this progressive Church—a young white woman and a black woman had begun an engaging friendship. The dialogue between the two women, as recorded here, serves as a model of what Jesus commissioned his followers to do upon his resurrection, and it exemplifies one of my pedagogical aims for the course. In all Jesus had taught his followers, indisputably their commission was to act the love that they had witnessed in his revolutionary, missionary activism. If his followers had learned anything from Jesus, it was to serve humbly for the good of all people—especially that of male *and* females, across boundaries of patriarchal power, generational differences and abilities, economic status, tribal affiliation, *and* dogmatic religious laws of exclusion.

Every time my students and I sat together in a circle during each evening class session, from one semester to the next in "The Bible as Literature," I experienced feelings of the healing effects of faith, hope, and love in my calling to remain on course to freedom. I close this chapter with a poem by Manisha Brown, a student in the spring 2018 offering of the course, about what she learned in it. Reflecting on the therapeutic implications of the circle seating formation, she titled the poem "Ode to My Therapy":

A circle where hearts share
A circle where tears release
A circle where there are enough words to say

Welcome to the night where the light creeps through
Every night's session is a breakthrough
Don't worry
Speak when it's your time
One of us will come to your rescue

Welcome to the night where the light creeps through
Here there is no blocked view or taboo
This is my preview
God cancelled my plans and placed me on this special Avenue

He brought people in my life
And gave me another value to His plans for me
He showed me who else He was and what He could do
Through people I saw once a week

Through my healing I found comfort through books and a feminist
Through my healing he pushed me to write every week
Stronger and stronger
Through my healing he failed me, so I could make corrections
Through my healing I sat in the dark with light still creeping through

He tossed me into water knowing I knew how to swim
But he also threw me a life jacket when waves sunk me under
So, I could walk on water
Instead of sinking away underwater

Note

[1] The interview Madison Frazier arranged with Muriel Brathwaite was recorded on Friday, September 21, 2018.

Acknowledgements

I would like to thank the following students (from the spring 2018 semester of "The Bible as Literature") whose responses I included in this chapter —Anthony Martinez, "GiGi" Jackson, Yesenia Schofield, Taylor Michael, "SLAM" (Tiffany Anderson), Kelly Prendergast, Keith Voney, Avram Wassef, Manisha Brown, and Madison Frazier; appreciation to my colleague Dr. Cheryl Rodriguez and Robert G. Yizar (both members of First United Church of Tampa); a special thanks to Dr. Bernice Powell Jackson (Pastor of FUCOT) for her partnership with me in allowing my students to present discussions of writings they produced in the course with FUCOT's Tuesday evening Bible Study sessions; finally, a "shout out" to Muriel Brathwaite for her engaging and inspiring *womanist* dialogue with Madison Frazier. It is a testament to the visionary and liberating power of love—across generations.

Works Cited

Averitt, Neil. *The Single Gospel: Matthew, Mark, Luke and John Consolidated into a Single Narrative*. Resource Publications, 2015.

Bessey, Sarah. *Jesus Feminist: An Invitation to Revisit the Bible's View of Women*. Howard Books, 2013.

Walker, Alice. *In Search of Our Mothers' Gardens: Womanist Prose*. Harcourt Brace and Co., 1983.

Chapter 12

Seated in the Circle of Love

Gary L. Lemons, Scott Neumeister, and Susie Hoeller

"So where do we go from here?" you ask. "Now what? ... How? What are our seven steps to equality? How do we make other people believe it? How do we change things for women in our church and in the world? What shall we do?"...Begin here: right at the feet of Jesus. Look to Love, and yes, our Jesus—he will guide you in your steps, one after another, in these small ways until you come at last to love the whole world.
Sarah Bessey, "Intimate Insurgency," *Jesus Feminist: An Invitation to Revisit the Bible's View of Women*

Womanist:...Committed to survival and wholeness of entire people, male *and* female...Not a separatist ...Traditionally universal, as in: "Mama, why are we brown, pink, and yellow, and our cousins are white, beige, and black?" Ans.: "Well, you know the colored race is just like a flower garden, with every color flower represented." Traditionally capable, as in: "Mama, I'm walking to Canada and I'm taking you and a bunch of other slaves with me." Reply: "It wouldn't be the first time." 3. Loves music. Loves dance. Loves the moon. *Loves* the Spirit. Loves love and food and roundness. Loves struggle. *Loves* the Folk. Loves herself. *Regardless*. 4. Womanist is to feminist as purple to lavender.
Alice Walker, *In Search of Our Mothers' Gardens: Womanist Prose* (1983)

Loving: From Concept to Pedagogical Practice—Gary's Closing Thoughts

Conceptually, as co-authors of *Let Love Lead on a Course to Freedom: A Study of "The Bible as Literature,"* Susie, Scott, and I embarked upon a collaborative journey recounting our experiences together as we labored to compose this book. We have written about our engaging, life-changing encounters with students and each other during the semesters I taught "The Bible as Literature" course, and we have documented the inspirational depth of its self-liberating classroom dialogues—across differences of gender, race, ethnicity, culture(s), sexualities, generation, and abilities. At the core of them—as we read, reviewed, and shared with each other students' writings from each semester—we would come to discover the profound thematic agency of *love* as a guiding moral, ethical, and social principle consistently expressed in writings students produced in the course.

Moreover, considering the biblical and literary implications of the book's title, I will always remember the enlightening conversation Scott and I had about it. One evening after class while he and I were walking to our cars parked on campus, as we discussed the vision for the book (to be co-authored by me, him, and Susie), he suddenly suggested we should think about the phrase—"let love lead" as a possible main title. It resonated deeply in my mind, even as we parted. I knew in that moment, this was the one. Yet it would be the phrasing for a subtitle that I would labor over and over again—interconnecting my pedagogical practice to Scott's visionary thinking. Finally, it came to me. Scott's idea of one submitting to the guiding power of love—as a conceptual agent of self-transformation—could simply be worded in a subtitle relating it to the journey the students and I had embarked upon in the "course" of our study of the Bible together in the classroom.

In the "Postscript" of my first book, *Black Male Outsider, a Memoir: Teaching as a Feminist Man*, I have a section titled "Teaching on the Margin and Loving." There I make the claim that black feminist pedagogy sustains, renews, and transforms space(s) for decolonization:

> For me, becoming a "professor" of feminism [teaching a course focused on the Bible as literature] has been about a personal life-sustaining journey toward self-love. I have learned to love myself again as a black male who has *chosen* to remain on the margin . . . I have determined to free myself from the bounds of patriarchy. (229)

As the visionary foundation for my pedagogical practice over the course of time, I have insisted that my students sit in a circle during our class meetings. Most classrooms in which I have taught (except for small graduate classes) have desks arranged in traditional rows. While this format works to mark the visual standpoint of the professor—situated at the front of the room—it focuses attention on the intellectual and authoritative power of this individual. Literally *and* symbolically, this format reinscribes and perpetuates institutionalized stereotypes of "professorship." Having written about my college teaching strategies over two decades, I have consistently labored to transform the classroom. Students literally become the center of what I think the space should look like. Rather than featuring my intellectual expertise (through lecturing), I purposely situate my intellectual standpoint in an all-inclusive, knowledge-building platform.

Creating a "face-to-face" seating arrangement in the classroom for a learning space promoting interactive dialogue between students and myself leads, I strategically become a part of the seating circle. At the beginning of each semester (after our first class meeting), I request that in our next session students assist me in arranging the desks in a circular setting. Once this task is accomplished, I sit in the circle with them. In this physical re-arrangement—not only is everyone's face clearly visible (to every person in the room), each one's voice is audibly empowered. The classroom is thus renewed and transformed. Personally, my three years of teaching "The Bible as Literature" was life-changing. Having embraced bell hooks' concept of "engaged pedagogy," rooted in an interactive student-teacher relationship, I have remained committed to her vision of it. hooks shares its transformative implications:

> Engaged pedagogy does not seek simply to empower students. Any classroom that employs a holistic model of learning will also be a place where teachers grow, and are empowered by the process. That empowerment cannot happen if we [professors] refuse to be vulnerable while encouraging student to take risks. (*Teaching to Transgress,* 21)

Not all my students were completely comfortable sitting in a circle. It made some of them more visible than they actually desired to be. Having to look at someone directly "face-to-face"—especially for "shy" students—was a potential issue that I would have to *engage*. Key to hooks' idea of empowered teaching is the critical importance of being "vulnerable" in the classroom. I absolutely agree. This is precisely where my transformation of the classroom seating lives. Here I not only challenge my students to be open but myself as well. It's all about risk-taking.

Seated together in a circle format each class session in "The Bible as Literature"—my students and I not only conversed about intersections between genders but collectively we faced each other's issues *inter*related to race, ethnicity, class, sexuality, cultures, and abilities. My pedagogical aim in the strategic employment of feminist/womanist thought in the study of the Bible as literature is to bridge theory and practice for "higher" education. Students came to know the critical importance of intersectional thinking.

In reality (as I have shared throughout *Let Love Lead*), when I first began teaching the life of Jesus in a feminist context, I clearly knew this would be a risk. Opening up about my pro-feminist and womanist positionality in the college classroom has always been about my taking a risk. Who would believe my story? This has always been a personal, political, and pedagogical issue for me. Yet when I determined to reject patriarchal and masculinist thinking as a black man, teaching for the first time at the New School University in 1994, the classroom became a critical site to put my life on the line of vulnerability. Sharing my struggle to become an advocate for women's rights called into question all that I grew up believing what a man should be. Telling my students the story about "how I made it over" (sexist *and* racist myths and stereotypes), I aim to enable them to open up. In this way, our interactive dialogue in the circle setting is life-changing for many students. For male students (who are most often gender "minorities" in my classes), such a space provides them the opportunity to engage openly in conversations related to manhood and masculinity.

In *The Will to Change: Men, Masculinity and Love*, bell hooks states, "It is not true that men are unwilling to change. It is true that many men are afraid to change. It is true that masses of men have not even begun to look at the ways that patriarchy keeps them from knowing themselves, from being in touch with their feelings, from loving. To know love, men must be able to let go the will to dominance. They must be able to choose life over death. They must be willing to change" (xvii). As a black man continually calling into question ideas of patriarchy (in and outside black/communities of color), I take to heart hooks' notion that "men must be able to let go the will to dominance," if we are to comprehend the life-saving power of love. The circle seating arranged classroom offers an all-inclusive space where male students can feel free to let go the fear of being vulnerable. Rather than being perceived as weak or less "manly"— male students can comprehend the freedom of self-actualization connected one's "willing[ness] to change." This idea resides at the center of my conceptual design for a liberatory classroom *re*-arrangement. As hooks notes in *Teaching to Transgress: Education as the Practice of Freedom*: "Professors who embrace the challenge of self-actualization will be better able to create pedagogical practices that engage students providing them with ways of knowing that enhances their capacity to live full and deeply" (22). I say let the student-teacher circle remain unbroken. In it, students have "enhance[d my] capacity to let love lead more "full[y] and deeply."

The Way Ahead Is In—Scott's Closing Thoughts

As I reflect on my writing for *Let Love Lead*, my experience working with Gary and Susie, and getting to know the students in

"The Bible as Literature," I cannot help but feel encouragement for the future. I see even more powerfully than when I first engaged with my colleagues and these undergraduates the efficacy of the autocritographical approach to merge standard, knowledge-based education with personal transformation, liberation, and healing within the English classroom. Back in 1995, in the middle of a career in information technology, I received my initial "calling" to be a teacher. A few years later, I took an interest in energy body work, and in an introductory course, I accepted another calling: to be a healer in any capacity I could. Not until 2009, five years after switching careers into teaching and two years after starting graduate school, did I encounter the perfect fusion of teaching and healing within Gary's "Feminist Theory" course, powered by autocritography. I began my own self-recovery process in that class, which was to extend throughout my graduate school years and continues to this day. I also started to implement autocritography as a strategy in my own classrooms—first at a middle school and eventually at the University of South Florida. While spiritual themes weave through many of the texts I have taught, I have never engaged my students as deeply in a work of holy writ as Gary has in "The Bible as Literature." Having witnessed the evidence of its power to "care for the soul," as Thomas Moore titles his book, I am inspired by the potential use of this vision of "higher education" as a means of sustaining and spreading the teaching/healing project to which I have allied myself.

A question arose as Gary, Susie, and I sat together discussing how we wanted to conclude the book, and it serves as the guide for my closing words—where do we go from here? The question evokes the obvious meanings of "How do we carry this work into the future?" and "What direction do we ultimately want our readers to take with them after reading our book?" Of course, the standard "direction" answers arose in my head: ahead, onward, and upward. Looking at our gathering into the small circle around Gary's table, however, a deeper, more intuitive answer emerged: inward. I began recollecting how powerful Gary's pedagogical technique is that he mentions above, in which his students—both undergraduate and graduate—sit in a circle for class, rather than the standard instructor up front/all students facing forward. Moreover, I thought about the autocritographical work of reader response itself and how it requires the merging of analytical thinking with inward-facing, self-reflective memory work. I therefore struck upon the two ways that going *in*, both into the circle of visible community and into our inner community of personal thoughts, feelings, and memories, is actually the way *forward*.

I recall with absolute clarity the evening (Dr.) Lemons and I first met: the opening meeting of his graduate "Feminist Theory" course in 2009. The University of South Florida facilities planners had placed our class in a small, semi-circular auditorium with ascending levels and fixed tables. Despite the fact that we students fit into this space, it did not "fit" Gary's vision of how our classroom community would work. He adamantly stressed to us that we had to "see" each other, and that intra-classroom, face-to-face dialogue was a lynchpin of his course. Our professor subsequently was able to arrange a different room for the rest of the semester, and we afterwards met in a space with individual chair/desks that could be arranged into a circle. Paradoxically, the room we moved into was not a good "fit" for student-to-chair ratio. It had seats for about forty students, and our small group of fifteen was dwarfed by the empty chairs around the edges of the room. For the university, it would have been more "efficient" to hold our class in a smaller classroom. Not for *efficiency* but for *community*, Gary had gone the extra mile—and I use that term with knowing reference to Matthew 5:4—to help create a community within the circle.

Although other graduate classes at USF did tend to operate in conference-style formats, Gary's insistence on being able to sit in a circle, even in his undergraduate courses, has true progressive underpinnings versus the efficiency reasons for those classroom setups. He is following the example and theoretical wisdom of one of his own mentors, bell hooks. "I still remember the excitement I felt," hooks recalls in *Teaching to Transgress*, "when I took my first class where the teacher wanted to change how we sat, where we moved from sitting in rows to a circle where we could look at each other. That forced us to recognize one another's presence" (146). Another presence-recognizing technique Gary employs is his insistence that students refer to each other by name when responding in dialogue. He reinforces this in his undergraduate courses at intervals during the first part of the semester by having "name quizzes"—in which each student must write down all the others' names—to sharpen the importance of their memorization. By facing faces and using names, Gary's students are not simply reproducing the isolation of normal classrooms, big or small; they are taking their "seat at the table," and Gary, following the title of another book by bell hooks, is teaching community.

Concomitant with her idea of the circle enabling recognition of all the others in the classroom, hooks also emphasizes that the instructor thereby decenters her/himself, initially just in a visual way—I was looking at peers far more often than the sole professor in that "Feminist Theory" classroom. But even more than just the line of sight factor, traditional seating organization reinforces classroom talk happening mostly as teacher to students as a group, student to teacher, or teacher in response to single student. In this scenario, even when one student may be responding to what another student has offered aloud, the response tends to be more aimed *at* the instructor than *to* the original speaker. The circle format tends to eliminate this construction of the power of speaking as mediated through the instructor. Gary further distances himself from classroom focus by only rarely speaking in a lecture mode and most often becoming one more voice in the dialogue propelled by students reading their autocritographical pieces aloud and getting feedback. Knowledge, therefore, becomes constructed, not dispersed, in a decentered classroom such as this—a space where the direction, as my theme is here in my concluding remarks, is "in."

Both the physical setup and the professor relinquishing the power center promote making the "invisible" student visible. On this point, I recall the words Ralph Ellison uses in his introduction to *The Invisible Man*: "I am invisible, understand, simply because people refuse to see me . . . When they approach me, they see only my surroundings, themselves or figments of their imagination, indeed, everything and anything except me" (3). I find that in the traditional classroom arrangement, all desks facing the instructor means that the human "surroundings" in the room, the other students, tend to become background to the "front and center" figure. The circle structure is a physical arrangement to create recognition. The fact that students read aloud then dialogue about their often very personal responses using each other's names empowers—or has hooks states, "forces"—even more intimate and personal visibility and recognition. By students facing inward, both in the physical/circular sense and the self-reflective writing shared within the circle, they grow in their humanity via one of the truest embodiments of what it means to study within the humanities.

This motif of seeing and visibility fits right into the discussion of "The Bible as Literature," especially as a theme of Jesus' ministry in the Gospels. Especially with women, as Sarah Bessey illustrates in *Jesus Feminist*, but also with other marginalized groups, Jesus went out of his way to "see" otherwise invisible people. For example, his breaking of double taboo to speak to the water-seeker at the well—both a Samaritan and a woman—in John 4 is one of the prime examples of his turning the invisible visible. Moreover, Jesus in multiple gospels not only scolds his disciples for trying to prevent children ("little ones" both in size and societal importance) from coming to him but also brings a child before his followers (and in Mark 9, hugs him) to illustrate childlike faith. When the humble centurion sends friends to ask Jesus to transmit healing to his servant from a distance, Jesus takes that moment to make the invisible Roman visible, announcing to the crowd, "I tell you, I have not found such great faith even in Israel" (*New International Version*, Luke 7.9). This instance is even more remarkable because natives of Israel would have hated and marginalized such a person, as part of an occupying force. Still, Jesus makes him visible at the core of his statement as an exemplar of faith, even to Israel's embarrassment. The prophet Isaiah foresaw the future messiah's life work of making visible the humble while de-emphasizing the proud, declaring in metaphor, "Every valley shall be raised up, every mountain and hill made low" (*New International Version*, Isa. 40.4). In this sense, a pedagogy that helps equalize the classroom as much as possible aligns with this messianic pursuit.

This theme of visibility, as well as the barriers to it, not only operates in the era of Christ; the Old Testament has such moments as well. When God calls to Moses out of the burning bush, sending him on the mission to win freedom for his fellow Hebrews, Moses attempts to become invisible: "Who am I that I should go to Pharaoh and bring the Israelites out of Egypt?" (*New International Version*, Ex. 3:11). The angel calls Gideon to deliver Israel from Midian, and Gideon's response echoes the invisibility-begging of Moses: "Pardon me, my lord,...but how can I save Israel? My clan is the weakest in Manasseh, and I am the least in the family" (*New International Version*, Judg. 6:15). Even David prays to the Lord in 1 Chronicles 17:16, "Who am I, LORD God, and what is my family, that you have brought me thus far?" But even more than this self-imposed invisibility, David encountered others who tried to prevent his "seat at the table," most vividly in the story of his encounter with Goliath. When David hears of Goliath's defiance of the Israelite army, the shepherd boy asks about the reward for killing the giant. "Why have you come down here?", David's brother Eliab scolds him for even inquiring, "And with whom did you leave those few sheep in the desert? I know how conceited you are and how wicked your heart is." To this scorn David counters, "Can't I even speak?" (*New International Version*, 1 Sam. 17:28-29). Saul treats David afterwards in a similar, discouraging manner. Ultimately, though, we know of the works of Moses, Gideon, and David. These figures who either felt unworthy or powerless to participate in a community or were discouraged from communal participation all left lasting legacies. Thus, both Old and New Testaments offer visions of individuals becoming visible, being invited to "the table," and making a difference for the better.

I hope, along with Gary and Susie, that *Let Love Lead* can be a text that inspires with its stories of students coming to personal transformation, liberation, and healing. Also, and especially for teachers or group leaders, I hope that many aspects of how "The Bible as Literature" course operated serve as a model for an efficacious method of facilitating the "higher education" I spoke of above. As I am writing this on Martin Luther King, Jr., day, I use his words to amplify the power of love as the highest educator: "I have decided to love. If you are seeking the highest good, I think you can find it through love...He who loves has the key that unlocks to the meaning of ultimate reality" King delivered these words in a speech whose title echoes the theme of this conclusion: "Where Do We Go from Here?" The best way *forward*, in my opinion, it to turn *inward* in love, both to those around us within the circle of whatever communal bonds we share and to our own experiences and memories that resonate with the stories of our humanity that transcend difference. While our differences cannot and should not be erased, we can assiduously seek to strengthen the "tie that binds our hearts our hearts in Christian love," as the old hymn goes. This loving bond is the goal of this course that we three authors have written about and that, we hope, can be reproduced in locations we could never personally reach. With an eye to the themes and wisdom that resonate across the ages and with a loving openheartedness to connecting to both literary individuals and individuals "within the circle" of the reading group, reading the Bible as literature can indeed embody a fundamental act of love.

Life-Changing Love—Susie's Closing Thoughts

It all seems so clear to me now. Is it just because I turned sixty-five this past July 2018 and can now be on Medicare instead of individual health insurance, with my monthly health care costs cut by 80%. Since sixty-five is the new forty-five, I have no plans to retire!

But making this life milestone is not the reason for my sudden burst of clarity. Here is the explanation about what is clear—what I am speaking about.

All my life, since my parents raised my brothers and me as Christians, I have known that Jesus commands us to love God and love my neighbor as myself. But in having to deal with nasty people in business, as neighbors and on the roads, I always found it impossible to love my neighbor as myself. I could love my family and my friends but not everyone around me. I know that Jesus said that even sinners love their friends. I know I am a sinner and can never perfectly imitate Christ. It is impossible. Even Peter, John and James fell asleep in the garden of Gethsemane while Jesus was praying to be spared the Cross.

In working with Gary and Scott on this book, I finally realized that if I could learn to "let love lead" me then I would be on the road to *freedom* from sin's power and guilt. Letting love lead means I would be able to substitute kindness for judgment and caring for indifference.

I have learned from Gary's students how to lessen pride and increase humility. As the class speaker on more than one occasion, I had walked in with a prideful attitude that I was there to impart my wisdom to them.

I know that Gary's students learned something from my presentations and from reading my book *Lean on Jesus*. But what I had not expected was how much I would end up learning from them—not just from their questions in class and class but in reading their papers about my book and *Jesus Feminist*. In their papers, the students expose their fears, their weaknesses, their struggles and their hopes. They bare their souls to the reader.

I learned from the students who were complimentary and from a small number who were critical of something I wrote. It was a great experience for me.

Pride is a huge problem for many highly educated people—it is too easy to look down on others with less education and life experience and dismiss them. I will never do that again . . . (as Canadians say) "for sure."

I saw firsthand how Gary's teaching methods can revolutionize learning by creating a circle of students who care about and trust each other. Learning is not a solitary pursuit. Learning is not the mastery of facts and figures alone. Learning is not the accumulation of grades, degrees and academic awards. It is not competing against other students; it is collaborating with them.

Letting love lead is the course to freedom for all of us—freedom from fear, freedom from sin.

The experience of collaborating with Gary and Scott on this book has been a life-changing experience for me. I never was in class with Scott, as we were separate guest speakers. I have had the privilege of his company at our planning meetings held at Gary's circular kitchen table. A beautiful table that Gary made with his own hands. Just like Jesus was a carpenter.

I use the term *life-changing* because I now understand why letting love lead puts us on the course to freedom:

> You, my brothers and sisters, were called to be free. But do not use your freedom to indulge the flesh; rather, serve one another humbly in love. For the entire law is fulfilled in keeping this one command: "Love your neighbor as yourself" (*New International Version*, Gal. 5.13-14).

Works Cited

Bessey, Sarah. *Jesus Feminist: An Invitation to Revisit the Bible's View of Women.* Howard Books, 2013.

The Bible. New International Version, Biblica, 2011.

Ellison, Ralph. *Invisible Man.* Modern Library, 1994.

hooks, bell. *Teaching to Transgress: Education as the Practice of Freedom.* Routledge, 1994.

---. *The Will to Change: Men, Masculinity, and Love.* Atria Books, 2004.

King, Martin Luther, Jr. "Where Do We Go from Here?" *Stanford University: The Martin Luther King, Jr. Research and Education Institute*, kinginstitute.stanford.edu/king-papers/documents/where-do-we-go-here-address-delivered-eleventh-annual-sclc-convention.

Walker, Alice. *In Search of Our Mothers' Gardens: Womanist Prose.* Harcourt Brace and Co., 1983.

Authors

Gary L. Lemons, PhD. is a professor in the Department of English at the University of South Florida. His areas of specialization are African American literature and feminist/womanist theory and criticism. He is also an abstract painter and graphic designer. His book publications include—*Black Male Outsider, a Memoir: Teaching as a Pro-Feminist Man. Womanist Forefathers: Frederick Douglass and W.E.B. Du Bois. Caught Up in the Spirit: Teaching for Womanist Liberation. Feminist Solidarity at the Crossroads: Intersectional Women's Studies for Transracial Alliance* (co-published with Kim Marie Vaz). *Building Womanist Coalitions: Writing and Teaching in the Spirit of Love.*

Scott Neumeister, PhD. is an adjunct professor at the University of South Florida in Tampa, where he earned his PhD. in English in 2018. His specialization in multiethnic American literature comes after careers as an information technology systems engineer and a teacher of English and mythology at the middle school level.

Susan L. (Susie) Hoeller is an international business attorney. She is a graduate of Colby College and Vanderbilt Law School. Susie was born in Chicago, Illinois, raised in Montreal, Canada, and currently lives in the Tampa Bay, Florida area where she practices and teaches part-time for the University of Tampa's Executive MBA program.

CPSIA information can be obtained
at www.ICGtesting.com
Printed in the USA
BVHW031932070322
630843BV00014B/70